I0022845

Articulating Media

Genealogy, Interface, Situation

Technographies

Series Editors: Steven Connor, David Trotter and James Purdon

How was it that technology and writing came to inform each other so extensively that today there is only information? Technographies seeks to answer
that question by putting the emphasis on writing as an answer to the large
question of 'through what?'. Writing about technographies in history, our contributors will themselves write technographically.

Articulating Media

Genealogy, Interface, Situation

James Gabrillo and Nathaniel Zetter

O

OPEN HUMANITIES PRESS

London 2023

First edition published by Open Humanities Press 2023

Copyright © 2023 James Gabrillo and Nathaniel Zetter, and respective authors

©①⊙

This is an open access book, licensed under the Creative Commons By Attribution Non-Commercial Share Alike license. Under this license, authors allow anyone to download, reuse, reprint, modify, distribute, and/or copy this book so long as the authors and source are cited, the use is not commercial, and resulting derivative works are licensed under the same or similar license. Read more about the license at creativecommons.org/licenses/by-nc-sa/3.0

Cover Art, figures, and other media included with this book may be under different copyright restrictions.

Cover Illustration © 2023 Navine G. Dossos

Print ISBN 978-1-78542-112-9
PDF ISBN 978-1-78542-111-2

◯

OPEN HUMANITIES PRESS

Open Humanities Press is an international, scholar-led open access publishing collective whose mission is to make leading works of contemporary critical thought freely available worldwide. More at http://openhumanitiespress.org

Contents

Introduction: Media and Articulation

JAMES GABRILLO AND NATHANIEL ZETTER

Archaeologists often delve into the debris of history, but William Rathje was particularly known for getting into other people's rubbish. In 1973, he mobilised his students from the University of Arizona to sort through what Tucson residents threw away, and then record the trash items against population data. Waste information unearthed habits Americans had concealed or misrepresented in surveys: they drank much more alcohol than they reported, and discarded alarming quantities of expensive beef. The 'Garbage Project' – as Rathje named it – slowly accumulated, and in 1987, he also began to dig in the city's landfills. As expected, the sites offered centralised densities of waste, but they also presented an unexpected methodological aid. 'Dig a trench through a landfill', Rathje and his team discovered, 'and telephone books can be seen to stud some strata like currants in a cake' (Rathje and Murphy 2001: 104). Each year, the residents of Tucson would receive new phonebooks and promptly dispose of them. Rathje found more every year, such that 'their expansion in number seems to know no bounds' (104–5). The yearly cycles of refuse could now be dated by the thick layers of sheets compacted in the rubbish. Media expiration offered temporal mediation. The discarded phonebooks segmented the past into clear layers of litter; as they grew in number, the phonebooks also mediated the evolution of Rathje's own archaeological method, which he christened 'garbology'.

The story of these compacted phonebooks in the landfill outside Tucson, Arizona, pressures our understanding of media obsolescence. When their contents cease to communicate, but their presence lingers, media can accumulate other means of speaking across the past and the present. These artefacts – these media – gather meaning and significance as we articulate the narratives and contexts that cling to them. Garbology and media archaeology meet somewhere among these many layers of paper discarded in the Arizona desert. For Rathje, the project revealed that the line between archaeology and litter collection had always been thin: 'Archaeologists work on material fragments [... that] are often what may be classed as garbage' (Shanks, Platt, and Rathje 2004: 72). Thus, 'archaeology is a practice of mediation, working between past and present' to establish 'questions of value', 'representation', and 'categorisation' that insistently inquire: 'what is fit to join an archive?' (72). Perhaps all archaeology is media archaeology. And much like garbage – the currency of archaeology – perhaps media can be excavated layer by layer, swabbed and appraised for category and value, and archived for further scrutiny.

This book intends to take seriously such problems of media and method. It considers the vernaculars of media to excavate those questions of value, representation, and categorisation that have become compacted within media history and media-critical writing. This delving must first locate the languages of media in certain places – whether they are the domestic spaces where phone numbers are dialled, or the subterranean landfills where academic dumpster-divers might discover old media's persistent traces. The contributions to this book thus twin an attention to language with an attention to location – the dual sense of our title, *Articulating Media*. The word *articulating* contains the sense of 'expressing' and that of 'uniting', 'connecting', or 'joining' – spatially and temporally. To articulate media means to express something about them by locating their connections in space and in time; it requires understanding the way they express by themselves connecting up spaces and times. Rathje's discarded phonebooks articulate something of this synchrony. Phonebooks are a medium for gathering expression: they guide the caller through the process of connecting up the space between the phones. Once obsolete, they come to express another set of connections: their accumulation in space marks out the time of their untimeliness. And their history traces this book's own historical trajectory. An old medium that was used to explain and classify the operation of the new medium of the telephone, phonebooks were rendered obsolete when the medium they had been used to connect, in turn, turned old. Their rise and fall from vital aid to shunned vestige of previous eras might therefore take us from Edison's 'Ahoy!' through telephone wires to today's wireless digital media. Meanwhile, their curious persistence articulates the afterlives of media that will also be of interest throughout this book. 'The avalanche of paper' the garbologists discovered in the dump expressed the urgent need to understand 'that paper and other organics […] tend not so much to degrade in landfills as to mummify' (Rathje and Murphy 2001: 105). The assumption that obsolescence means degradation appears to lead, in fact, to media accumulation. In this case, mummified paper both clogs up and marks out the waste record.

Perhaps it is unusual to think of media *mummifying*, but this book assumes that unsettling some of the typical words that have become entombed within media theory today might be helpful to unsettle, too, some of its encased assumptions. *Articulating Media* seeks to trace, and perhaps to reorient, a few of the conventions mummified into the media vernacular and the vernacular of media theory. Our contributors exhume media materialities and situations both familiar and unexpected. Following previous volumes in the *Technographies* series, media technologies will be understood not as mute objects addressed through language, but as processes and devices situated in the very grammars and vocabularies of their address – training our focus, too, on 'the varying degrees to which all technologies have been written into being' (Pryor and Trotter 2016: 16). To situate media in their articulation, we must examine the situations both of media and of the media-critical writing in which they have been conceptualised. Where might media theory *take place*? What does it mean for media theory that this taking-place often occupies the space of media itself? What materialities might survive media's multiple articulations and associations?

Media, Metaphors, Matter

Even if all archaeology turns out to be media archaeology, the persistence of archaeological metaphors in media theory and history remains striking. 'Media archaeology' – the method itself – draws directly on Michel Foucault's metaphor of an 'archaeology of knowledge' (Huhtamo and Parikka 2011: 2, 8–9). From this influence, however, the method inherits a practice of the archival rather than the earthy digging up of artefacts. 'Archaeology', for Foucault, 'describes discourses as practices specified in the element of the archive' (Foucault 1972: 131). A cluster of spatial metaphors are deployed to signal the 'never completed' activity of 'uncovering' traces from that archive, but explicitly, in fact, 'it does not relate analysis to geological excavation' (131). Still, media archaeology delves into excavational metaphors quite readily. It 'has been interested' – Jussi Parikka, one of the contributors to this volume, explains in his *What Is Media Archaeology?* – 'in excavating the past in order to understand the present and the future' (Parikka 2012: 2). 'Media archaeology sees media cultures as sedimented and layered', he continues, 'a fold of time and materiality where the past might be suddenly discovered anew, and the new technologies grow obsolete increasingly fast' (3). Indeed, such is the metaphor's popularity and enduring hold that as soon as Wolfgang Ernst mentions 'archaeological layers' he admits, repentantly: 'the "archaeological" metaphor, as already mentioned, is hard to resist' (Ernst 2011: 241).

All this talk of digging up the media dirt has run through other 'excavational' methods and other archives. Diving through the history of literary 'close reading', Barbara Herrnstein Smith strikes the 'oddness of some of the language used to describe the activities' of both the close and 'distant' approaches (Smith 2016: 70). On the side of the Digital Humanities, she chides the use of 'the rather violent "extract" or the creepy "excavate"', since 'such language makes the practices so described sound distinctly unpleasant, rather unnatural, and certainly very alien' – as if the objects are approached 'like teeth, oil, or corpses' (70–1). Parikka himself knowingly puns on the last of these resonances in applying the vocabulary of death and decay to media that resist their own obsolescence. 'In the midst of talk of "dead media" by such writers as Bruce Sterling', he muses, 'it was clear that a lot of dead media were actually zombie-like media: living deads, that found an afterlife in new contexts, new hands, new screens and machines' (Parikka 2012: 3).

Perhaps the very spatial properties of this archaeological trope can help us to understand its rhetorical appeal. Intriguingly, the theory of 'cultural techniques' (*Kulturtechniken*) that represents another of media theory's current vocabularies turns out to be just as compelled by the archaeological metaphor. Bernhard Siegert, another contributor here, defines the intellectual turn towards media as such, at least in Germany, as 'an attempt to overcome French theory's fixation on discourse by turning discourse from its philosophical or archeological head onto its historical and technological feet' (Siegert 2015: 3). Nevertheless, shortly thereafter, that very turn from 'the Foucauldian "archive" to media technologies' itself becomes an 'archeology of cultural systems of meaning' that derives from the material pleasures of an 'archival obsession' rather than a 'passion for theory' (3). According to Siegert, the theory of cultural techniques is focused on isolating the 'inconspicuous technologies of knowledge' (2) that make possible the structure and regulation of such systems. In short, thinking like a cultural technician means taking Foucault's archival metaphor seriously enough that the archive itself, and not what it holds, can become one's fixation. 'The history of paper only turns into a media history', Siegert tells us, 'if it serves as a reference system for the analysis of bureaucratic or scientific data processing' (5). Perhaps the archaeology of the rubbish dump only turns into a media archaeology when its mummified paper sediments become a reference system for the culture, economy, and media apparatuses that made such vast garbage heaps necessary in the first place.

The theory of cultural techniques has other linguistic alliances, too. One of these is language itself, which serves as a tactical metaphor for their operations. 'Cultural techniques define the agency of media and things', writes Cornelia Vismann (2013: 83). 'If media theory were, or had, a grammar, that agency would find its expression in objects claiming the grammatical subject position and cultural techniques standing in for verbs' (83). The theory of cultural techniques thus crystallises the active relations between objects and habits. For Siegert, it tracks those 'media, symbolic operators, and drill practices' that generate 'distinctions: inside/outside, pure/impure, sacred/profane, [...] and so on' (Siegert 2015: 2, 14) – and to this list, we might add those waste-management operations that generate the distinction between useful objects and litter.

The language of language runs through this approach, formulating grammatical rules and administering lexical sorting offices. But it also joins this language of language with the language of machines. 'In other words (those of Lacan)', Siegert clarifies, 'cultural techniques point to a world of the symbolic, which is the world of machines' (Siegert 2015: 193). Jacques Lacan's threefold 'methodological distinction' among the real, the imaginary, and the symbolic, which was so centrally coded into Friedrich Kittler's

(1999: 15) media history, also inhabits cultural techniques, such that media now seem ceaselessly to pass in and out of the doors of the symbolic in order to operationalise 'distinctions in the real' (Siegert 2015: 14). Transcoding the symbolic and the machine turns out not only to draw Lacan's words into Siegert's vocabulary, but also those of the machines that inspired him. Opening or closing a door works to 'perform, observe, encode, address, and ultimately wire the difference between inside and outside' (14). For Vismann, these operations are 'almost algorithmic', while their theorisation seeks 'to derive the operational script', which means 'to extract the rules of execution from the executed act itself' (Vismann 2013: 87). This terminology alternately embodies and formats, articulates and solders, but ultimately the distinction that makes a distinction dwells in the lexical network of information theory, cybernetics, and digital computing technologies.

Siegert's contribution to this volume places that metaphorical knot in its larger historical situation. Unravelling the evolution of media in German philosophy, he asks 'how the writing of media history is affected by the media of history'. The question takes us from Hegel to Claude Shannon – from history as the 'narrative time' of written records to the mid-twentieth-century induction of 'switching time', through which circuit diagrams withdrew the 'real' from human experience. Two epistemological divides emerge from Siegert's media/history archive: the first marks a diachronic divide between an older notion of history and the emergence of 'history' as a collective singular; the second marks a synchronic divide between conscious sensory data and unconscious signal processing in the body. 'History' in this sense is held within the history of history-writing's own various media technologies. Media theory's insistence on machinic metaphors might thus re-emerge as one way the field has attempted to process its own historical conditions of possibility.

There is, moreover, a long history to media writing's animation by emergent technical vernaculars, and some of media theory's basic distinctions were born in that lexical encounter. 'The electric light is pure information', wrote Marshall McLuhan (2005: 8) in 1964. 'It is a medium without a message, as it were, unless it is used to spell out some verbal ad or name. This fact, characteristic of all media, means that the "content" of any medium is always another medium' (McLuhan 2005: 8). The words 'information' and 'message', and the singling out of 'content', were not incidental. McLuhan's self-rearticulation as media sage was electrified by reading Norbert Wiener's *Cybernetics* (1948) and *The Human Use of Human Beings* (1950). In 1951, he had written to Wiener to note the 'special attention' he gave the two books and to gush with his ideas for a cybernetic re-reading of Modernist literature (Martin 1998: 109, 125).

Indeed, when Kittler drew on Lacan's three keywords, he was also siphoning from Lacan's own animation by the cybernetic vernacular (see Liu 2010). Kittler further charged this vocabulary with historical and cultural energy, while also drawing explicitly from the mains of Claude Shannon's 'information theory' in the afterword to *Discourse Networks 1800/1900*'s second printing. 'The term *discourse network*', he writes, 'as God revealed it to the paranoid cognition of Senate President Schreber, can also designate the network of technologies and institutions that allow a given culture to select, store, and process relevant data' (Kittler 1990: 369). Indeed, in Kittler all the metaphorical tropes of media theory already mentioned can be found compacted: Foucault's 'concept of the archive' is 'synonymous with the library' and thus 'discourse-analytic studies had trouble only with periods whose data-processing methods destroyed the alphabetic storage and transmission monopoly, that old-European basis of power' (369). 'Archeologies of the present', by contrast, 'must also take into account data storage, transmission, and calculation in technological media' (369). Kittler, in short, rewires discourse into information.

Information networks can be described only when they are contrasted with one another. The source, sender, channel, receiver, and drain of streams of information, Shannon's five functions, in other words, can be occupied or left vacant by various agents: by men or women, rhetoricians or writers, philosophers or psychoanalysts, universities or technical institutes. [...] Whether data, addresses, and commands circulate among pedagogy, Poetry, and philosophy, or among media technologies, psychophysics, and literature, the difference changes the place value of each word. (370)

If such differentials constitute the media history of writing, Kittler felt that the influence of his book was similarly differential: '*Discourse Networks 1800/1900* has become part of an information network that describes literature as an information network' (371). Once one has entered the cybernetic language game, it is circuit boards all the way down.

This description of the intellectual field as an information network articulates the extension into contemporary media writing of what Bernard Dionysius Geoghegan has called 'the cybernetic apparatus': that frenzy of inventive vernaculars that galvanised interdisciplinary research in the middle of the last century by liquifying the lexicon of mathematical and machinic logic (Geoghegan 2011: 97). It is thus pressing that we scrutinise, as Geoghegan formulates it, 'the ability of material instruments [...] to transform into epistemological figures that coordinate, suspend, or rationalize difference'; this is an 'ambiguity characteristic not only of the cybernetic apparatus but of much media-related inquiry and commentary' (Geoghegan 2011: 99). In his contribution to the present volume, Geoghegan further investigates such affinities of technology and knowledge. Here, he traces the ways information theory was channelled beyond communications engineering into variously creative and political applications in other fields, where the theory's preference for 'systems over statements, patterns over meaning, combinatorics over authorship, relay over articulation, conveyance over composition, reproduction over interpretation, infrastructures over individuals' was used to authorise the re-conception of human beings in equivalently technical terms. We must also be wary, then, of what else media theory inherits when it inherits the vernaculars of information theory and cybernetics.

If media theory's vocabulary is insistently spatial, then – whether digging, archiving, or wiring and rewiring – these spatial articulations are both historical and historicising: they trace an era's animating technical diction; they coordinate the in-betweens where devices, actions, and people are deemed to meet; and they devise the lines that situate media and technology in particular times and places.

Genealogy, Interface, Situation

In Silicon Valley, apparently, one does not have a profession but a 'space'. Corey Pein reports that '"What's your space?" meant "What does your company do?" […] If you were a writer, you would never say "I'm a writer". You would say "I'm in the content space", or, if you were more ambitious, "I'm in the media space"' (Pein 2018). If media theory is to account for such a chilling extraction of 'media space' from writing, it might do so by attending to its own forms of writing media and space as such. Into the media-theoretical 'space' of spatial metaphors and metaphorical spaces enters the project of technographies. Both cultural techniques and media archaeology 'find echoes', according to Sean Pryor and David Trotter (2016: 14), in this approach – their word, 'echoes', uses the mixing of sound reverberations in space as a metaphor for media-theoretical intermixing. The present collection continues this project by laying the technographic cables of media writing across the expanse of media history's forms of language. Through the lens of articulation, the essays address the vernaculars of media from the nineteenth century to the rise of digital technologies and uncover consequences for the historiography of media inquiry and the many forms it takes today. These diverse contributions map particular articulations of media and perform the articulations involved in the technographic writing of media theory and history. Distinctly varied in object and technique, our contributors stand at various intersections of design studies, feminist theory, the history of science and technology, literary criticism, musicology, and sound studies. Collectively, they mark out the vernaculars that have intersected media and location, while unsettling familiar ways of contemplating the interaction between media technologies and their localisation. Our ambition is to encourage a reappraisal of three of the field's fundamental operations: the *genealogy*, or tracing, of media; the *interface* as both a technical and cultural in-between; and the institutional *situating* of media devices. The book is thus divided into three parts, each taking its provocation from a verb that articulates the dual linguistic and spatial problem at play: *tracing, interfacing*, and *situating*.

'Tracing Media' refers to the activity of genealogy; it draws on the distinction between Foucault's archaeological phase, which has often been the inspiration for media theorists, and his later 'genealogical' phase, which has perhaps less frequently been excavated for its undergirding metaphors. The chapters in this part focus not on particular devices, machines, or systems, but on the family trees of lexis, the branches of which run through the development of the media concept and its associated vernaculars since the nineteenth century. The contributions from Siegert and Geoghegan already mentioned fall into this part. The other chapter in this section also traces those mediations that variously iterate immediacy, perception, and otherness. Melle Jan Kromhout reveals the long history of using the metaphor of 'the dark side of the moon' to describe acoustic mediation. From Wagner to Pink Floyd, Kromhout shows how the metaphor pervades both sonic innovation and its theoretical writing – across Kittler, Michel Serres, and others. He proposes to depart from imagining the relationship between music and the cosmos in terms of an ideal harmonic order, and instead to account for the physical complexity and randomness of technological processes, the speed and scale of which remain inaccessible to sensory perception. Across the book's first part, then, the genealogy of media vernaculars reveals those situations that media elide, implode, or imagine as unreachable.

One way to account for those elisions and implosions is to scrutinise the interfaces through which media become sensible, and through which media writing has often sensitised itself to them. The book's second part, 'Interfacing Media', thus focuses on the interface – its discursions and localities. In his preamble to *The Interface Effect*, Alexander R. Galloway affirms that: 'Interfaces themselves are effects, in that they bring about transformations in material states. But at the same time interfaces are themselves the effects of other things, and thus tell the story of the larger forces that engender them' (Galloway 2012: vii). Yet interfaces can also be ineffectual. Louisa Shen opens *Articulating Media*'s second part by locating a turning point in the history of computational interfaces. The arrival of a proto-graphical user interface, developed for the operating system of the Alto computer at Xerox PARC in 1973, required much written guidance. Teaching users how to be users involved mythologising the machine even as it was explicated. A barrier emerged between user and code that demanded careful coordination; the computer was made usable by at once revealing and hiding its alternately effective and ineffective interface effects. If today's devices, as Galloway puts it, 'foreground the interface like never before' (Galloway 2012: 30), then a moment when the interface's foregrounding needed explanation can also query the standard procedures of media-theoretical foregrounding.

Advancing two decades in interface history, Caroline Bassett revisits the largely extinct Multi-User Domain 'LambdaMOO', to recover a strand of cyber-feminism that might help us re-think what 'being a digital being' can mean. Resisting the 'presentist' and 'correctionist' tendencies of more recent feminist accounts of the interface, Bassett theorises LambdaMOO not as a rudimentary form of digital culture, but as a vitally-present instantiation of gender performativity. Here, Bassett offers another sense of technography: the performative writing of the digital self emerges as a way to revisit the tropes of cyberculture. Re-visualising ostensibly outdated media categories plays out the interface's processual dynamic; it is actively formed in the negotiation between users and the uses to which they put the technology – between language and code, the symbolic and the material.

Obsolescence can hold uncanny counter-valences, then – as we saw earlier in Rathje's mummified phonebooks. Indeed, 'cyberspace' itself has come to seem a curiously old-fashioned term for Bruce Sterling's '"place" where a telephone conversation appears to occur' (Sterling 1992: 10). In 2007, McKenzie Wark was already able to mark the word's obsolescence, and efficiently so, by replacing the 'now archaic term cyberspace' with 'gamespace' in quoting from K-Punk/Mark Fisher's blog (Wark 2007: 223). The tidy word 'replaced' signals that media theory might follow the same cycle of new and old that has been used to characterise media as such. The newer term, 'gamespace', designates a mode of interfacing with digital media that no longer seems to offer a window into a mediated space of ephemeral interactions that is bounded by un-mediated zones on all sides. There is now, for Wark, no unique space between the phones – only a digitised spatial topology everywhere meshed by material communications and constantly articulated by 'restrictions and hierarchies, firewalls and passwords' (Wark 2007: 66).

Emma McCormick-Goodhart concludes the book's second part by reflecting on a different way to theorise this form of spatial constitution – one inscribed by material interfaces. Reflecting on 'Deaf space', and the way it re-articulates sonic categories, she presses the concept of hearing beyond the merely aural into a media ecology of tactility and haptic architecture. The media-technographic project gains an urgent question: what are the technological dimensions of a language that is not written, but performed? If technographies articulate 'those transformative occasions on which writing confronts its own enabling opposite internally' (Pryor and Trotter 2016: 16), what might it mean for that 'enabling opposite' to be constituted by the thresholds McCormick-Goodhart discovers in embodied language? Collectively, part two offers an account of the interface that also acts as a theoretical interface between digital media's past and present embodied histories, leading into the collection's third part: 'Situating Media'.

A certain counter-history of phonebooks and of Sterling's place between the phones opens this final part – which considers the institutional and other situations formed by media, and those that inform media's particular effects. Renée Farrar situates *Dial-a-Poem*, a sound installation first shown at the New York Museum of Modern Art in 1968, in which visitors listened to contemporary poets recite their work by dialling a telephone and hearing an automated answering service. Farrar isolates one poet's performance – Ted Berrigan's 'Telegram to Jack Kerouac' – to recover its gesture towards the intricacies of reconstructing and accessing older media, especially recorded sounds, through digital archives. Poetry in its mediated, yet situated, performance articulates, perhaps, a technographic mode of its own, one that renders untimely the typical cycles of media obsolescence. Indeed, the discarded phonebooks in the dump have more recently been joined by all manner of other neglected technological guidebooks – once essential to navigating screen media ecologies. As David Hesmondhalgh and Amanda Lotz observe in a recent article, from the 1950s to the 1980s television audiences gained access to programming schedules with the aid of newspaper listings and special publications, such as *TV Guide*. The subsequent rise of cable and satellite services reconfigured televisual interfaces from these linear navigation aids – printed channel listings – into electronic programme guides that were themselves navigable; eventually, these too were reconfigured into today's programme selection platforms, which are distributed not only across menus within devices, but also across multiple devices – televisions, computers, tablets, phones (Hesmondhalgh and Lotz 2020: 393). Television might now be navigated, not with a television guide that resembles a phonebook, but with a phone, the image on which itself offers a television in miniature. But television guides were in some sense designed for obsolescence: they were only a brief capture of the temporal onrush of programming, momentarily guiding the viewer's channel-hopping. Their replacements are inversely designed – to sustain audience attention, perpetually, through habitual use and integrated interfaces that reach television out into the domain of Wark's digitally enmeshed 'gamespace'.

Navigating the currents of online streaming, then, requires information-rich indexing tools that situate users in feedback loops beyond the television set. Writing of the spatial forms present in the fantasies of knowledge, Steven Connor notes the popularity of this navigation metaphor to describe 'moving through spaces of information, physical or virtual' (Connor 2019: 293). Since the ocean has 'little in the way of landmarks', 'one must always employ accessory grids of reference'; both seascape and mediascape are thus placed under 'the net of abstract knowledge' (293). The collection's final two chapters are concerned with such symbolic and infrastructural accessory grids for crossing between the expanse of knowledge and its abstract function of discoverability. In her essay, Rebecca Ross cuts across the functions of discoverability and digitisation in analysing Google's use of language – particularly, its conversion of writing into 'big data' projects. She considers what it might mean for this immense producer of spatial data to align its corporate identity with the alphabet, and the challenges studying such a move poses for situated media theory. Expanding the problem of writing to its own expansion in the ocean of data, Ross probes the limits of traditional media-theoretical vernaculars for writing about Google's extraction of the alphabet, which processes printed books into a haphazardly-coded database of 'de-situated fragments'.

While such cloud databases may seem to render media access placeless, they do so only by coordinating devices ever-more-efficiently, expanding their reach into and forcing their requirements onto every site where the user's attention may be held. The more one goes wireless, in other words, the more one relies on the affordances of a particular situation for effective interfacing – from Wi-Fi 'hotspots' to ergonomic seating. As Connor articulates it, the 'capacity to be ubiquitous or indifferent to place is concentrated in particular places' (Connor 2019: 299). Distributed media are in fact gatherers or collectors, since they attract people and devices to those densities where the network is smoothest, fastest, or cheapest to access. There is a certain symmetry here with the project of an essay collection, which itself seeks to assemble one such density in order to provoke intellectual contiguity through textual proximity, and thus to generate new branches of the network. *Articulating Media*'s gathering began in a particular institutional situation – a pair of conferences at the University of Cambridge – and finally, it re-gathers in these pages. During the second conference, Jussi Parikka posed the question: 'where does media theory happen?' If it happens in lecture rooms and classrooms, and in books like the one you hold – or have 'opened' on an electronic device anywhere Open Access can be accessed – then it happens in the folding of its own object, media, into the scene of its articulation. This articulation is thus a concentration of the 'media space' itself, one which navigates those institutional signs and situations that preface the expansion of media technologies from devices into epistemological figures and knowledge infrastructures.

Aptly, then, Parikka's essay here delves into a media archaeology of the British Library, gathering the media-theoretical fragments and concluding the collection. The contemporary infrastructural situations of data production and management are dialled into Richard Wright's 'Elastic System' artwork, the situation of which was the Library itself. 'An articulation of a thing or a meaning is always, at least partly', Parikka writes, 'already premised by the fact that a system articulated it to be discoverable.' Data transfer that is designed to rise to the surface involves an articulation that goes 'all the way down' – an infrastructure to structure the infrastructure, to bring it into the visibility that is its function. The book's final part thus presses into the terrain of data abstractions, while arguing collectively that these abstractions must be understood according to their enfolding of histories and temporalities, infrastructures and institutions. It is a well-worn trope that 'data' derives from the Latin for what is given or gifted, but today, Parikka suggests, what is given by data is not just information but the articulating property of those institutional situations in which it is held.

William Rathje's systematic sifting of urban garbage offered us an opening metaphor to articulate this volume's excavation, sorting, and scrutinising of forms of media and articulation. After decades of garbological investigation, he too reflected on the vernacular of landfills: not only 'vast composters' they are also 'vast mummifiers' (Rathje and Murphy 2001: 112) requiring the mediation of space and time. In a 2011 interview, Rathje reminisced that 'when you walk on a landfill, and one of those compactors or a garbage truck or anything drives within a hundred feet of you, the whole thing feels like you are standing on Jello. The whole thing shakes' (Lane 2011: 82). The wobbling landfill expressed the incomplete transaction of the merely thrown away into the truly wasted. Since 'part of the compaction process is to have the heavy machinery vehicles driving on the landfill', the cultural technique of mummification itself registered the industrial effort to make the landfill into a particular location. It was only after the Second World War that the U.S. Army brought their newly acquired landfill knowledge home and applied it to the widening expanse of commercial waste. For Rathje, the rise of landfills thus expresses the military's ability to standardise absolutely everything – even waste (Lane 2011: 81). Compacting garbage in this form was itself a compact process; it was localised and repeatable. The cultural technique of mummification produced not only the distinction between waste and useful object, but between errant litter and situated or contained refuse. Like other kinds of containers, landfills produced a particular sort of space – one that called out to be filled. And, as Rathje was forced to conclude, with exasperation: 'garbage expands to fill up the space that's provided for it' (81).

An essay collection is not quite a compaction or a mummification of media or thought. Its internal variety and divergences flow through many voices and objects of study. If readers will sometimes feel the result wobbling or shaking beneath their feet, then this should only indicate that the essential work of gathering is safely underway. They are asked to excuse the unstable ground, to press on as variety and divergence work to trace, interface, and situate the remarkable media effects of untimely compactions and timely resurgences. Such trembling is necessary to begin unearthing media's many forms of articulation, and to articulate media theory in some striking new poses.

Works Cited

Connor, Steven. 2019. *The Madness of Knowledge: On Wisdom, Ignorance, and Fantasies of Knowing*. London: Reaktion Books.

Ernst, Wolfgang. 2011. 'Media Archaeography: Method and Machine versus History and Narrative of Media'. In *Media Archaeology: Approaches, Applications, and Implications*, 239–255. London: University of California Press.

Foucault, Michel. 1972. *The Archaeology of Knowledge*. New York: Pantheon Books.

Galloway, Alexander R. 2012. *The Interface Effect*. Cambridge: Polity.

Geoghegan, Bernard Dionysius. 2011. 'From Information Theory to French Theory: Jakobson, Lévi-Strauss, and the Cybernetic Apparatus'. *Critical Inquiry* 38: 96–126.

Hesmondhalgh, David, and Amanda Lotz. 2020. 'Video Screen Interfaces as New Sites of Media Circulation Power'. *International Journal of Communication* 14: 386–409.

Huhtamo, Erkki, and Jussi Parikka. 2011. 'Introduction: An Archaeology of Media Archaeology'. In *Media Archaeology: Approaches, Applications, and Implications*, 1–21. London: University of California Press.

Kittler, Friedrich A. 1990. *Discourse Networks 1800/1900*, trans. Michael Metteer, with Chris Cullens. Stanford, CA: Stanford University Press.

Kittler, Friedrich A. 1999. *Gramophone, Film, Typewriter*, translated by Geoffrey Winthrop-Young and Michael Wutz. Stanford, CA: Stanford University Press.

Lane, Matthew R. 2011. 'A Conversation with William Rathje'. *Anthropology Now* 3: 78–83.

Liu, Lydia H. 2010. 'The Cybernetic Unconscious: Rethinking Lacan, Poe, and French Theory'. *Critical Inquiry* 36: 288–320.

Martin, Reinhold. 1998. 'The Organizational Complex: Cybernetics, Space, Discourse'. *Assemblage* 37: 102–27.

McLuhan, Marshall. 2005. *Understanding Media: The Extensions of Man*. London: Routledge.

Parikka, Jussi. 2012. *What is Media Archaeology?* Cambridge: Polity.

Pein, Corey. 2018. 'How to Get Rich Quick in Silicon Valley'. *The Guardian*, 17 April. https://www.theguardian.com/news/2018/apr/17/get-rich-quick-silicon-valley-startup-billionaire-techie.

Pryor, Sean, and David Trotter. 2016. 'Introduction'. In *Writing, Medium, Machine: Modern Technographies*, 7–17. London: Open Humanities Press.

Rathje, William, and Cullen Murphy. 2001. *Rubbish! The Archaeology of Garbage*. Tucson: University of Arizona Press.

Siegert, Bernhard. 2015. *Cultural Techniques: Grids, Filters, Doors, and Other Articulations of the Real*, translated by Geoffrey Winthrop-Young. New York: Fordham University Press.

Smith, Barbara Herrnstein. 2016. 'What Was "Close Reading"? A Century of Method in Literary Studies'. *The Minnesota Review* 87: 57–75.

Sterling, Bruce. 1992. *The Hacker Crackdown: Law and Disorder on the Electronic Frontier*. New York: Bantam Books.

Vismann, Cornelia. 2013. 'Cultural Techniques and Sovereignty'. *Theory, Culture & Society* 30: 83–93.

Wark, McKenzie. 2007. *Gamer Theory*. London: Harvard University Press.

Part I: Tracing Media

I

Narration Time, Switching Time, Given Time

BERNHARD SIEGERT

How and why do we historicise media?

Any writing of media history which is aware of its own conditions of possibility should ask how the writing of media history is affected by the media of history. In the wake of the Anthropocene debate and especially with reference to geological deep time one could witness in various places the emergence of a manner of referring to the practice of historians as 'excavating' (Parikka 2015: 30; Zimmerman 2008). Although Parikka has written about excavating rotten telegraph cables and electronic waste in the literal sense of the word, the main intention in using the term, I guess, is to point out a certain tension between archaeology and historiography.

Hence, as the idea of excavation as well as the concepts of media archaeology or media paleontology (Sterling 2006) seems to critically relate to the practice of historians, I would like to share some thoughts concerning the relationship between history and media. I am guided by two basic ideas. The first concerns the difference between historiography and genealogy in the Nietzschean sense. This brings up the question of relevance, which Jussi Parikka raised in an interview in 2010. The genealogical mode of media-historical research is guided by the question of what the relevance of excavating media might be. The danger, as Parikka has pointed out, is 'a curiosity cabinet way of doing media history that indeed is interesting, but does not necessarily reach out towards issues in politics, or even explicate how to bring in fresh theoretical perspectives' (Garnet and Parikka 2010). As Michel Foucault noted, genealogy stands in opposition to a historiographical method that asks for origins and developments, and which follows an inborn logic of perfection. I would not be even as polite as Parikka, who concedes that this way of doing history is interesting in itself. It is hard to find Heinrich von Stephan's *History of the Prussian Post Office* from 1859 interesting if you do not know how to turn that book into an explosive device.

Second, and more relevant here, I am guided by the idea that the concept of history which has been common in Europe since the end of the eighteenth century is not independent from 'media', whatever we mean by this or whatever was meant by the term 'media' in the past. Here, I draw on Reinhart Koselleck, whose numerous investigations of the historical semantics of the concept of history and of historical time-concepts have paved the way for metahistorical reflections on media history. But we have to go beyond Koselleck and relate his transcendental determinations to empirical media concepts, asking ourselves what changes are invoked by such a turn from the transcendental to the empirical.

I. Narration Time

Since early modern times, history has been based on a contract: whatever deserves the label 'historical' occurs in a format that is compatible with the medium in which history is narrated. *Quod non est in actis non est in mundo* ('What is not in records is not in the world') was the motto of Isabella of Castile, which Philipp II, her great grand-child, later made the maxim of his state (de Ferdinandy 1977: 32). It was not by chance that it was Spain, the first state in Europe to give its entire administration over to writing, that claimed the ontological power of data – what is registered in files – over the things that are and that were. Only that which is registered in files and recorded by archives can turn into experience and so become the basis for horizons of expectations. The baroque thought experiments on the 'Eternal Return of All Things' are based in principle on precisely this Spanish maxim, which makes bureaucracy rule over history (Fichant 1991: 130). Leibniz's '*Apokatastasis panton*' fragment, for instance, correlates past and future history with the media format of books, pages and lines as it begins with the number of all possible different books of limited volume. If we assume that the annual public history of the world can be written down in a book that contains one hundred million letters, then by consequence the different public histories will be finite and will start to repeat themselves one day (Leibniz 1921: 28; see Blumenberg 2003: 133–49). An analogous argument works for the history of individuals, too.

> If you would measure one year by ten thousand hours, ten thousand letters would suffice to narrate any hour in the life of any human being, that is one page of one hundred lines, each line calculated to consist of one hundred letters. [...] Hence, in order to write a book which contains the annalistic history of the entire human race in all details, the required number of letters would not have to exceed one hundred thousand million millions [in numbers: 100,000,000,000,000,000]. (Leibniz 1921: 29)

The precondition of such an argument is: everything that happens can also be narrated. However, Leibniz's aim is not to prove the Eternal Return. Rather, he argues that the infinitesimal calculus that he himself invented necessitates the assumption that there are and will always be imperceptibly small changes within the continuum of the world, changes which remains below the threshold of description of the medium of the book. 'There will always be imperceptible differences, which cannot be sufficiently signified in books' (28). Leibniz introduces a difference between the phenomena that can be linguistically articulated and written, and the Real, which persists in the small perceptions, but cannot be experienced consciously – and which therefore defies any historiographic narration (Blumenberg 2003: 141).

One can find an early notion of the 'media of history' in Friedrich Schiller's inaugural lecture, 'What is, and to What End Do We Study, Universal History?' However, and typical for his time, Schiller does not use the term 'media' to refer to writing but, in analogy to air and water, uses the word to refer to the medium of the orally passed-down lore: '*Von Munde zu Munde pflanzte sich eine solche Begebenheit [...] fort, und da sie durch Media ging, die verändert werden und verändern, so musste sie diese Veränderungen mit erleiden*' ('From mouth to mouth, such an event was transmitted [...] and since it passed through media which are changed, and do change, it too necessarily suffered these changes') (Schiller 1988: 266). Because the elements of oral speech, the sounds, suffer all the changes of the medium by which they are propagated, oral speech is not a medium of history. More precisely: there are no media of history. The notion that writing could be a *medium* was inconceivable for Schiller. History could only exist after it became independent from media in the old sense. Hence, Schiller links history and writing: '*Die lebendige Tradition oder die mündliche Sage ist daher eine sehr unzuverläßige Quelle für die Geschichte, daher sind alle Begebenheiten vor dem Gebrauche der Schrift für die Weltgeschichte so gut als verloren*' ('Living tradition, or the myth by word of mouth, is thus a highly unreliable source for history; all events prior to the use of the written word, therefore, are as good as lost to world history') (Schiller 1988: 266).

In Hegel, the contract between narrativity and history takes on the form of a back-coupling between Spirit and history: 'Universal History [...] is the exhibition of the divine, absolute development of Spirit in its highest forms – that gradation by which it attains its truth and consciousness of itself' (Hegel 2001: 69). Therefore, Hegel can only pitifully look back to Schiller, because Schiller had already pronounced, 'with the deeply melancholy conviction' (50), that the ideals which mankind proposes can never be realised. Schiller could only dream of a utopian future in which ideal and history might coalesce. For Hegel, by contrast, the process of history is nothing but the Universal Spirit making explicit its own nature. But Universal History initially pursues that purpose totally unconsciously, which is why the whole business of Universal History is nothing but rendering the Spirit conscious of itself (39). With this back-coupling Hegel is finally able to conceptualise history in media theoretical terms: 'In our language the term *History* [Geschichte] unites the objective with the subjective side, and denotes quite as much the *historiam rerum gestarum,* as the *res gestae* themselves; on the other hand it comprehends not less what has *happened,* than the *narration* of what has happened' (76). The fact that everything relevant which happens obeys the laws of representability in the form of narration is anything else but a happy coincidence: 'This union of the two meanings we must regard as of a higher order than mere outward accident; we must suppose historical narrations to have appeared contemporaneously with historical deeds and events; it is an internal vital principle common to both that produces them synchronously' (76).

Therefore, for Hegel, history begins with the appearance of states, where for Schiller history begins with the invention of writing. Only the State 'presents subject-matter that is not only adapted to the prose of History, but involves the production of such prose in the very progress of its own being' (76–77; translation modified). The State is subject and object of history at the same time because inasmuch as it requires 'formal commands and laws – comprehensive and universally binding prescriptions' it also produces 'a record [... of] intelligent, definite – and, in their results – lasting transactions and occurrences; on which Mnemosyne [...] is impelled to confer perpetuity' (77). The periods 'that were passed by nations before history was written among them – which may have been filled with wild revolutions, nomadic wanderings, and the strangest mutations – are on that very account destitute of *objective* history, because they present no *subjective* historical narration' (77; translation modified). In contrast to Schiller, the problem of lost historical narrations does not exist for Hegel: 'We need not suppose that the records of such periods have accidentally perished; rather, because they were not possible, do we find them wanting' (77). In other words: if some historical *record* has perished, it has not been an *historical* record.

At the beginning of the nineteenth century the semantics of history changed in a radical sense. What becomes visible in Schiller and terminates in Hegel is the discovery of history as such. As Reinhart Koselleck was able to demonstrate, history (*Geschichte*) had been a plural until the 1770s; around 1800 it became a collective singular. This collective singular again turns into a transcendental category, which conflates the condition of possible history with the condition of its possible knowledge. Since then, one has had to define (as Schiller did) the conditions by which 'history is brought to speech'. These conditions for Koselleck are categories that must exist in the 'life-world' (*Lebenswelt*) – perhaps the most critical term in this essay – i.e. 'experience' and 'expectation'. These categories are appropriate to thematise historical time, because they entangle past and future' (Koselleck 1989: 349–75).

Although Koselleck talks of 'experiences' and 'expectations' as 'the medium' in which history becomes concrete, he nevertheless does not mean by that term writing, or any other kind of technology of storing, transmitting, or processing data. Because of this media blindness we have to combine

Koselleck's historical hermeneutics with the systems theory of his colleague from Bielefeld, Niklas Luhmann. Luhmann's book on *The Reality of the Mass Media* begins with a sentence that can be read straight away as a full-frontal attack on Koselleck's media blindness: 'Whatever we know about our society, even about the world we live in, we know through mass media. This is not only true for our knowledge of society and history, but also for our knowledge of nature' (Luhmann 1996: 9). The point of the title of Luhmann's book, *Die Realität der Massenmedien*, is of course its ambiguity: the reality, which mass media are, is the same as the historical reality, which mass media produce. In this respect Luhmann is a true Hegelian. Mass media 'consist of their own operations. Printing happens. Broadcasts happen. Reading happens. Programs are received' (12). But, although Luhmann admits that 'the mode of operation' of technologies 'conditions and limits what is possible as mass communication' (13), he excludes the 'Materialities of Communication' from his notion of media – with explicit reference to the volume edited under that very same title by Hans Ulrich Gumbrecht and Karl Ludwig Pfeiffer, to which he himself had contributed (see Gumbrecht and Pfeiffer 1994). This is a self-exclusion which appears as bizarre as the exclusion of the materialities of communication from the concept of media appears to 'hardware oriented' media historians. 'Nevertheless we do not want to consider the mechanical or electronic interior life as operations that belong to the system of mass media' (Luhmann 1996: 13). What is more: 'While we exclude the technological apparatuses, the "Materialities of Communication", from the operations of communication, *because they are not communicated*, we include the reception which understands or misunderstands [*verstehender oder mißverstehender Empfang*]' (13; my emphasis). What Luhmann means by that is a reception that always already makes sense of what it receives. Only that which can be understood of what media communicate can be reality or history; in other words, that which addresses human consciousness.

Gumbrecht has recently reminded us that the temporal structure of consciousness undergirds understanding and communication, a structure which, according to Husserl, consists of 'retention' (a fraction of a second of memory) and 'protention' (a fraction of a second of anticipation). The entire problem of 'How to Historicise Media' boils down to the fact that the temporal structure of the materialities of communication in the digital age differs from the temporal structure of consciousness. What escapes understanding, what cannot be part of the *Lebenswelt*, life-world, is neither part of history nor of reality at all. Luhmann is not only a Hegelian, he is also a Leibnizian, if a negative one. For him the argument for the *Apokatastasis panton* (Universal Restitution) would have worked. He accepts the Leibnizian divide but decides to take the other side. Moreover: only the exclusion of the materialities of communication, only the exclusion of hardware operations, includes the 'reception which understands'. What became apparent between Leibniz and Luhmann is that experience – and hence history itself – has been limited to what, since Husserl, has been called *Lebenswelt*, life-world. Interestingly, Gumbrecht, as editor of the *Materialities of Communication* volume (which stressed the shortcoming of all theories of communication – or the humanities in general – which neglect the technological apparatuses), also seems to subscribe to this point of view, when he concedes, on the one hand, that there might be a kind of temporality which exists outside of human consciousness, but argues, on the other hand, that this temporality is irrelevant since the perception of the environment is always already affected by the temporal structure of consciousness (see Gumbrecht 2017). Gumbrecht still identifies environment with life-world, which is exactly what needs to be questioned today, as our environment is a 'computing environment', itself constituted by billions of hardware operations per second. For Koselleck, who uses the term *Lebenswelt* explicitly, the life-world describes the totality of experience and expectation, and therefore the possibility to thematise history (Koselleck 1989: 351). For Luhmann, the life-world is set under media conditions, but in his opinion the notion of the medium can be limited to what can be understood – that is, *to contents*. McLuhan, despite the title of his most notorious book, would be out. As would Kittler. Media history would consist of the history of all the content that was communicated by media. A history of hardware and how it determines understandability first of all does not and cannot exist, because it is not covered by the life-world, it does not enter the *Lebenswelt*.

Obviously, the radical limitations of Luhmannian media theory derive from the sub-clause: 'because they are not communicated' (i.e. the operations of communication are not communicated). They are not given. Media Archaeology as well as the Theory and History of Cultural Techniques take decidedly other and different positions with regard to this critical point. Media Archaeology draws the conclusion from Luhmann that all media history comes to an end as soon as the inner operations of media – in analogy to the small perceptions of Leibniz – are no longer understandable and hence no longer lend themselves to narration. The Theory of Cultural Techniques, on the other hand, questions the non-communicability of the inner operations, (a) with regard to the destination of that communication, and (b) with regard to what is communicated, i.e. reality or history. If, on the one hand, both Luhmann and Koselleck accept as a fact that the only subject of history is human consciousness, which has the ability to understand, the Theory of Cultural Techniques reckons with other non-human or unconscious receivers, who are able to process communications which cannot be understood. On the other hand, the Theory of Cultural Techniques presupposes that the non-communication of the inner operations of media is also somehow communicated insofar as it structures what is communicated. What constitutes the life-world – especially today – are billions and billions of hardware operations per second, which escape, but nevertheless format, our experience. We must become Leibnizians again.

II. Switching Time

History is a function of media, the history of media included. This is not a problem as long as we reduce media to the communications that run through it (to quote Luhmann again), that is: to its content. But it becomes a basic aporia of media history if we limit ourselves, as historians, not to the communications of media that we are able to experience within our mediatised life-world, but to the materialities of communication.

In the case of one of the earliest examples of media historiography in Germany, the Hegelian ideal that the *res narratae* are co-extensive with the *res gestae* could turn into reality. According to Johann Gottlob Immanuel Breitkopf's project of a monumental history of the art of printing, the sources of media history are identical with the medium of historiography. When Breitkopf published the plan for his history in 1779, his aim was to defend Gutenberg's right to the title of the original inventor of mass printing, against the illegitimate claims of nefarious Dutch, Belgian, and Italian authors. The history of the art of printing itself consisted in a narrativisation of antiquarian book catalogues. The book was at the same time the medium of the *res gestae* and of the *res narratae*.

The Hegelian concept that everything that is an historical fact happens under the transcendental condition that it can be narrated means that history becomes a collapse of the difference between *res gestae* and *res narratae*. This was informed by the fact that philosophy in Hegel's time refrained from explaining perception and ideas on the level of a theory of nerves and the brain, as had been the case in the days of Leibniz and Kant. Leibniz acknowledged that there is something that constitutes the primary qualities of perceptual data (colours and sounds) but which can never be experienced as such, i.e. the analogue noise of small perceptions. Kant identified the divide between given data and that which gives the data. On the one hand, Kant referred in his *Critique of Judgement* to the mathematician and physicist Leonhard Euler, accepting the theory that colours and sounds consist of 'sequential beats [*pulsus*] of the ether' or of 'the air concussed by sound' (Kant 1974: 140). But on the other hand, Kant could not continue to accept that the perception of colour and sound worked in such a way that 'the mind' would count these beats, which are in the case of sound between 16 and 16,000 per second, and trillions in the case of colours.

It is along the border of this divide between conscious sensory data and unconscious signal processing in the body that the humanities were established in the 19th century (Kittler 2006). While Hegel interpreted sensory data as cultural data on the level of natural language, Gustav Theodor Fechner, the founder of psychophysics, started to decode these cultural data on the basis of natural science. However, in order to discover facts like that of Fechner's law, which contains the physiological conditions of what can be consciously perceived, human beings had to be stripped of their humanity.

The test subjects (including the experimenters themselves) were subjected to conditions that excluded the use of natural language from the very beginning (Kittler 2006: 42). What Fechner's law states is that 'the amount of sensation is proportional to the logarithm of the stimulus, if that stimulus is referring to its threshold value' (Fechner 1907: 10, 12–13). The nature of what can be consciously perceived, and what is 'understandable', is that all understanding or misunderstanding is limited by a certain threshold value. As a result, philosophy could no longer claim that it was compatible with the results of psychophysical tests. Husserl's phenomenology was the first attempt to 'work around' that problem successfully by inventing the '*Lebenswelt*' as a philosophically autonomous category (Kittler 2006: 42).

In this life-world that humans inhabit no psychophysical facts exist. All cultural techniques, from perception to memory and thinking, are identical with their appearance or phenomenality; they are given by introspection. From this moment on the humanities could claim independence from scientific methods and the data that they produced. Relevant data – 'relevant' in the sense of 'relevant for the human being as an inhabitant of the life-world' – are given by the sensorial and intellectual faculties of the human being itself, i.e. are independent from the interior operations of media, physiological or technical. Heidegger's writings before the so-called *Kehre* derived the most rigorous consequences from this reduction of science to the life-world. In *Being and Time*, Heidegger did not deny the facts that had been produced by psychophysics and experimental psychology; but he reduced them to dependent variables of life-worldly experience.

> Hearkening, too, has the mode of being of a hearing that understands. 'Initially' we never hear noises and complexes of sound, but the creaking wagon, the motorcycle. We hear the column on the march, the north wind, the woodpecker tapping, the crackling fire (Heidegger 1996: 153).

In his 'The Origin of the Work of Art' he insisted again on the immediacy of a 'hearing that understands':

> In immediate perception, we never really perceive a throng of sensations, e.g. tones and noises. Rather, we hear the storm whistling in the chimney, the three-motored plane, the Mercedes which is immediately different from the Adler. Much closer to us than any sensation are the things themselves. In the house we hear the door slam – never acoustic sensations or mere noises. (Heidegger 1993: 151–2)

According to Heidegger ears that inhabit the life-world are born hermeneuts: they interpret not only human or natural languages, but also trade marks.

Hence, it is our so-called humanity that separates us from the real. This means that the real, the signal processing that is going on in the nerves, can only be short circuited with machines if the human being is excluded from this connection. It is here where Wolfgang Ernst's Media Archaeology ties in, and can in this perspective be seen as an ascetic exercise in transcending one's own humanity. Ernst's exercise allows humans to experience something that the *Dasein* is unable to experience, namely signals as such, because it always already interprets what it hears. In *Being and Time*, Heidegger adds that 'it requires a very artificial and complicated attitude in order to "hear" a "pure noise"' (Heidegger 1996: 153). In other words, it requires media which allow the subject to bypass its own hermeneutical automatisms.

That is in a nutshell the historical epistemology which stands behind Luhmann's conviction that the operations of communications, 'because they are not communicated', must be excluded from the system of mass media and, in consequence, from the reality of mass media. They are not communicated: we never hear acoustic sensations or noises, but always already meaning. The question is, whether we draw from this the conclusion with Husserl, Heidegger, Luhmann and the rest of the Humanities, that we should exclude hardware operations from the history of media, or whether we accept with Leibniz the fact that an ocean of operations, although the single waves it consists of are not communicated, formats the communications of the media. Claus Pias once wrote in a text, entitled 'Synthetic History', that *'Medien formatieren das, was sie bloß neutral aufzuzeichnen vorgeben und produzieren ihre je eigenen Limitationen und Ausschlüsse'* ('Media format precisely that which they pretend to only record in a neutral way and thereby produce their very special own limitations and exclusions') (Pias 2001: 182). In other words, because media are not communicated, data, which is communicated by digital media – be it symbolic, optical, or acoustical data – becomes communicable, formattable, compressible, scalable in the first place, and finally perhaps even understandable. It is the 'non-givenness' of the hardware operations which performs the act of giving. For this reason, everything that is narratable in digital technical media is no longer subjected to narration time, but to *given time*. Given time is the structure of life-worldly time, or historical time, respectively, which is produced by switching time, without the latter being communicated.

The aporia of narration time and narrated time (which is based on switching time) – the time of the *res narratae* of the media and the time of the *res gestae* of media – can neither be technically performed nor brought together by intellectual synthesis. Nevertheless, we can reflect on it by using a double perspective on one and the same thing.

Let us have a look at the original circuit diagram, which visualises the inner operations of the very first digital switching circuit, the 'Eccles-Jordan trigger' (fig. 1.1); today better known as 'flip-flop'. Basically, this is a digital

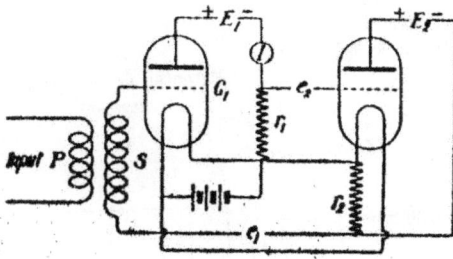

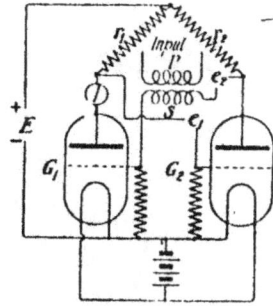

FIG. 1.   FIG. 2.

Figure 1.1: 'Eccles-Jordan trigger relay'. Eccles, William H., and F.W. Jordan. 1919. 'A Trigger Relay Utilising Three-Electrode Thermionic Vacuum Tubes'. *The Electrician* 83: 298.

memory capable of storing exactly one bit, one atom of the *Lebenswelt* so to speak, or one atom of history.

How do you communicate this? As a matter of fact, circuit diagrams like this one had to be communicated in narrative form in order to be accepted as patents. Hence, all patent applications had to include not only a diagram, but also a narration of what is going on in the represented circuit. The question is: does the narration of the interior operations communicate what the device communicates? All narration treats what it narrates as an analogue device because narration adheres to the temporal structure of consciousness. Thereby the very conditions of narrativity enable you or even force you – if you are an historian of electronic media – to realise that this diagram is part of the history of analogue media, i.e. of radio. After all, what we have here is basically a grid electrode which is modulated by a signal. The similarity with Edwin Armstrong's 'Audion' amplification circuit of 1913 is striking (fig. 1.2) (and Eccles and Jordan were fully aware of it [1919: 298]).

Armstrong himself described in his patent abstract this apparatus in terms of two coupled circuits: the grid circuit, connecting the aerial to the grid of the triode, and the wing (anode) circuit, connecting the anode of the tube, the battery, an autotransformer T and a telephone receiver. The two circuits are interlinked at the junction point O in such a way that a part of the output signal is coupled back to the input circuit, thereby causing an amplification of the feeble input signal. The principle is that of a relay: the feeble input signal that is applied to the grid is amplified by a feedback of the strong oscillations in the anode circuit. A highly unstable device, though: if the feedback became too strong the whole apparatus turned into an oscillator, that is, a transmitter. Armstrong (1914: 2; my emphasis) himself already noticed a pathological bias of his circuitry: 'Signals that are scarcely audible with the ordinary audion connection can be amplified to a point where they are too strong for, *and "paralyze" the most stable audions'*.

E. H. ARMSTRONG.
WIRELESS RECEIVING SYSTEM.
APPLICATION FILED OCT. 29, 1913.

1,113,149.

Patented Oct. 6, 1914.
3 SHEETS—SHEET 1.

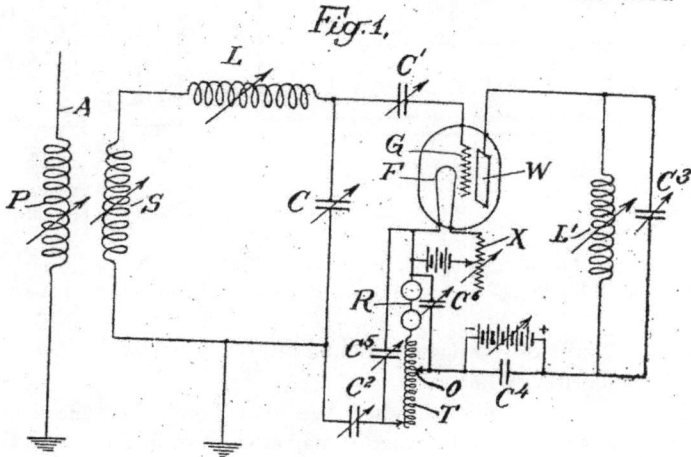

Figure 1.2: Edwin H. Armstrong: Wireless Receiving System, Specification of Letters Patent, Serial No. 797.947, United States Patent Office, Oct. 6, 1914 (A = Aerial, C = Capacitance, F = Filament, G = Grid, L = Inductance, O = ?, P = Primary, R = Receiver, S = Secondary, T = Transformer, W = Wing, X = ?)

In the Eccles-Jordan triggers, this pathological bias became the one and only purpose. What made the Armstrong amplifier dysfunctional – positive back-coupling – was used to trigger a second positive back-coupling which had the exact opposite effect. Because Eccles and Jordan used resistance back-coupling instead of inductances, the retroactive current applied to the grid is exactly opposite in phase to the original alternating current. The result is 'a one-stroke relay, which, when operated by a small triggering electrical impulse, undergoes great changes in regard to its electrical equilibrium, and then remains in the new condition until re-set' (Eccles and Jordan 1919: 298). What we have here, when we look only at the inner operations, are two Armstrong amplification circuits that paralyse each other. One circuit is driven by back-coupling to its maximum, the other, also by back-coupling, to its minimum. In this state, the entire device remains stable until a new input is introduced. If that happens the entire wonderful cross-coupled back-coupling would start again until the device arrives at the exact opposite state. As long as we narrate the inner operations the trigger relay appears as an entirely analogue device which with great speed arrives at a limit value of paralysis. But precisely these inner operations, which can be narrated, the trigger relay must not communicate in order to work as a digital device, which communicates what it has to say: one bit of information. As a device that produces a digital atom of a narration that is accessible in the life-world, it has to blackbox its mode of operation and to withdraw from perception the archaeology that is readable when we look at it as an analogue device. The archaeological level of media analysis contradicts the phenomenological level on which we have a digital object that is able to store exactly one atom of information, which can be communicated or narrated. The switching time of the digital device presupposes a withdrawal of media history in order to enable the communication of history. Either you know what the technology does, cut off from the data it communicates, or you know the data that it communicates, which excludes you from the Real of its operations. The symbolic is based on the absence of the Real.

Hence, the gap between machines and life-world, between experimental science and phenomenology, the nonhuman and the human, becomes constitutive for history (if history is taken in the modern sense that was established around 1800 as the unity of *res gestae* and *res narratae*).

III. Given Time

Eccles-Jordan trigger relays were used in the Colossus at Bletchley Park and in John von Neumann, John Mauchly and J. Presper Eckert's ENIAC. But the theoretical concepts of the analog and the digital had not yet been clarified at all at that time. They were discussed at length during the Macy Conferences between 1946 and 1953, the papers and protocols of which form the founding documents of cybernetics. The minutes of the discussion that followed a paper by the physiologist Ralph Gerard at the 1950 conference document the fundamental uncertainty of the participants concerning the question of whether the digital should be considered part of the Real or part of the Symbolic. While von Neumann as a mathematician clearly expressed that he was in no way interested in how the digital was implemented within the analogue Real, the neurophysiologists tried desperately to localise the digital within the Real, which explains why the physiologists and psychologists tended to identify the analog with the continuous and the digital with the discrete – and even, as did J.C.R. Licklider, demanded to replace the former with the latter (Pias 2003: 188).

Of special interest is Norbert Wiener's position. Wiener declared that the basis of the digital is the creation of a 'certain time of non-reality' (Pias 2003: 158), which lies between two stable states. Wiener's 'time of non-reality' corresponds exactly to Luhmann's 'what is not communicated [*was nicht mitgeteilt wird*]'. What is not communicated, or what must not be communicated, is the non-real: it absconds from Koselleck's 'space of experience' (1989: 354–9). It must not be communicated, because if it were, nothing would be communicated any more, nothing would be given in experience. Switching time must operate below the (Fechnerian) threshold of perception time and below the threshold of narration time, because otherwise narrated time (the *res gestae*) would dissolve into noise. Under the conditions of the digital, narrated time, history, is based upon declaring the switching time non-real, in which a bi-stable element – be it a neuron or a flip-flop – switches from one state (zero or nothing) to another (one or all), or as non-existent, as did the psychologist John Stroud: 'You treat them as if these transition states did not exist' (Pias 2003: 184). The Symbolic is based on the absence of the Real, once more. The schizophrenic ontology, which the Eccles-Jordan trigger performed, now becomes cybernetic theory. Switching time is Real only in the frequency domain *f*, but not in the time domain *t*. Phenomenological time is discrete since human consciousness exists in computing environments, notwithstanding the philosopher's clutching to the allegedly fundamental 'retention' and 'protention'. Whatever happens between two stable states escapes reality – and hence history.

Digital switching time appeared as given time in 1936 on the first pages of Claude Elwood Shannon's MIT master's thesis, titled 'A Symbolic Analysis of Relay and Switching Circuits'. Shannon tried to define, in the most elementary way, a switching circuit. Much in the spirit of the Eccles-Jordan-Trigger Shannon defined the Symbolic as the limiting value of the real. Between both terminals of a circuit, Shannon assumes, there is either infinite impedance or zero impedance. A variable X, which is a function of time, shall be named the 'hinderance' of the two-terminal circuit *a-b*. Zero designates the 'hinderance' of a closed circuit, and One, the 'hinderance' of an open circuit. The variable X can take as a function of time exactly two states: 'At any given time either $X = 0$ or $X = 1$' (Shannon 1936: 6).

What does that mean: 'At any given time'? 'At any given time' means not at any time, which is not given because it is withheld, withdrawn, or forbidden. If the life-world consists of atoms, which are given by the switching time of flip-flops or transistors, then it is constituted by the permanent ban on or withdrawal of the Real – in the sense of the impossible, of 'what is not communicated', of that which must not become part of the life-world of human consciousness, and is not part of a media theory that clings to the Hegelian idea of a transcendental solidarity between the human mind (or the Spirit) and what possibly can happen in history. But if media events are back-couplings between a history of media and the media of history, then media events are events of a writing that cannot be caught up by any writing of humans. This will be the price to pay for the permanent media-technological augmentation and reproduction of the life-world, which is more and more a ubiquitously computed life-world. Then 'to historicise media' would not mean the narration of the history of apparatuses; it would mean the narration of a writing of history, the switching times of which – in order to render this writing event-making – must be impossible to narrate. Not only must media history be the history of the first writing; it must be, and far more urgently, also the history of the last.

Works Cited

Armstrong, Edwin. 1914. Specification of Letters Patent No. 1,113,149, Patent Abstract. United States Patent Office.

Blumenberg, Hans. 2003. *Die Lesbarkeit der Welt*. Frankfurt am Main: Suhrkamp.

Breitkopf, Johann Gottlob Immanuel. 1779. *Über die Geschichte der Erfindung der Buchdruckerkunst: Bey Gelegenheit einiger neuern darüber geäußerten besondern Meynungen. Nebst vorläufigen Anzeige des Inhaltes seiner Geschichte der Erfindung der Buchdruckerkunst*. Leipzig: Breitkopf.

de Ferdinandy, Michael. 1977. *Philipp II.: Größe und Niedergang der spanischen Weltmacht*. Wiesbaden: Pressler.

Eccles, William H., and F.W. Jordan. 1919. 'A Trigger Relay Utilising Three-Electrode Thermionic Vacuum Tubes'. *The Electrician* 83: 298.

Fechner, Gustav Theodor. 1907. *Elemente der Psychophysik*, vol. II, 3rd ed. Leipzig: Breitkopf und Härtel.

Fichant, Michel. 1991. 'Plus Ultra'. In Gottfried Wilhelm Leibniz, *De l'horizon de la doctrine humaine, Apokatastasis panton (La Restitution Universelle)*. Paris: Librarie Philosophique J. Vrin.

Gumbrecht, Hans Ulrich, and Karl Ludwig Pfeiffer, ed. 1994. *Materialities of Communication*. Stanford: Stanford University Press.

Gumbrecht, Hans Ulrich. 2017. 'Zeitbegriffe in den Geisteswissenschaften heute', plenary address to the Austrian Academy of the Sciences, 23rd June 2017. https://www.oeaw.ac.at/fileadmin/NEWS/2018/PDF/Akademie_im_Dialog_10.pdf

Hegel, G.W.F. 1986. *Vorlesungen über die Philosophie der Geschichte*. Frankfurt am Main: Suhrkamp.

Hegel, G.W.F. 2001. *Lectures on the Philosophy of History*, translated by John Sibree. Kitchener, Ontario: Batoche Books.

Heidegger, Martin. 1993. 'The Origin of the Work of Art'. In *Basic Writings*, edited by David Farrell Krell, 139–202. San Francisco: Harper.

Heidegger, Martin. 1996. *Being and Time: A Translation of Sein und Zeit*, translated by Joan Stambaugh. Albany: State University of New York Press.

Hertz, Garnet, and Jussi Parikka. 2010. 'CTheory Interview: Archaeologies of Media Art'. *CTheory*, 1 April 2010. http://www.ctheory.net/articles.aspx?id=631.

Kant, Immanuel. 1974. *Kritik der Urteilskraft: Werkausgabe*, vol. X, edited by Wilhelm Weischedel. Frankfurt am Main: Suhrkamp.

Kittler, Friedrich. 2006. 'Thinking Colours and/or Machines'. *Theory, Culture & Society* 23: 39–50.

Koselleck, Reinhart. 1989. *Vergangene Zukunft. Zur Semantik geschichtlicher Zeiten*. Frankfurt am Main: Suhrkamp.

Leibniz, G.W. 1921. *Apokatastasis panton*. In Max Ettlinger, *Leibniz als Geschichtsphilosoph*, 27–34. Munich: Kösel and Pustet.

Luhmann, Niklas. 1996. *Die Realität der Massenmedien*, 2nd edn. Opladen: Westdeutscher Verlag.

Parikka, Jussi. 2015. *A Geology of Media*. Minneapolis: University of Minnesota Press.

Pias, Claus. 2001. 'Synthetic History'. *Archiv für Mediengeschichte* 1. https://www.uni-due.de/~bjoo63/texte/history.pdf

Pias, Claus, ed. 2003. *Cybernetics. The Macy Conferences 1946–1953*, vol. I. Zürich: diaphanes.

Schiller, Fredrich. 1789. *Was heißt und zu welchem Ende studiert man Universalgeschichte?* Inaugural Lecture, Jena; 26 May 1789. Jena: Akademische Buchhandlung.

Schiller, Friedrich. 1988. *Poet of Freedom*, vol. II, edited by William Wertz, trans. Caroline Stephan and Robert Trout. Washington, DC: Schiller Institute.

Shannon, Claude Elwood. 1936. 'A Symbolic Analysis of Relay and Switching Circuits'. MIT: M.A. thesis. https://dspace.mit.edu/bitstream/handle/1721.1/11173/34541425-MIT.pdf

Sterling, Bruce. 2006. 'Media Paleontology'. In *The Book of Imaginary Media: Excavating the Dream of the Ultimate Communication Medium*, edited by Eric Kluitenberg, 56–73. Amsterdam and Rotterdam: NAi.

Zimmerman, Virginia. 2008. *Excavating Victorians*. Albany: State University of New York Press.

2

'I Hear a New World': Moon Metaphors and Media Music

MELLE JAN KROMHOUT

Post-Human Music Theory

Ideas about the relation between the sound of music and the structure of the universe go back a long time. At least since the sixth century BC, when Pythagoras and his followers related the mathematical ratios of musical intervals on a monochord to the position of the seven heavily bodies – the five known planets, the sun, and the moon – such conceptual relations have played a role in Western music and music theory. They run from Plato and Aristotle in the fifth and fourth centuries BC, via Cicero's famous 'Dream of Scipio' in the first century BC and the influential work of Boethius in the sixth century AD, all the way to Johannes Kepler's seventeenth-century *Harmony of the World* and beyond. Even today, as Peter Pesic and Axel Volmar describe, the popular discourse on highly advanced string theory – often called a potential 'theory of everything' – frequently resorts to musical metaphors like the Harmony of the Spheres to convey the supposed elegance and symmetry of this late twentieth-century physical theory (Pesic and Volmar 2014).

In this chapter, I argue that the invention of technological sound media in the late-nineteenth century not only reiterated such longstanding ideas about the conceptual relation between music and the cosmos, but also added a new, less idealistic dimension to its discourse. In an essay commemorating the fortieth anniversary of the launch of the two Voyager spacecraft, each carrying a golden record containing – among other samples of human civilisation – a selection of music from across the globe, musicologists Alexander Rehding and Daniel Chua argue that the very existence of these records, as they travel beyond the borders of our solar system, raises questions about what an alien civilisation might possibly make of the sound data they contain. Taking such questions seriously and considering possible answers, they write, first requires a critical reconsideration of what defines sound, music, hearing, and listening down here on earth (Rehding and Chua 2017).

A similar shift away from an anthropocentric perspective informs the issues I want to address in this chapter: how can we think and write about music in the age of technological sound reproduction; or how should we deal with music that is not, or at least not entirely, produced by human beings, but by media-technological operations that are based on physical processes that often surpass and escape our sensory and mental capabilities? Specifically focusing on the use of the moon as a metaphor for sonic and musical practices, I argue that the changing conceptual relation between outer space and the sound of music can provide a way to think about these questions pertaining to the production and reception of sound and music beyond human experience. Firstly, because both technological sound (re)reproduction and the age of human space exploration are the products of advances in technical media; and secondly, because both challenge and transcend the borders of human perception and the physical limitations of life on earth.

'Technical media', Friedrich Kittler writes in 'Towards an Ontology of Media', 'are but the visible side of some moon whose dark side would be mathematics and physics' (Kittler 2009a: 29). For readers of Kittler's work, such references to classic rock group Pink Floyd and their 1973 blockbuster album *Dark Side of the Moon* quickly become a somewhat tiresome reminder of the media philosopher's intellectual coming-of-age in the 1960s. Kittler's almost monomaniacal love for the work of Pink Floyd notwithstanding, I want to argue that this idea of the dark side of the moon does provide a vivid figure for the otherness and inaccessibility of outer space, which in turn, through the logic of the metaphor, allows us to better apprehend the ways in which the operations of technical media shape the sound of music in the twentieth and twenty-first century.

Kittler's reading of Pink Floyd's *Dark Side of the Moon* allows us to think through the complex relations between music, media, and outer space. At various instances, he refers to post-war popular music – produced in the highly-mediatised environment of the music studio – as an 'other music' (*eine andere Musik*). As I explain more extensively elsewhere, this 'other music' can be described as the product of a gradual transition over the course of the nineteenth century from the symbolic grid of Western musical notation as the main mode of musical representation to the reign of media technologies that process physical sound signals directly (Kromhout 2021). This 'historical transition from intervals to frequencies, from a logic to a physics of sound', as Kittler calls it, not only caused a shift from symbolic representation to technical reproduction, but, more generally, a shift from a culture that conceived of (written) music as the pure, unmediated expression of the author's interiority to a culture in which the exteriority of physical sound itself – objective and impartial to subjective meaning – became the focal point of musical articulation (Kittler 1999: 24).

The earliest reference to this idea of an 'other music' is in an essay titled 'The God of Ears', first published in 1984, which closes with the following paragraph:

> The media explosion of our days [...] should not only be heard in the media-theoretical manner of its prophets. According to Marshall McLuhan, the message of the synthesizer is simply the synthesizer. But even if the darkness is so overwhelming that no dark side of the moon exists, electronic media might yet invoke a still darker presence (Kittler 2015: 16).

To me, this passage on the one hand emphasises how the physical materiality of sound, as it is produced, reproduced, shaped, and transmitted by the channels of technical media, became an increasingly important part of musical articulation. Because 'the message of the synthesizer is simply the synthesizer', sound media did away with the representational logic according to which musical sounds represent anything other or deeper than what they already are. On the other hand, however, by pointing to the 'still darker presence' invoked by electronic media, Kittler signals that the impact of technical media also goes beyond this clear-cut McLuhanian logic. By introducing the metaphor of the dark side of the moon, he prompts a move away from age-old imaginations in which sound, music, and cosmos are determined by some form of harmonic order. Instead, the 'still darker presence' suggests a media-theoretical update through which this conceptual relation between sound and space is no longer defined by an ideal of pure ratios and perfect order, but by the uncomfortable truth that human agency and sense-making have become increasingly arbitrary in the face of media-technological processes whose speed, scale, and complexity largely escape rational grasp and sensory perception.

When confronted with the physical materiality of sound waves, ideas of an ever-present-but-inaudible celestial harmony were replaced by the infinitesimal approximations of mathematical analysis. Although this analytical approach no longer allowed for dreams of complete symbolic representation, it did enable the technical reproduction of physical sounds. In the following, this transition is exemplified by a series of brief case studies that track the way in which the emerging relation between music and sound media is addressed through a changing metaphorical relation with the moon: from a bright and illuminating source of Romantic inspiration to the dark and foreign celestial body that modern science revealed it to be.

By the Light of the Moon

On 9 April 1860, French inventor Édouard-Léon Scott de Martinville sang a song into his *phonautograph*, a device he developed around 1857 to inscribe and visually represent physical sound waves (Feaster et. al. 2008). The idea behind the machine was ultimately to enable users to 'read' the waveforms as one would read conventional musical scores. The phonautograph could thus inscribe, but not acoustically reproduce, sound (Feaster 2010: 43). For more than one-and-a half centuries many of Scott's recordings 'lay silent and forgotten in venerable French institutions' (Feaster et. al. 2008). In 2008, however, a team of American researchers from the First Sounds project led by Patrick Feaster used digital scanning technologies to reconstruct the sound waves inscribed on the phonautograms and get them 'to speak and sing' for the first time (Feaster et. al. 2008).

Thanks to this procedure, which Feaster calls 'eduction,' we can now retroactively push the beginning of the age of technological sound reproduction back from the year Edison invented the phonograph (1877) to the late 1850s (Feaster 2010: 47). Although a number of older phonautograms exist, the oldest known recording of a human voice of which a reliable reconstruction could be made up to now is Scott's twenty-second rendition of 'Au clair de la lune' (by the light of the moon) (Feaster 2017):

Au clair de la lune,	By the light of the moon,
Mon ami Pierrot,	*My friend Pierrot,*
Prête-moi [...]	*Lend me* [...]

Listening to this reconstructed recording for the first time, even my over-sensitised twenty-first century ears were struck by this miracle of sound reproduction. The experience might not be unlike that of listeners in the earliest days of sound technology in the late-nineteenth century: the sheer amazement of hearing a sound that was heard before return exactly as it was; the disbelief that a fleeting moment in time can be captured and replayed. 'As long as a turntable is spinning or a CD is running', Kittler describes this experience in 'Lightning and Series – Event and Thunder', 'an old magic emerges despite the fading of years, hair and strength. Time stops, what more do hearts want?' (Kittler 2006: 68). Scott's reconstructed phonautogram recording might be the best illustration of this aspect of sound recording. Emerging from heavy layers of noise and static, the voice has an ethereal, ghostly quality; and exactly because of this crudeness, the almost incomprehensible twenty-second recording underlines how unbelievable this feedback loop between 1860 and the present remains. This is a voice singing to us from the past. This is, as Wolfgang Ernst calls it, a 'sonic time machine' (Ernst 2016).

However, only focusing on this 'magical' aspect of sound reproduction is a rather uncritical and limited interpretation of the technology, because it inherently invokes a *myth of perfect fidelity*: the idea that complete similitude between originals and copies is the ideal of any process of sound reproduction, and that this ideal can ultimately be achieved by preventing, eliminating, or maximally reducing every acoustic trace of the reproduction medium itself (Kromhout 2021). When one remains dazzled by the sheer magic of the sonic time machine, the history of technological sound reproduction seems to be a slow, but steady progression toward the ideal of entirely noiseless, purely transparent reproduction, ultimately culminating in the final collapse of the difference between original and copy, input and output. Such a perspective reduces the complexity of the physical processes that are performed by technical media to construct a symbolic model in which the idea of perfect reproduction seems, if not possible, at least conceivable.

Only with an idealised, infinitely precise device that is capable of unlimited accuracy, could input and output remain identical; only an idealised device captures an event and physically reproduces it in its totality. In *The Parasite*, Michel Serres describes the rationalist, positivist ideal that such a device presupposes:

> The philosophies about which I have just spoken come into play in this imaginary world where there is only one system and where this one system is constructed on only one norm or one principle. [...] They come into play in an ideal world of light and dark where there is only one exterior and one interior, only one shadow and one light. (Serres 1982: 69)

This clear-cut, unambiguous 'world of light and dark', he continues, would be a world 'without any atmosphere, where a screen separates space into black and white, furnace and glacier, blinding light and opaque night' (69). This is a world where no medium disrupts the perfect transmission of physical signals through space and time. Such a world does not exist anywhere on earth. Instead, Serres concludes, 'this imaginary world is on the moon' (69).

In Serres's account, then, perfect transmissions and perfect reproductions are not of this world. To imagine their possibility requires the idea of a place where earthly uncertainty and instability do not apply. It is this play of light and dark, of clarity and obscurity, of earthly atmosphere and heavenly vacuum, of symbolic representation and media technological reproduction that Scott's recording invokes as well. With the phonautograph, Scott wanted to circumvent the cumbersome symbolic system of music notation in favour of a more direct representation of sound that was supposed to make its intrinsic physical logic directly legible. The visual inscriptions produced by his device, however, revealed a physical complexity that cannot be interpreted like symbolical forms on paper, but only reproduced technologically. Processed by a combination of nineteenth-century and twenty-first-century technologies, the reproduction of Scott's own voice singing 'Au claire de la lune' unwittingly and presciently encapsulates this confrontation. By combining lyrics about moonlight – the quintessential Romantic symbol of inspiration for poets to write words on paper – with the uncannily *real* sound of Scott's voice, it highlights the distance between the unambiguous world of rationalist models and the fuzzy borders of the physical world.

Born from this confrontation between rational, scientific control over physical laws by means of technical media, and its continuous subversion by the fact that the physical processes inside our media black boxes escape such full control, Scott's phonautogram anticipated what Kittler calls the 'other music'. This duality of the concept, which came to light more and more clearly over the course of the nineteenth century, is further illustrated by the passage from Nietzsche's *Beyond Good and Evil* on which Kittler based his concept. Here, Nietzsche contrasts the music of Georges Bizet's *Carmen* with the later works of his former idol Richard Wagner. Unlike Wagner's 'Parsifal music', he writes, the music of Bizet incites a dream of

> a more profound, more powerful, perhaps more evil and more mysterious music, a supra-German music which does not fade away, turn yellow, and grow pale at the sight of the blue voluptuous sea and the brightness of the Mediterranean sky. (Nietzsche 2009: 173)

This more profound, powerful, evil, and mysterious music is marked by the duality between what Nietzsche calls 'southern' and 'northern', or lighter and darker tendencies. On the one hand, it showcases an Apollonian straightforward emphasis on form, clarity, and order. Indeed, such clarity and order also apply to sound and music inscribed on the hardware of technical media. Operating directly in physical reality, technological reproductions do not rely on imitations of nature, because they do not symbolically represent, but physically (re)produce what Kittler calls the inextricable and continuous 'noise source' called nature (Kittler 1997: 7). Hence, like Nietzsche's 'more profound, more powerful' music, technologically reproduced music does 'not fade away, turn yellow, and grow pale' in comparison to the sounds of the natural world. Instead, it can be repeated over and over again, always sounding, as Kittler puts it, 'just as rich, colourful, and bright as nature itself' (7).

On the other hand, however, the idea of the 'other music' runs counter to this Apollonian clarity and tends toward a darker, Dionysian side of Nietzsche's musical philosophy. Like a shadow cast by the white light of the moon, this Dionysian side emphasises the inherent irrepresentability and transience of the 'noise source called nature' that can never be reproduced in its entirety. Like the rational positivism of scientific models or symbolic representations, the colourful lucidity of an Apollonian order conceals the complexity and irregularity of the physical reality that lies underneath. 'Media', Kittler argues, 'are the visible sides [...] of a world that science invokes as the dark side of the moon' (Kittler 2012b: 383). Whereas the mathematical analysis of sound made its physical complexity symbolically representable, it did so by lumping it, as Serres puts it, 'under the numberless thickness of successive orders of integration' (Serres 1995: 20). Similarly, whereas Scott's phonautograph inscribed physical sound waves directly on paper without the detour of human symbolisation, the outcome of this procedure only more forcefully emphasises the irrepresentability of sound in any other form but itself.

Hence, because the complexity of physical sound can never be articulated in full, but can only be approximated mathematically or technologically, we can never completely determine or control what happens in between the input and output of our media systems. This is why, as Kittler stresses, in the case of sound media, the supposed 'reproduction' of sound is actually a case of 'production' (Kittler 2015: 8). Instead of *reproducing* input signals (with the ideal of perfect fidelity as the ultimate horizon) technical media always *produce* new signals, in all their irrepresentable complexity. The colourful and bright sounds of the 'other music' are produced by the physical operations of media that keep slipping from our control; and the clarity of the rationalist 'ideal world of light and dark' is always already negated by this 'darker presence' at the heart of the media, which is born from the mathematical operations that enabled the conceptualisation of such clarity in the first place. Because of the irrepressible presence of that which cannot be represented, perfect reproduction remains fundamentally impossible.

Music Machines

Taking Serres's 'imaginary world on the moon' and Kittler's metaphor of the dark side of the moon as my guide, I want to trace the emergence of this new musical sensibility throughout the music of the past 150 years. Step by step, the moon stopped being a light in the darkness and source of Romantic inspiration, because science and music increasingly shifted the attention to its dark side. In Kittler's analysis, even before the possibility of technological sound (re)production emerged, the first signs of the 'other music' had been apparent in the 'pure dynamics and pure acoustics' of Richard Wagner's music dramas in the second half of the nineteenth century (Kittler 1994: 224). Parallel to developments in physical acoustics and early sound technologies, he argues, Wagner was 'the first who truly wrote out the noise-source called nature' by acoustically approximating physical sounds in all their spectral and temporal complexity (Kittler 1997: 7). Instead of merely representing and imitating non-musical sounds through the language of music, Kittler writes, Wagner's singers and orchestra operate as 'a machine' that reproduces rather than representing the physical characteristics of natural sounds (7).

Although Wagner's acoustic reproductions are still transcribed in a written score that uses the Western diatonic scale to approximate natural sounds, his music machine, as Kittler sees it, reproduces the sounds of nature as closely as possible (Kittler 1997: 7). Most exemplary, in the opening of *Das Rheingold* (and thus the *Ring des Nibelungen*-opera cycle as a whole) 'all the harmonics of

E-flat appear one after the other, as if in a Fourier analysis; only the seventh is missing, because it cannot be played by European instruments' (Kittler 1999: 24). By composing this approximate Fourier series, Wagner was on par with the latest physical and psychoacoustic insights regarding the spectral nature of physical sound. The possibility of analysing the overtone structure of sounds using the Fourier Theorem was first suggested by Georg Simon Ohm in 1843 and confirmed and fully developed by Hermann von Helmholtz in *On the Sensations of Tone as a Physiological Basis for the Theory of Music*, published in 1863 (Kittler 1994: 96).

Earlier in the century, in the preliminary discourse to his *Analytical Theory of Heat*, physicist Jean-Baptiste Joseph Fourier wrote that he believed his mathematical theorem, which he formulated in the context of the analysis of heat propagation, would be applicable to the analysis of many other phenomena as well:

> It is recognised that the same principles regulate all the movements of the stars, their form, the inequalities of their courses, the equilibrium and the oscillations of the seas, the harmonic vibrations of air and sonorous bodies, the transmission of light, capillary actions, the undulations of fluids, in fine the most complex effects of all the natural forces (Fourier 2009: 1).

A few pages later, he remarked that 'if the order which is established in these phenomena could be grasped by our senses, it would produce in us an impression comparable to the sensation of musical sound (*resonance harmoniques*)' (Fourier 2009: 8). However, contrary to this confirmation of the ideal of natural harmony (from the movements of the stars to rhythm of the tides to the logic of sonic vibrations), the application of Fourier's theorem to the analysis of sound, first by Ohm and subsequently by Helmholtz, revealed a split between the idealised concept of harmonic organisation and the physical complexity of the phenomena at hand. Although Ohm was right to assume that complex sound waves can be represented through series of sine and cosine values, his famous dispute with acoustician August Seebeck – on the correct definition of a tone – already indicated that because this representational model does not take the temporal factor into account, Fourier analysis provides a rather one-sided representation of sound waves (Turner 1977).

The visual representation of sound by Scott's phonautograph reveals that the direct physical inscription of natural signals will not necessarily make them legible and opaque, but will instead only deepen the problem of grasping their full nature. The same ultimately goes for the Ohm-Helmholtz-model of sound based on Fourier's Theorem: although it suggests a comprehensive order, it does so only on the basis of a mathematical approximation that reduces the full complexity of the physical phenomenon. Hence, the materiality of sound as Helmholtz conceives does not reflect or articulate some deeper natural order or cosmic harmony. Instead, it 'foreshadows', as Veit Erlmann puts it in *Reason and Resonance*, a 'loss of absolute certainty and [...] the often invoked death of the subject' (Erlmann 2010: 270). Notably, Erlmann illustrates Helmholtz's lifelong attempt to reconcile his materialist scientific approach with a persisting believe in neo-Kantian idealism with a verse from Goethe's 'An den Mond' (To the Moon) that 'appears [...] in an "autobiographical sketch" in which Helmholtz, now at age seventy, reflected back on his life and career: *That which man had never known / Or had not thought out, / Through the labyrinth of mind / Wanders in the night'* (248).

Several decades later, in 1911, the composer Arnold Schoenberg closed his monumental *Harmonielehre* with the novel idea of 'tone-color melodies' or '*Klangfarbenmelodie*': organising musical material based on relations between tone colours instead of relations between pitches or the logic of harmonic progression. Carl Dahlhaus and Julia Kursell argue that, like Wagner's shift toward the materiality of sounds, Schoenberg's new concept might very well have been influenced by emerging theories on the physical nature of tone colours and the logic of overtone series (Dahlhaus 1987; Kursell 2013: 191–211). Prior to finishing his treatise on harmony, Schoenberg had already put the idea of *Klangfarbenmelodie* into practices in the third of his *Five Pieces for Orchestra*, Op. 16. 'The sound' of this piece, Kursell writes,

> changes without taking a detour through the domain of tonal relations. The role of the instruments is similar to that of the simple tones in Helmholtz's experimental synthesis. Their sounds merge into one, such that the components can no longer be recognized (Kursell 2013: 211).

Piece by piece, between Wagner and Schoenberg, the traditional organisational logic of tonal harmony made way for a stronger focus on the physical characteristics of individual sounds. So, as Kittler puts it, 'by the time Schoenberg, in 1910, produced the last analysis of harmony in the history of music, chords had turned into pure acoustics,' to be analysed, studied, pulled apart, and reconfigured into new sonic territories (Kittler 1999: 24).

In Schoenberg's case, Scott's moonlight also reappeared in *Pierrot Lunaire*, a melodrama based on the German adaptation of a set of poems by Belgian poet Albert Giraud. It was first performed in 1912, three years after the premiere of *Five Pieces for Orchestra* and one year after the publication of the *Harmonielehre*. Widely regarded as one of the high points of Schoenberg's freely atonal period prior to his formulation of the twelve-tone system, the expressionist *Sprechstimme* (literally, 'speaking voice') at the heart of the piece performs a reversal of traditional musical logic not unlike the *Klangfarbenmelodie* three years earlier. In *Pierrot Lunaire*, Phyllis Bryn-Julson and Paul Mathews write, 'Schoenberg wanted the *Sprechstimme* to sound primarily as the timbre of speech' (Bryn-Julson and Mathews 2009: 50). In contrast to the disembodied melodic purity of the classical singing voice, the *Sprechstimme*-technique takes the timbral, bodily materiality of the speaking voice as its focal point (Brinkman 2011: 153). Consequently, as Schoenberg himself remarked in a letter in 1912, both vocally and instrumentally, in *Pierrot Lunaire* 'the colours mean everything and the notes nothing' (Brinkman 2011: 141).

Significantly, this reversal is reflected in the lyrical content of the piece as well. Whereas in the first of its three sections, the moon is still very much the nineteenth-century symbol for expressive subjectivity and romantic interiority, the progression of Schoenberg's piece exemplifies, as Reinhold Brinkman describes in his essay on the evolution of the Pierrot-figure throughout the nineteenth century, the transformation of the romantically 'moon sick' Pierrot into 'a model of identification for the late artist of modernity, for the problematic state of subjectivity, for the crisis of identity and cohesion of the I' (Brinkman 2011: 154). As Brinkman cites Verlaine's early poem *Pierrot* (1868), which stands as an exemplary of this shift in character from Romantic poet to modernist artist: 'You are no longer the lunar dreamer of the past' (152).

Whilst meaningful words are traded in for pure sounds and tonal harmony makes way for sound colour melodies, the moon thus turns into a symbol for the end of the classical subject as well. Ferruccio Busoni, pianist, composer, and author of the proto-futurist manifesto 'Sketch of a New Esthetic of Music', describes *Pierrot Lunaire* as being 'assembled from crumbled ingredients from a big music machine' (Brinkman 2011: 157). Like Wagner's acoustic machine, this machine produces music about music: music that speaks not *through* but *of* sound. This is what Busoni's admirer Edgar Varèse would go on to call the 'liberation of sound' (Varèse 2004: 17).

Throughout his career, Varèse believed that the advance of electronic media would ultimately allow music to break free of its representational restraints to articulate 'an entirely new magic of sound' (Varèse 2004: 18). In 'Ionisation' – a piece for thirteen percussionists composed in 1929 and 1930 – Varèse used the wailing sounds of a siren: an instrument that about a century earlier had been one of the preferred devices to put new ideas regarding the nature of physical sound and the physiology of human hearing to the test, as it seamlessly glides from the highest to the lowest sonic register. The music of the future, Varèse predicted, would no longer be limited by the whimsicalities of musical performers and the necessity of notation, because it could be 'automatically put on a machine that will faithfully transmit the musical content to the listener' (18). Around the time he first formulated these thoughts in a lecture in Santa Fe in 1936, Varèse was working on a major composition that would go through various iterations and names from the 1930s to the 1950s: from *The One All Alone*, through *The Astronomer* to *Espace*. The piece ultimately remained unfinished, whilst portions of it were reworked into other compositions, but Varèse intended it to be the ultimate musical marriage between his interest in scientific and technological progress and his mystical ideas about the cosmos (Hering 2009: 154). As he put it in 1936:

> We have actually three dimensions in music, horizontal, vertical, and dynamic swelling or decreasing. I shall add a fourth, sound projection – that feeling that sound is leaving us with no hope of being reflected back, a feeling akin to that aroused by the beams of light sent forth by a powerful searchlight – for the ear as for the eye, that sense of projection, of a journey into space (Varèse 2004: 18).

Music becoming a journey into space; this is where the age of technical media truly takes hold of musical expression: 'the music of our century', Kittler writes as well, 'leaves earth or the living environment behind' (Kittler 2015: 13). As Scott unknowingly anticipated with his phonautogram in 1860, when it is no longer necessary to represent the sound of music symbolically, because it can be stored and reproduced directly, one no longer needs the light of the moon to provide inspiration from afar – a light in the darkness for poets to pour out their hearts on paper. Instead, while down on earth, electrical lighting began illuminating the cities, the moon became a destination in and of itself and its otherworldly terrain a source for new sounds and an 'other' music that is no longer limited by the earthly atmosphere and the restraints of human subjectivity. Still, when looking for the light, one tends to find shadows as well.

'I Hear a New World'

From writing in romantic moonlight to a journey to the dark side of the moon – I suggest this transition provides a figurative shorthand for the emergence of the 'other music' from the mid-nineteenth century onwards. In his 1934 composition *Ecuatorial*, Varèse used the ethereal sound of two newly invented theremins. The theremin, build by Russian inventor Lev Theremin (or Termen) in the late 1920s, was one of the first fully electrical musical instruments and thus perfectly suited for Varèse's new sound worlds. Indeed, James Wierzbicki writes that, after the Second World War, the theremin became the go-to instrument for 'depicting alien "Others" in Hollywood films', and to provide a sonic sense of outer space more generally (Wierzbicki 2014). As Trevor Pinch remarks as well, on Harry Ravel's 1947 album *Music out of the Moon*, conducted by Les Baxter, the

> eerie wailing sound of the Theremin, representing the sounds of space, contrasts with the sound of the earthbound human orchestra, which eventually conquers and dominates the sound of the aetherial and seductive space sirens (Pinch 2014).

As the title of this record shows, by 1947, it was no longer the light *of* the moon, but music *out of* the moon that stimulated the senses of human listeners. Ten years before the launch of the Sputnik and twenty-two years before Neil Armstrong set foot on the moon, the otherworldly sounds of electronic media had already begun to conjure otherworldly perspectives. Subsequently, in the 1950s and early '60s, the development of magnetic tape recording in combination with the invention of stereo and hi-fi sound equipment enabled big leaps in the creative flexibility of sound engineers, music producers, and recording artists. These ever more advanced technologies produced sounds that no longer imitated, but went beyond nature entirely: sounds that defied the laws of physics and became, in Kittler's words, 'completely free from the barriers that nature and acoustical physics impose on us' (Kittler 2005: 25).

Kittler, although a child of the post-war generation, was not all that excited by the revolutionary spirit of 1968. Instead of rallying on the street, he listened to music (Kittler 1992). Besides the acoustic machine of Richard Wagner, the young Kittler recognised a new musical sensibility in the howling feedback of Jimi Hendrix's guitar and the cosmic echoes and spatial effects of early Pink Floyd records. These were musical articulations that were no longer formed and communicated by means of the symbolic mode of musical notation, but shaped, produced, manipulated, and transmitted through sound itself – material, physical, real. Wagner's music had shown the first signs of this new sensibility, but the popular music of the 1960s truly established its reign. Produced in sound studios and pressed on records, music no longer holds the pretence of fixed meanings beyond or behind the sound itself. Idealistic and immaterial ideas of music as the expression of the author's soul are traded in for what Kittler calls a 'single and positive feedback between sound and the listener's ears' (Kittler 2015: 13).

Around 1967, Pink Floyd experimented with early sound-spatialisation technologies on stage, as well as tape manipulations, artificial reverberation, and extreme echo effects in the studio. On the band's debut album, *The Piper at the Gates of Dawn,* and especially on its opening song 'Astronomy Domine', frontman Syd Barrett thereby 'exposes rock 'n' roll to the domain of astronomy' (Kittler 2015: 5). About six years later, the band continued this astronomical legacy of their troubled co-founder and former leader, who left the band due to severe mental instability in 1968, in the form of the multimillion-copy-selling musical journey to the *Dark Side of the Moon.* However, Pink Floyd was not the first pop act to travel to the moon. In 1960, groundbreaking British record producer Joe Meek had already explored its terrain by writing, recording, and producing an album called *I Hear A New World.* From its enticing title to its strange and alienating music, this largely ignored record is the perfect illustration of the relation between lunar fantasies, sound technology, and an 'other music'.

By the time Meek began working on the project, he had already been involved in the production of a few hit records, either as sound engineer or producer. One of his earliest successes was the 'Bad Penny Blues', released in 1956 by jazz combo Humphrey Lyttelton and his Band (Cleveland 2015: 30). Otherwise a relatively unremarkable bluesy jazz tune, both Lyttelton and session's producer Dennis Preston recall how Meek's novel recording techniques made the song into a hit. During the sessions, Lyttelton describes, Meek 'over-recorded the drum brushes, and he also did something very peculiar by distorting the left hand of the piano' (30). He thereby created a sound that 'made a hit out of what would otherwise have been another track on a jazz EP. And it was purely a concept of sound' (30). Through this concept of sound, Preston remarks as well, Meek 'was anticipating the future [...]. Joe had a concept of sound I really and sincerely think was ten years ahead of its time' (49). His ear for sonic detail, combined with his willingness to experiment with the technology explains Meek's initial success, but also caused clashes with executives and colleagues at International Broadcasting Company (IBC), the studio where he worked. In 1957, after suffering depressive episodes because of the persistent harassment from superiors and colleagues over his homosexuality, he quit his job and ventured out on his own (Cleveland 2015: 42–43).

Although it is possible that some of the sessions for *I Hear A New World* took place at Lansdowne, the studio he and Preston subsequently built and ran, most of the recording was probably done at home (Cleveland 2015: 79). This was Meek's pet project, which he had dreamed about for years. He called it '"an outer space music fantasy" about life on the moon'. More elaborately, he described the record as

> a picture in music of what could be up there in outer space. I can already see and hear in my imagination from the studies I have made on outer space what wonderful new sights and sounds are in store for us. (Cleveland 2015: 74)

Experimenting with all the engineering tricks and sound effects that were available to him, Joe Meek's song suite about life on the moon committed these ideas about the wonderful sounds on the moon to magnetic tape, to be transported to the ears and brains of listeners around the world.

To bring it to life, he went, as one of his co-workers describes, 'pretty far out of his way' (Cleveland 2015: 78). The result is thirty-three minutes of spaced-out sound effects, heavy reverberation, eerie high-pitched vocals, technologically treated instrumentation, and the processed and manipulated sounds of, among other things,

> running water, bubbles blown through drinking straws, half-filled milk bottles being banged by spoons, the teeth of a comb dragged across the serrated edge of an ashtray, electrical circuits being shorted together, clockwork toys, the bog being

flushed, steel washers rattled together, heavy breathing being phased across the mics, vibrating cutlery, reversed tapes, a spot of radio interference, [and] some, well-quirky percussion (Cleveland 2015: 78).

To fully bring the lunar sound world to life, all these sounds were subsequently manipulated. Meek added early versions of echo and distortion effects. He compressed the dynamic range and equalised the sound spectrum in ways that would only become standard practice several years later. He also used 'extreme stereo-panning' (placing sounds in the far right or far left channel) and slowed down, sped up, and reversed the tape. Ultimately, many sounds on the record were 'so deeply immersed in reverb and echo as to be unrecognizable' (Cleveland 2015: 78). As a consequence, although the song structures and harmonic and melodic material on *I Hear A New World* are not groundbreaking or highly innovative, the record as a whole sounds like nothing else at that time; and it still comes across as fresh and exciting more than fifty years later.

Around the same time, similar techniques for processing sound were being explored and developed in the famous experimental sound studios for electronic and electroacoustic music in Cologne and Paris. In contrast to the highbrow avant-garde composers and highly trained engineers in those studios, however, Joe Meek did not have any formal compositional or musical training; even as engineer and record producer, he was largely an autodidact. Meek therefore was a true child of the media age: he just listened and experimented, because he realised that with recorded music, the sound itself is always primary. When you are working with technical media, the sounds are always already there, to be repeated, shaped, manipulated, changed, or discarded without passing through the additional symbolic layer of written notes on paper. Using all the technology at his disposal and fully embracing the serendipity of their physical operation, Joe Meek created a type of music that could only have been produced in the music studio. By committing the imaginary sounds of the moon to the material carrier of magnetic tape, he produced truly otherworldly music.

Black Boxes

Joe Meek called the machines he built himself — to realise the sound effects and manipulations he was after — his 'black boxes' (Cleveland 2015: 55). The name draws attention to the darker presence that his 'other music' invokes. In the age of technical media, it is no longer possible to rely on symbolic modes of representation that assume the possibility of total, rational control over mind and matter. Instead, following Claude Shannon and Warren Weaver's model of communication, when sound signals are fed to the input of black boxes and come out at the other end, what happens in the channels in-between always randomly affects their specific sonic contours, if ever so slightly. Despite ideals of an imaginary world of light and dark and the suggestion that the advance of technical media amounts to ever greater control over the laws of physics, the operations of black media boxes do not create perfect copies and infinitely exact representations. No matter how hard we try to get them to *re*produce reality, they continuously produce it anew.

In Kittler's analysis, the post-Pythagorean interpretation of the Harmony of the Spheres assumed an ideal cosmic order connecting planetary trajectories to musical harmony. This is how Plato, he writes, 'moved music and number to the heavens for almost 1600 years, where nobody heard and interrupted them' (Kittler 2009b: 144). Modern mathematics and modern acoustics, on the other hand, revealed this order to be nothing but a symbolic simplification of a more complex and noisier reality. As the physical implementation of mathematical sound analysis, technical media do not deal with symbolic clarity and cosmic harmony, but with this ungraspable complexity of physical signals itself. Like the Harmony of the Spheres, what Kittler calls the 'other music' articulates ideas of the universe, but no longer in the form of the symbolic order that determined Western musical cultures for centuries. Instead, as Pesic and Volmar write in their article on musical metaphors of string theory: 'the complexity and turbulence of the cosmos suggests a much noisier and more avant-garde 'symphony' [...]. Even if the possible vibrational states of the primal strings generate the properties of all the observable particles, their combined sound would be largely dissonant and aleatoric' (Pesic and Volmar 2014).

Hence, 'the universe that is simulated' in twentieth-century music studios, using space echoes, guitar feedback, artificial reverberation, and countless other sound effects, 'is an acoustic illusion beyond compare' (Kittler 1997: 9). By processing real, physical sounds signals through the black boxes of contemporary media, the 'other music' produced by musicians like Meek, Hendrix, or Pink Floyd does not care for traditional concepts of musical signification and representation. Although sound media offer ever more advanced possibilities for the technological production and reproduction of physical signals, the very processes that produce these signals in the first place remain beyond our control. The faster and the more detailed our media become, the more sharply they reveal this fundamental irrepresentability, this 'darker presence' at their heart. Consequently, it is no longer possible to assume an unambiguous relation between moonlit inspiration, the interiority of the artist and the expression thereof in the form of inherently meaningful works of art.

In contrast to these pre-technological ideals, the music of the media age is not based on the symbolic ordering processes carried out by human subjects. In Wagner's music dramas, the orchestra functions as a loud speaker *avant-la-lettre* to physically reproduce, and not represent, natural sounds as closely as possible, albeit still within the constraints of the Western diatonic system. In the early twentieth century, Schoenberg left this system behind and turned toward musicalising physical sound analysis in the form of *Klangfarbenmelodie* and *Sprechstimme*. With Varèse's music, which he called nothing but 'organized sound', the transformation was almost complete; but only in post-war sound studios did the 'other music' fully come into its own (Varèse 2004: 20).

As Abbey Road Studios-doorman Gerry O'Driscoll postulates at the very end of *The Dark Side of the Moon*, in the age of space exploration and the 'other music', 'there is no dark side of the moon, really; matter of fact, it's all dark', because we know very well – as he adds in the part of the quote that did not make the album – that 'the only thing that makes it look light is the sun' (Pink Floyd 2011; Harris 2005: 135). Similarly, the sonic identities produced by sound technologies take shape in black boxes that remain as unknown and foreign to us as the dark side of the moon. Because the channel always affects the output of the reproduction chain, sound media do not represent nor reproduce the so-called input signal. Instead, they produce what Kittler calls 'unforeseeable, unthinkable, unimaginable acoustic events' (Kittler 2013: 40). *Unforeseeable* in that they are as temporally contingent as any other sound; *unthinkable* in that they do not result from rational compositional choices; and *unimaginable* in that they do not require the creative impetus of human authors to impact listeners.

As was already evident from Scott's phonautograms, which revealed this irrepresentability of sound beyond the realm of the sonic itself, everything that happens in the black boxes along the recording chain maintains a level of contingency that defines the specificity of their output. 'Nothing and nobody', writes Kittler, 'limits the possibilities of electronic media. There is always, beyond any angst of delusion, the possibility of making different music' (Kittler 2015: 12). Such music is borne from the complete malleability of physical sound courtesy of the operations of technical media; but just as well from the fundamental ungraspability of its moment of production inside the black box itself. Hence, the sound of the 'other music' shines bright like the moon, but just as the moonlight is only a reflection of the sun, it invokes the much darker presence of its other side as well: 'I hear a new world / calling me / So strange and so real / Haunting me / How can I tell them / what's in store for me?' (Meek and The Blue Men 1991).

Acknowledgements

Many thanks to Melissa van Drie and Simon Ferdinand for their invaluable commentary, advice, and suggestions.

Works Cited

Brinkman, Reinhold. 2011. 'The Fool as Paradigm: Schönberg's *Pierrot Lunaire* and the Modern Artist'. In *Schönberg & Kandinsky: An Historic Encounter*, edited by Konrad Boehmer. New York: Routledge.

Bryn-Julson, Phyllis and Paul Mathews. 2009. *Inside* Pierrot Lunaire*: Performing the* Sprechstimme *in Schoenberg's Masterpiece*. Plymouth, UK: Scarecrow Press.

Cleveland, Barry. 2015. *Joe Meek's Bold Techniques*, second edition, version 3. Oakland, CA: ElevenEleven Music.

Dahlhaus, Carl. 1987. 'Schoenberg's Orchestral Piece Op16 No3 and the concept of *Klangfarbenmelodie*'. In *Schoenberg and the New Music*, translated by Derrick Puffett and Alfred Clayton. Cambridge: Cambridge University Press.

Erlmann, Veit. 2010. *Reason and Resonance: A History of Modern Aurality*. New York: Zone Books.

Ernst, Wolfgang. 2016. *Sonic Time Machines. Explicit Sound, Sirenic Voices, and Implicit Sonicity*. Amsterdam: Amsterdam University Press.

Feaster, Patrick. 2010. 'Édouard-Léon Scott de Martinville: An Annotated Discography'. *ARSC Journal* 41 (1): 43–82.

Feaster, Patrick. 2017. 'Speed-Correcting Phonautograms Without Pilot Tones'. *Griffonage-dot-com* (blog), December 10. https://griffonagedotcom.wordpress.com/2017/12/10/speed-correcting-phonautograms-without-pilot-tones.

Feaster, Patrick, David Giovannoni, Richard Martin and Meagan Hennessy. 2008. 'The Phonautograms of Édouard-Léon Scott de Martinville'. 2008. *First Sounds*. www.firstsounds.org/sounds/scott.php.

Fourier, Jean Baptiste Joseph. 2009a. *The Analytical Theory of Heat*, translated by Alexander Freeman. Cambridge: Cambridge University Press.

Harris, John. 2005. *The Dark Side of the Moon: The Making of the Pink Floyd Masterpiece*. Cambridge, MA: Da Capo Press.

Hering, Willem. 2009. 'The-One-All-Alone: Notes on *Espace* and *Désert*'. In *Varèse 360O*, edited by Willem Hering and Lieve Bertens. Amsterdam: Holland Festival.

Kittler, Friedrich. 1992. 'Wenn Die Freiheit Wirklich Existiert, Dann Soll Sie Doch Ausbrechen', interview by Rudolf Maresch, *Rudolf-maresch.de*, April 4. www.rudolf- maresch.de/interview/16.pdf.

Kittler, Friedrich. 1994. 'World-Breath: On Wagner's Media Technology'. In *Opera through Other Eyes*, edited by David J. Levin. Stanford: Stanford University Press.

Kittler, Friedrich. 1997. '"Vernehmen, Was Du Kannst": Über Neuzeitliche Musik als Akustische Täuschung'. *Neue Zeitschrift für Musik* 158: 4–9.

Kittler, Friedrich. 1999. *Gramophone, Film, Typewriter*, translated by Geoffrey Winthrop-Young and Michael Wutz. Stanford: Stanford University Press.

Kittler, Friedrich. 2005. 'Echoes; ein Prolog'. In *Hörstürze. Akustik und Gewalt im 20. Jahrhundert*, edited by Nicola Gess and Florian Schreiner. Würzburg: Königshausen & Neumann.

Kittler, Friedrich. 2006. 'Lightning and Series – Event and Thunder'. *Theory, Culture & Society* 23: 63–74.

Kittler, Friedrich. 2009a. 'Towards an Ontology of Media'. *Theory, Culture & Society* 26: 23–31.

Kittler, Friedrich. 2009b. *Musik und Mathematik*, vol. 1, part 2. München: Wilhelm Fink Verlag.

Kittler, Friedrich. 2012a. 'Dionysios Revisited: Vom Patriarchalischen Ideenhimmel und dem Reich der Irdischen Liebe. Friedrich Kittler im Gespräch mit Frank M. Raddatz'. In *Das Nahen der Götter Vorbereiten*. München: Wilhelm Fink Verlag.

Kittler, Friedrich. 2012b. 'The Cold Model of Structure', interview by Christoph Weinberg. *Cultural Politics* 8: 375–384.

Kittler, Friedrich. 2013. 'Bei Tanzmusik Kommt Es Einem in die Beine'. In *Auditive Medienkulturen. Techniken des Hörens und Praktiken der Klanggestaltung*, edited by Jens Schröter and Axel Vollmar. Bielefeld: Transcript.

Kittler, Friedrich. 2015. 'The God of Ears'. In *Kittler Now, Current Perspectives in Kittler Studies*, edited by Stephen Sale and Laura Salisbury. Cambridge: Polity Press.

Kromhout, Melle Jan. 2021. *The Logic of Filtering*. New York: Oxford University Press.

Kursell, Julia. 2013. 'Experiments on Tone Color in Music and Acoustics: Helmholtz, Schoenberg, and Klangfarbenmelodie'. *Osiris* 28: 191–211.

Meek, Joe and The Blue Men. 1991. 'I Hear A New World'. *I Hear A New World*, RPM Records.

Nietzsche, Friedrich. 2009. *Beyond Good and Evil: Prelude to a Philosophy of the Future*, translated by Ian Johnston. Arlington: Richer Resources Publications.

Pesic, Peter and Axel Volmar. 2014. 'Pythagorean Longings and Cosmic Symphonies: The Musical Rhetoric of String Theory and the Sonification of Particle Physics'. *Journal of Sonic Studies* 8. https://www.researchcatalogue.net/view/109371/109372/0/53.

Pinch, Trevor. 2014. 'Space is the Place: The Electronic Sounds of Inner and Outer Space'. *Journal of Sonic Studies* 8. https://www.researchcatalogue.net/view/108499/108500.

Floyd, Pink. 2011. 'Eclipse'. *The Dark Side of the Moon*, EMI.

Rehding, Alexander and Daniel Chua. 2017. 'Earth Music'. *Musicology Now*, 10 July. http://musicologynow.ams-net.org/2017/07/earth-music.html.

Serres, Michel. 1982. *The Parasite*, translated by Lawrence R. Schehr. Baltimore: John Hopkins University Press.

Serres, Michel. 1995. *Genesis*, translated by Geneviève James and James Nielson. Ann Arbor: University of Michigan Press.

Turner, R. Steven. 1977. 'The Ohm-Seebeck Dispute, Hermann Von Helmholtz, and the Origins of Physiological Acoustics'. *The British Journal for the History of Science* 10: 1–24.

Varèse, Edgard. 2004. 'The Liberation of Sound'. In *Audio Culture. Readings in Modern Music*, edited by Christoph Cox and Daniel Warner. New York: Continuum Group.

Wierzbicki, James. 2014. 'The Imagined Sounds of Outer Space'. *Journal of Sonic Studies* 8. https://www.researchcatalogue.net/view/109621/109622.

Winthrop-Young, Geoffrey. 2006. 'Implosion and Intoxication: Kittler, a German Classic, and Pink Floyd'. *Theory, Culture & Society* 23: 88.

3

The Statistical Order of Discourse: How Information Theory Encoded Industrial and Political Discipline

BERNARD GEOGHEGAN

All the repetition and incarnation of the sanitized term
information, with its cleansing cybernetic properties, cannot wash
away or obliterate the fundamentally dirty, semiotic, semantic,
discursive character of the media in their cultural dimensions.

(Hall 1989: 48)

In the 1934 chorus to his play *The Rock*, T.S. Eliot conjured visions of a modern world animated by the frenzy of invention but impoverished of meaning, asking the memorable question, 'Where is the knowledge we have lost in information?' Hardly a decade later Claude E. Shannon, an admiring reader of Eliot and a 29-year-old mathematician in the employ of the Bell Telephone Laboratories, offered an economical answer. Charged with evaluating the security of SIGSALY, an encrypted telephone connecting U. S. President Franklin Roosevelt with British Prime Minister Winston Churchill, Shannon proposed its analysis in terms of information transmitted (Rogers 1994). An informational analysis, such as he proposed, ignored many familiar features of human communications. 'A natural language such as English', he explained, 'can be studied from many points of view – lexicography, syntax, semantics, history, aesthetics, etc. The only properties of a language of interest in cryptography are statistical properties' (Shannon 1945: 10). As philology, grammar, poetics, and meaning receded from this mathematical view of language, a new measure of its consistency took shape: '"Knowledge" is thus identified with a set of propositions having associated probabilities. We are here at variance with the doctrine often assumed in philosophical studies which consider knowledge to be a set of propositions where are either true or false' (Shannon 1945: 3). The knowledge lost in information was that of truth and falsehood. In its stead emerged another value: the statistical order of discourse.

In 1948, Shannon published a heavily revised account of his memorandum, substituting the analysis of ciphers for a more general analysis of the codes used by communication engineers to compress messages into more economical signals. The resulting article, 'A Mathematical Theory of Communication', launched the new field of information theory, dedicated to the analysis of conditions governing the efficient and error-free transmission of signals in communication systems. Information named the statistical patterns of messages and provided a theoretical guide to how to economically match its encoded signal to its conveying infrastructure. Shannon's analysis of communications in terms of its statistical properties captured the mid-century scientific imagination. Along with his former professor and colleague Norbert Wiener's *Cybernetics: or, Control and Communication in the Animal and the Machine* published that same year, Shannon's information theory set in motion a new scientific strategy according to which the natural, cultural, and technical worlds could be described in terms of statistically patterned data flows. Armed with a toolbox of provocative concepts for describing these flows in terms of *code, entropy, senders, receivers, message, channel, signal, noise,* and *bits,* information theory permitted a far-reaching resignification of the natural and human sciences as so many provinces of a vast empire of *communications.* Interpreters applied Shannon's findings to the analysis of phenomena as diverse as human memory, schizophrenia, kinship, spoken language, the arts, and psychotherapy in informational terms.

The mid-century proliferation of communication theories across the sciences, including Wiener's cybernetics, represented the far-reaching generalisation of a new logic of the trace made possible by industrial communications. Yet the uniformity of that trace – the apparently universal and standard operations it disclosed within communications – also encouraged specific forms of power. Communication theories accommodated political, economic, and cultural communications to the discipline of a single 'signal economy'. Its search for an integrated and monopolistic management of communications served empires and nation-states positioned to command vast technoscientific infrastructures. It likewise consolidated a broader set of epistemological transformations that rested on the widespread circulation of statistics, printed numbers, and territorial ambitions of imperial, national, and colonial powers. These powers embraced a technoscientific strategy that downplayed the significance of origin, intention, and meaning in communications in favour of a new conception of the traces of the world in terms of immanent relations among discrete, serial, and standardised elements. Pushed to its logical extreme, it encouraged an uncanny conception of humans as the channels – rather than the authors – of data streams that subtended machines, nature, economics, and language. As human intentions waned, information theory positioned a new authority that rose to the fore, residing in the technoscientific authority of national and industrial infrastructure.

A Non-Arbitrary Economy of the Signifier

What exactly was information theory a theory of? A few words about the theory itself are in order. In the first instance, Shannon's account was an analysis of communications according to a very specific set of features. In the opening pages of 'The Mathematical Theory of Communication', he offered the following memorable explanation:

> The fundamental problem of communication is that of reproducing at one point either exactly or approximately a message selected at another point. Frequently the messages have meaning; that is, they refer to or are correlated according to some system with certain physical or conceptual entities. These semantic aspects of communication are irrelevant to the engineering problem. The significant aspect is that the actual message is one selected from a set of possible messages. The system must be designed to operate for each possible selection, not just the one which will actually be chosen since this is unknown at the time of design. (Shannon 1949: 3)

Admirers and critics of the theory have lavished attention on Shannon's exclusion of semantics, occasionally noting its passing resemblance to linguist Ferdinand de Saussure's remarks on the relative autonomy of linguistic representations from the concepts they represent. It would appear a common interest in the arbitrariness of signifiers inflects both theories. In and of itself, however, Shannon's distinction between the materiality of a representation and its meaning was the least remarkable aspect of his (and, for that matter, Saussure's) theory of the sign. This notion of the relative autonomy of language on the one hand and meaning on the other is a hallmark of language theories dating back at least to Aristotle (Weber 1976: 918). Shannon's point, in fact, was that signifiers were neither arbitrary nor, at least in relationship to one another, autonomous. Rather, they formed statistically determined chains available for infrastructural exploitation.

The significance of Shannon's exclusion of semantics rests upon its status as one element within a set of interrelated positions tied to industry, economy, and technocracy. How these claims fitted together to define an entire stance for communication had radical implications, particularly in how they enlisted longstanding philosophical notions – such as the gap between signifier and signified – in a new schema of industrial and technocratic governance. Whereas philosophers of language typically noted this gap to turn their attention towards the psychological problem of meaning or the linguistic problem of signification, Shannon's information theory – rather like Saussure's linguistics – focused on the differential relations among signifiers. Putting aside the contingency of any particular representation, he instead began asking into correlations among signs divorced from their underlying meaning.

Furthermore, whereas the relative autonomy of signifier and the signified often troubled Western thought, Shannon found in this division a promising opportunity to extract a commercial surplus, for example using short codes for frequently appearing signals. By way of example, Shannon cited the use in Morse code of shorter symbols to represent frequent letters such as 'e' and more involved symbols to represent infrequent letters such as 'q', 'x', and 'z'. The search for greater economy by telegraph firms prompted the development of such schemes. 'This idea', he noted, 'is carried still further in certain commercial codes where common words and phrases are represented by four- or five-letter code groups with a considerable saving in average time' (Shannon 1949: 10). By showing how to measure the frequencies of signs and calculate improved codes for their representation information theory rendered this gap between signifier and signified the basis for a new science of industrial economy. This approach represented a canny exploitation of a phenomenon that inspired apprehension among his predecessors in natural philosophy and hermeneutics.

Another aspect that bore on Shannon's exclusion of semantics was the presumption that communication concerned conveyance rather than expression. As the 'Mathematical Theory' put it, communication involved 'reproducing at one point either exactly or approximately a message selected at another point' (Shannon 1949: 3). This framed communication in terms of a problem of the reproduction rather than expression, communion, understanding, or correctness of a representation. Shannon's information theory treated communication as a problem of continuity, identity, and fidelity of messages, with particular emphasis on the reproduction of an already existing 'message'. The exclusion of meaning reflects, in part, the fact that expression and formulation of the message are already outside the system – i.e. 'selected at another point' – before being handed off to the communication system. Communication is first and foremost a problem of technical service, which a mathematical theory of communication analyses to better facilitate. In contrast to classical theories of rhetoric that often focused on the composition or interpretation of messages, Shannon's theory identified with its mythical emissary, the Greek god Hermes, and the practicalities of his successful delivery.

Key to Shannon's theory was its inclusiveness of messages beyond human expression. Whereas classical rhetoricians often restricted their analysis to the messages of humans, animals, or divinities, Shannon approached informational analysis from the perspective of a technician indifferently processing a far broader array of 'signals'. This inclusiveness partly reflects the rise of a technocratic world view that construed an ever-wider array of phenomena in terms of their amenability to machine-like governance. As we will consider in greater detail below, with the rise of industrial communications, the realm of the world's affairs subject to representation as signals appeared to multiply exponentially; engines, nerve impulses, electrical transformers, even stars in the sky seemed to be transmitting electrical and magnetic signals. 'Information is interpreted', Shannon explained in a summary paper, 'in its broadest sense to include the messages occurring in any of the standard communication media such as telegraphy, radio or television, the signals involved in electronic computing machines, servo-systems and other data-processing devices, and even the signals appearing in the nerve networks of animals and man' (Shannon 1972: 12.246B). Developing a theory that covered all these examples made sense for a firm such as Bell Labs, which had a hand in the design of computers, artillery weaponry, and other systems that frequently transmitted non-representational signals internal to a system, with no recourse to human consciousness or intentionality. As Shannon put it in the longer passage cited above, 'Frequently the messages have meaning; that is, they refer to or are correlated according to some system with certain physical or conceptual entities' (Shannon 1949: 3). Indeed, Shannon's own Ph.D. research on genetics affirmed the fact that even non-machinic systems often featured information-like relay. Only by excluding semantics could a general theory of information suitable to these diverse systems be devised.

A corollary to the rejection of communication was the expression of an interior in favour of a more technical conception of selection from pre-defined possibilities. A message was 'selected from a set of possible messages' whose possibilities were predefined by shared conventions. Communications as the expression of a free and autonomous, subjective interior gives way to communication as an articulation within a mathematically governed system of probabilities. Yet even the term 'selected' can lead one astray. For purposes of devising economical codes, these probabilities – rather than individual senders – played a major role in selection. By way of example Shannon cited the letters in standard written English, which he described as being around 50% redundant. 'This means that when we write English half of what we write is determined by the structure of the language and half is chosen freely' (Shannon 1949: 26). From the perspective of information theory, speakers of a language are playing something equivalent to Scrabble, wherein communication as creative expression must compromise with communication as correlating possible expressions with the availability of a set, with a pre-structured field of articulation. (Shannon makes a similar point in noting the bearing of redundancy on the composition of crossword puzzles, emphasising the problem of accommodating a mathematically determined string of signs to a predetermined field where articulation must accommodate the presence of intersecting strings [Shannon 1949: 26].) The 'source' of a message does not simply generate freely, according to a situation at hand; instead, it operates as a kind of algorithmic transformer, fixing stable possibilities between a virtual set and the possibilities for its enactment in a circumscribed real space. As any player of Scrabble (or solver of crosswords) knows, in these kind of language games meaning takes a backseat to the establishment of stable relations among constraints that structure what is and is not communicable.

Shannon's decision to use printed natural language for several key analyses further contributed to the powers of the theory to travel across disciplines. These analyses amounted to a new theory of authorship in terms of stochastics and were governed by an invisible infrastructure of industrial economy (Hookway 2014: 97). Applied to natural language, information theory suggested that English and other languages come equipped with their own systems for generating letters, words, phrases, and entire sentences. In a 1950 lecture at the Macy Conferences on Cybernetics, Shannon offered the following mathematical approximations of English, drawn from his 1948 theory of communication:

1. xfoml rxkhrjffjuj zlpwcfwkcyj ffjeyvkcqsghyd

2. ocro hli rgwr nmielwis eu ll nbnesebya th eei

3. on ie antsoutinys are t inctore st be s deamy achin d ilonasive tucoowe at teasonare fuso

4. in no ist lat whey cratict froure birs grocid pondenome of demonstures of the retagin is regiactiona of cre.

5. representing and speedily is an good apt or come can different natural here he the a in came the to of to expert gray come to furnishes the line message had be these.

6. the head and in frontal attack on an english writer that the character of this point is therefore another method for the letters that the time of who ever told the problem for an unexpected. (Shannon 2004: 249)

Where sample one offers randomly selected English characters, sample two employs statistical probability of specific letters, sample three and four extended statistical likelihood to include pairs and trigrams of letters, leading to a loose approximation of vowels and consonants. Five extends this method to words and six to pairs of words. Shannon remarked that these passages 'show that it is perhaps reasonable to represent English text as a time series produced by an involved stochastic process' (Shannon 2004: 249). Much like the transatlantic transmissions of SIGSALY, or for that matter television broadcasts, printed English appeared to have mathematically recurrent patterns that could – with the aid of sophisticated computing – be mapped out and predicted, either to economise transmissions or obscure their content.

With these economies in mind, Shannon's exclusion of semantics (and his corresponding descriptions of communication systems) becomes intelligible as industrial strategy. His theory of information proposed an orderliness of discourse corresponding to signal economies legible from within the dictates of industrial political economy directing the activities of Bell Labs and its sponsor American Telephone and Telegraph. These values found particularly concise expression in Shannon's celebrated schematic representation of communication that defined communication in terms of a *source* and *destination*, relaying a unilinear *message*, coded by a *transmitter* into a *signal* encountering potential *noise* as the *receiver* converted it back into a *message*. The only allowance for modifications, for example encoding, served the faithful delivery of a message according to conventions already specified by the techno-economic constraints of a physical infrastructure. Perhaps more than any other element of Shannon's theory, this diagram profoundly distorted analysis as it travelled to other disciplines (Schmitz 2018). Adapted in fields such as psychology, communication studies, and design, it imposed a peculiar new diagrammatic logic on objects of study. Communication as a social act and language as a social product, where individual utterances often resonate with polylogical circumstances of enunciation and reception, had no place within this schema. The theorist of information dealt, in the first instance, with the study of more or less unified and self-contained sources emitting unambiguous messages for reception by unified and self-contained receivers.

The upshot of these conditions is a subtle but profound dislocation of communications from sites of social struggle to structures of technocratic governance. Writing in the cryptography memo, Shannon explained: 'We consider a language, therefore, to be a stochastic (i.e. a statistical) process which generates a sequence of symbols according to some system of probabilities' (Shannon 1945: 11). Any ergodic source (i.e. an entity that emitted signals with statistical patterning) could be said to produce a language suitable for analysis by this theory. Genetic sequences, long-term patterns in stock prices, recurring weather patterns, and even behaviours themselves all assumed the properties of a language. It was not so much that these myriad sources mirrored human speech. On the contrary, human speech manifested the qualities of ergodic sources, a semblance that only emerged when conveyance was itself determined by mathematically governed reading- and writing-industrial machines. Shannon's claim that knowledge be 'identified with a set of propositions having associated probabilities' reflected the epistemic affordances of these machines, devised in the context of industrial conveyance and adapted to the exigencies of war.

From this new alignment of political, economic, and discursive orders emerged a seductive account of information in terms of statistically quantifiable selections. These selections indexed the possible states of a well-defined and standardised system of representation (i.e. code) and the infrastructure responsible for its transmission. With an eye to the most radical economic quantification, Shannon proposed measuring these selections in terms of the number of binary selections to produce a particular pattern. As a selection required more steps (and less predictable outcomes) the quantity of information increased. Highly unpredictable (i.e. disordered) signals were said to contain a greater rate of information. The greater the number of selections required to produce a signal, and the lower their likelihood, the higher their informational value. Shannon proposed to measure these selections on a base of two that corresponded to 'bits', a portmanteau from *binary digits*. Combined with a method of measuring the semi-predictable statistical likelihood (i.e. stochastics) of particular data series, Shannon's analysis permitted the development of codes that would abbreviate the most frequently appearing clusters of signs, thereby permitting economisation through the elimination of redundancy (or the selective deployment of redundancy to combat anticipated noise).

Paired with his schematic diagram, Shannon's theory mapped out an assembly line of functions that formed the basis for professional specialties and specialised instruments, corresponding to the most efficient distribution of labour among humans and machines. The coding schemas he theorised, for example, might represent human messages but – like SIGSALY – they depended on reading and writing machines to realise the coding techniques that his analysis suggested would increase efficiency. Actually, realisation of many of these schemes exceeded the computational power widely available in Shannon's day, and, except in specialised cases – for example, 1960s satellite transmissions – it was generally more economical to expand bandwidth than compress signal relay. Nonetheless, Shannon's theory offered a loose rubric for quantifying these kinds of trade-offs relevant to largescale industrial infrastructures of communication. His much-remarked exclusion of semantics from communications analysis enabled him to specify better the task of the AT&T: namely, the reliable transformation of speech into a well-defined commodity for management, distribution, and reproduction.

Statistics, Standardisation, and Governance

An indispensable element of Shannon's theory, and the wider communicative materialism to which it belonged, was a novel analytical framework enabled by the emergence of statistics, standardised industrial communications, and what historian of science Ian Hacking has termed 'the avalanche of printed numbers' (Hacking 1982). Functionaries and insurance adjusters shepherded forth the rise of statistical reason. As far back as the sixteenth century, when government administrators in London began tracking mortality rates to cope with the plague, natural philosophers began to discern uncannily stable patterns within these numbers (Hacking 1971: 211–12). In his 1662 tract *Natural and Political Observations Made upon the Bills of Mortality*, John Graunt noted with interest that factors such as the sex ratio, suicide rates, the lifespan among particular social groups, and the changing population of London could be predicted with relative reliability. It was as if a stable and invariable calculus subtended the most intimate individual decisions concerning life and death. Building on existing research into the probabilities of gambling, Jacob

Bernoulli's *Ars Conjectandi* or 'art of conjecturing' (published posthumously in 1713) introduced the weak law of large numbers which partially quantified how the size of a sample shaped the statistical inferences that could be drawn from it. Not one to reify the numerical significance, Bernoulli explained in a letter to Leibniz that his delay in publishing the work related, partly, to the need to elaborate on the most important aspect of his findings, that is, its 'civic, ethical and economical' import (Mattmüller 2014: 285). Insurance contracts, missing persons cases, detentions pending trials, and elections were among the events he suggested would be statistically predictable in this manner (Mattmüller 2014: 285). Bernoulli's work laid the foundations for modern actuarial practice by permitting diverse chance events to fall under the sway of rational economic analysis. Firms equipped with the infrastructure necessary to collect and analyse data on the problem at hand – fires, crashes, suicides, disease – could predictably distribute risk over large pools that met losses while earning reliable profits.

Servants of the British, American, French, Prussian and other Western states likewise embraced statistics (the term, statistics, literally denoted a 'science of the state'). State clerks devised everything from education policy to the control of disease to the structuring of state pensions and the appropriate measures to counter criminality by means of mathematical glosses of printed records. This closely bound statistics and record keeping to information processing: for example, the use of punched cards and mechanical computers to process census data, work that in the United States prompted statistician and census taker Herman Hollerith to found the Computing-Tabulating-Recording Company (later renamed IBM). A long-time employee of the U.S. Coast Survey, C.S. Peirce (better remembered for his 'theory of signs' that he dubbed 'semiotic') roundly rejected principles of determinism and championed statistical methods such as randomisation in scientific experiment (Hacking 1990: 200–15). Francis Galton, who established the statistics of regression and correlation, likewise developed innovative methods of photography to produce models of standard human bodies, invented the method of fingerprinting as a tool of criminology, spearheaded the use of questionnaires to survey human populations, and championed eugenic sciences. Allying these diverse methods was less a unified ideology than an uncanny knack for allying record keeping, mechanical reproduction, and mathematical analysis with the goals of managing an unwieldy modern state characterised by startling scale and diversity.

These developments laid the foundation for Russian mathematician Andrei Markov's discovery of 'Markov chains' and 'Markov processes' through the analysis of large series of printed literature, a key component of Shannon's later work on information. In a 1913 essay commemorating Bernoulli's work on the law of large numbers, Markov analysed 20,000 consecutive characters in the poem *Eugene Onegin* by Alexander Pushkin, showing a statistical regularity in the distribution of vowels throughout the text (Markov 2006).

He furthermore showed that these printed characters formed a special class of statistical series in which future states (i.e. letters) depended on current states. A subsequent study by Markov of 100,000 letters in *Childhood Years of Bagrov's Grandson* by Sergey T. Aksakoff confirmed these initial findings and demonstrated that such patterns operated independently of the author (Link 2006: 563). The significance of this finding for communications theory stemmed from its transposition of the law of large numbers from the mere study of a generic population and its probable distribution across the whole to events unfolding in time, where time and state of the system structured future events. Shannon would recognise that messages fitted this generic structure, where the appearance of one symbol or sign often conditioned the likelihood of future signs.

Equally importantly, Markov radicalised the divorce between signs and intentions. His analysis was decidedly not of speech or human expressions. As Saussure stressed in his celebrated and nearly contemporaneous lectures, conventional writing systems of the sort employed by Western culture have no fixed and natural relation to the spoken word. For the purposes of linguistics, the meaningful units of speech corresponded to other units, such as the phoneme (for Saussure) or grammars (for Chomsky). This seemed to contrast with the kinds of data systematically gathered by demographers or criminologists, who might maintain that their records of sexual ratios or fingerprints of criminals reflected traits embodied prior to their inscription. Markov, by contrast, measured the inscription itself, valuing it as a neutral data set that did not directly reflect either consciousness or language. His analysis extracted, from standard printed texts, the patterns that inhered in the relations of the signs themselves. Treating the very pinnacle of Russian literary culture, the poetry of Pushkin, in this manner dangled the tantalising prospect that nearly all artefacts of human culture were amenable to treatment as a kind of big data. All that was wanted was a sufficiently expansive system for capturing the results of human action and expression in stable and standardised data points for comparison to one another. The link to Bernoulli offered the fascinating prospect that such varied phenomena as human communications, mortality rates, and crop yields might operate according to common mathematical laws. These patterns belonged to the printed Russian itself. If purposefulness had anything to do with this account, it was that of Russian itself which employed human speakers as the medium for its statistically patterned expressions.

As the aforementioned examples suggest, mechanical reproduction acted as a technological a priori to the rise of informational analysis. With the rise of telegraphy, wire services, and fiction for the masses, a new set of determinations came to bear on language, and with it a new set of techniques – scientific and industrial – for extracting value from communications. The supple expressiveness of language and the terseness of industrial economy corresponded not merely to styles or expressiveness but also to compression schemes reflecting conditions of production. Charles Dickens and Ernest Hemingway are often cited as embodying these two extremes of signal economy: the former is said to have embellished his writing in response to periodical policies that paid freelancers by the word; the latter, it is said, developed his curt writing style from long habit of reporting for wire news services that encouraged compact prose due to high costs of turning in stories by transatlantic telegraphy. 'I had to quit being a correspondent', Hemingway once remarked. 'I was getting too fascinated by the lingo of the cable' (cited in Carey 2009: 163). According to the conventions of 'cablese' devised by news agencies, a story telegraphed by its correspondent as 'Wales Parisward smorning omnistation cheered stop he said friendship proFrance unceasing' could be translated by its recipient into 'The Prince of Wales left for Paris this morning. All those present at the station cheered him wildly. He said: "My friendship for France will always be with me"' ('Cablese' 1928: 45). Less important than how or if a particular medium impacted one or another author are the changing linguistic sensibilities to which these stories' widespread circulation attests. The submission of ever-greater classes of communications to the imperatives of machine inscription and industrial economy created a new sense of the materiality of writing itself.

Encoded within the standardized economy of signals were not only industrial but also political preferences. Semantics, intention, and origin slipped to the margin of intelligibility, replaced by a new axis of machinic patterning in service to infrastructural power. *The Handbook of the Telegraph* published in London in 1862 illustrates how telegraphy tended to turn all communications into standardised, quantifiable traces. The guide advises would-be telegraphic clerks that excellent handwriting and basic competency in mathematics (skills associated with creating a standardised and quantified chain of reproduction) will aid them in their quest to become communications professionals. Most remarkable is the one skill it identifies as *non-essential*: the ability to speak or understand the language being telegraphed. 'An "instrument clerk"', the manual explains, 'may be quite competent to telegraph or receive a dispatch in a foreign language and yet not understand a single world of it' (Bond 1862: 1). What matters is the ability to process discrete letters and patterns with machine-like efficiency and total indifference to the social, cultural, and geographic specificities of clients. These standardised traces, in turn, coincided with the standardisation of the nation along new infrastructural principles: 'Constant practice', the manual explained, 'enables [the telegraph clerk] to signal, *i. e.* to send and receive messages [...] with the rapidity of lightning, hence annihilating distance and concentrating time, conveying tidings of the movements of an army, the rise and fall of dynasties, or the desires of a peasant, with like facility and marvelous speed' (Bond 1862: 1). The creation of standardised technical traces in Morse code enacted an adequation not only of language, but also of nations, dynasties, and the very bodies of operators to industrial infrastructures (Bond 1862: 1). In telegraphy, the order of discourse, signal economy, and political economy coincided.

Bell Labs researchers consolidated these various trends into a single programme of communicative materialism. In 1924, while in the employ of AT&T's Department of Development and Research, Harry Nyquist published 'Certain Factors Affecting Telegraph Speed'; it outlined how to extract new efficiencies from the transmission of 'intelligence' through the improvement of coding and signal-shaping schemes. A leap forward in the analysis of coding schemes, Nyquist showed that '2.2 times as much intelligence' (i.e. messages) could be transmitted via telegraph simply by improving signal encoding mechanisms. In the 1928 essay 'Transmission of Information' his colleague Ralph Hartley of Bell Labs scientifically formalised the divorce between signal and semantics by discarding the anthropocentric term 'intelligence' in favour of the more technical term 'information' to describe the patterning of transmissions. Scrubbing away psychology allowed Hartley to offer a mathematical definition of information applicable to all serially patterned transmissions. He posited that

$$H = n \log s$$

wherein H designated the quantity of information associated with n selections and s stood for the total number of possible selections for a given symbol. This equation defined communication as the unidirectional transmission of serial and discrete messages from a predefined set of symbols. This definition was intuitive for telegraphy but, Hartley observed, 'when we attempt to extend this idea to other forms of communication certain generalizations need to be made' (Hartley 1928: 542). In analyses of media including telephony and television Hartley showed how communications could be construed as serial representations from a predetermined range of representational options. In one of his more peculiar examples of information structures (and the relative patterns and freedoms of such selection), Hartley asserted that 'in the sentence, "Apples are red", the first word eliminates other kinds of fruit and all other objects in general' (Hartley 1928: 536). In this analysis, spontaneous, ostensibly non-coded and natural language ceded its expressive kernel to the problem of machine-like structural selection among a fixed set of differential elements. The laws of economy and industrial standardisation dictated a new order of discourse.

Information as Infrastructural Power

Shannon refined and generalised the work of Nyquist in his 1948 two-part article 'A Mathematical Theory of Communication', published in *The Bell System Technical Journal*, the in-house research journal of Bell Labs. The journal boasted a small-but-influential audience of engineers, mathematicians, and physicists, mostly at industrial laboratories and research universities (Shannon 1948). Drawing on the work of Markov, he added demonstrations of the statistically predictable character of communication signals. He showed how redundancy and variable transmission rates could ensure error-free communications; specified the capacity of communication channels; identified information with entropy; and postulated that discrete alternating units represented in terms of bits offered the most economical measure of transmissions. Implicit in his analysis, and particularly his examples applied to natural language, were a wide range of assumptions embodied in the alliance of scientific, technical, and political methods that informed his analysis: that natural language itself could serve as a source of data interchangeable with other products of machine artifice; and that human communication could be explained in terms of the values of efficiency, schematic abstraction, formalisation, and iterability drawn from industrial research methods.

For the champions of technocracy, this notion of information often carried one meaning. Information was a neutral technical good, shorn of history, won by scientific and technological collaboration: an accumulation of data points vouchsafed by technological abundance, infinitely reproducible independent of its contexts, disclosing significance that transcended the intentions of its generating agents and conditions of capture. The practitioners of technocracy, however, saw a second set of implications to information theory. Here, information became the strategic exploitation of an infrastructure, adapted to select interests, and amenable to remote planning. While the meaning of individual messages was extrinsic to the engineering problem, the engineering problem itself was rife with political significance. These practitioners recognised in information theory a tool for the macro-governance of meaning-making, beyond the scope of the individual 'user'. Viewed in this light, information theory took on the trappings of a tool not only for the streamlining of industrial infrastructure but also for the streamlining of industrial ideology.

A more fundamental alignment of ideological, infrastructural, and epistemological unities underlay the promise of the Bell Labs' search for a universal-communications techniques. Much as the telegraphers' handbook recognised the close alliance of telegraphic infrastructure with the fate of dynasties, armies, and classes, the aptly named American Telephone & Telegraph viewed its research as part of a national political project. The search for more efficient and universal theories of communication belonged to that project. Bell Labs owed its existence to a government-sanctioned monopoly granted to American Telephone & Telegraph that underwrote (in the form of higher consumer prices) the vast expenses of maintaining its research activities. With a unified and integrated infrastructure, so the theory went, came a unified and integrated nation. AT&T celebrated outwardly this alliance of infrastructural, national, and epistemological unity: the entrance to Bell Labs headquarters in Manhattan featured a triumphant granite relief of the United States united by telegraph wires mounted above a headphone-wearing titan flanked by the message 'SERVICE TO THE NATION IN PEACE AND WAR'. The bold message celebrated the equation of national unity and infrastructural unity that justified the firm's existence. A similarly conceived 1920 public service advertisement for AT&T depicted Columbus and his men on a beach with the title, in bold, 'Our Many-Tongued Ancestors' (fig. 3.1). The text below explained that although the United States had been 'Born of the diverse nations of the earth', its inhabitants today realised the necessity for national unity under a single flag, a single purpose, and a single 'form of patriotic understanding'. It continued:

> A confusion of tongues makes for a confusion of ideas. Everything which goes toward the up-building and maintenance of a one language people makes for national strength and national progress. It is in such service that the Bell Telephone has played so vital a part. Its wires reach every corner of the country, making intimate, personal speech between all kinds of people a matter of constant occurrence. (American Telephone & Telegraph Company 1920: 715)

Echoing a common early twentieth-century theme, the advertisement imagined that the unified Bell System would cut through the linguistic and cultural differences of the nation to produce a single transcendent national people. Eliding a multiracial heritage that included, for example, native Americans or enslaved Africans, the Bell System positioned itself as the neo-colonial inheritor of a European ancestry. The technical infrastructure, as it were, fitted within a larger narrative of progress and improvement – i.e. the myth of a self-made American people built through ingenuity and hard-work – aligned with self-effacing European background. This promise fitted within a larger program of 'one policy, one system, universal service' that promised to meet the varied and diverse needs of the nation through a single unified system (fig. 3.2). In lieu of the historical and traditional inheritances said to lend European nation-states a natural unity springing from shared heritage, America would turn towards the power of communication infrastructures to produce unity that abolished conflict, difference, and the weight of history itself.

This political project formed an inextricable element in the signal economies and discursive orders elaborated by Bell Labs researchers. It spoke the words of Nyquist's analysis when he took the phrase 'United States' as the exemplar for comparing the efficiencies of encoding schemes. The definition of communication guiding information theory conflated economy and national strength. Shannon's favoured industrial standards of economy, efficiency, iterability, elegance, systematicity, formalism, and fidelity offered an account of communication as coincident with the maintenance of frictionless

Our Many-Tongued Ancestors

Born of the diverse nations of the earth, Americans appreciate, now more than ever before, the necessity for national unity; one flag, one purpose, one form of patriotic understanding.

A confusion of tongues makes for a confusion of ideas and principles. Everything which goes toward the up-building and maintenance of a one language people makes for national strength and national progress.

It is in such service that the Bell Telephone has played so vital a part. Its wires reach every corner of the country, making

intimate, personal speech between all kinds of people a matter of constant occurrence.

But the telephone is no interpreter. If its far reaching wires are to be effective, those who use them must speak the same language. The telephone best serves those who have become one with us in speech.

Yet uniformity of language is not enough from those who would gain the greatest good from the telephone, neither is financial support enough; for complete service makes essential true co-operation on the part of every subscriber.

AMERICAN TELEPHONE AND TELEGRAPH COMPANY
AND ASSOCIATED COMPANIES

One Policy   One System   Universal Service

Figure 3.1: 'Our Many-Tongued Ancestors' was one of dozens or more advertisements in the early decades of the twentieth century presenting AT&T and the Bell Telephone System infrastructure as a vehicle of cultural unification and homogenisation. American Telephone & Telegraph Company, 'Our Many-Tongued Ancestors', *The Survey* XLIII, no. 19 (6 March 1920): 715.

One Policy
One System
Universal Service

THAT the American public requires a telephone service that is universal is becoming plainer every day.

Now, while people are learning that the Bell service has a broad national scope and the flexibility to meet the ever varying needs of telephone users, they know little of how these results have been brought about. The keynote is found in the motto—"One policy, one system, universal service."

Behind this motto may be found the American Telephone and Telegraph Company—the so-called "parent" Bell Company.

A unified policy is obtained because the American Telephone and Telegraph Company has for one of its functions that of a holding company, which federates the associated companies and makes available for all what is accomplished by each.

As an important stockholder in the associated Bell companies, it assists them in financing their extensions, and it helps insure a sound and uniform financial policy.

A unified system is obtained because the American Telephone and Telegraph Company has for one of its functions the ownership and maintenance of the telephones used by the 4,000,000 subscribers of the associated companies.

In the development of the art, it originates, tests, improves and protects new appliances and secures economies in the purchase of supplies.

It provides a clearing - house of standardization and thus insures economy in the construction of equipment, lines and conduits, as well as in operating methods and legal work—in fact, in all the functions of the associated companies which are held in common.

Universal, comprehensive service is obtained because the American Telephone and Telegraph Company has among its other functions the construction and operation of long distance lines, which connect the systems of the associated companies into a unified and harmonious whole.

It establishes a single, instead of a divided, responsibility in inter-state connections, and a uniform system of operating and accounting; and secures a degree of efficiency in both local and long distance service that no association of independent neighboring companies could obtain.

Hence it can be seen that the American Telephone and Telegraph Company is the active agency for securing *one policy, one system,* and *universal service*—the three factors which have made the telephone service of the United States superior to that of any other country.

American Telephone & Telegraph Company

Figure 3.2: American Telephone & Telegraph Company, 'One policy, one system, universal service', *American Home and Gardens* (November 1908): xii.

exchange among elements in a technological collective. Struggle, to the extent that it appeared within Shannon's account of information, corresponded to an impersonal confrontation between the efficacy of a system and the natural forces of noise and disorder. Information, in turn, embodied these values, displacing alternate values of communication such as inclusiveness of parties, evocativeness of significance, meaningfulness or expressivity, adequacy to a situation, and historical situatedness. In the initial wartime memorandum Shannon had acknowledged as much with his aforementioned remark that he bracketed traditional criteria for analysing communications, including 'lexicography, syntax, semantics, history, aesthetics, etc.' (Shannon 1945: 10). Concepts introduced in their stead, such as redundancy, code, information, and entropy, emptied communications of historical struggle in favour of functionalist economic values. Individual subjective expression ceded ground to statistical relations subtending mathematical sets of possible messages available to senders.

This political subtext to the order of informatic discourse became manifest as it circulated outside narrow engineering contexts. The schemes employed to forge unity in the nation by means of communication infrastructure became elements in the forging of epistemological unities among researchers and peoples of diverse stripes. 'While the central results are chiefly of interest to communication engineers', Shannon remarked in a 1950s talk he gave on information theory, 'some of the key concepts have been adopted and found useful in such fields as psychology, linguistics, and the like' (Shannon ca. 1954: 1). By recasting familiar terms such as communication, code, signal, message, entropy, and bit in accordance with the dictates of what he termed 'the engineering problem', information theory invited broad and often creative application beyond the confines of industrial engineering. This resulted in new relays across the disciplines: Shannon's close friend and long-time supervisor, John R. Pierce of Bell Labs, once wrote that thanks to information theory 'engineers, psychologists and linguists can, at their best, talk a common language and understand what the other is saying' (Pierce 1957: n. p.). This was true, so long as communication engineering defined the terminology and framework of the conversation. Understanding and commonality rested, in this sense, on the unquestioned acceptance of the concepts of communication engineering as a neutral interdisciplinary medium of exchange.

The political connotations became even more marked as engineering theories of communication became social theories of communication. In his 1955 essay 'How Communication Works' Wilbur Schramm, one of the founders of communication studies, explained how information theory could be adapted for social scientific use. The essay developed from his work for the bureau of U.S. international propaganda, the United States Information Agency, following Schramm's communications research for the U.S. military in the Korean conflict. In it he argued that: 'It will be easier to see how mass communication works if we first look at the communication process in general.' He offered up Shannon's model as a stand-in for communication writ large: 'Communication always requires at least three elements – the source, the message, and the destination' (Schramm 1954: 3). Following a quick gloss on Shannon's diagram and general remarks on coding and statistical predictability, Schramm remarked that 'Perhaps, the most important thing about such a system is one we have been talking about all too glibly – the fact that the receiver and sender must be in tune. This is clear enough in the case of a radio transmitter and receiver, but somewhat more complicated when it means that a human receiver must be able to understand a human sender' (Schramm 1954: 5–6). He proposed to account for this by adding two intersecting elements to Shannon's diagram, titled 'field of experience', that referred to the coordination of meaning between sender and receiver. 'If we have never learned any Russian, we can neither code nor decode in that language. If an African tribesman has never seen or heard of an airplane, he can only decode the sight of a plane in terms of whatever experience he has had. The plane may seem to him to be a bird, and the aviator a god borne on wings' (6). Conceived as a tool of social influence, the task of coding took on the political project of bringing linguistic and racial others into alignment with the dominant schema conceived by communicators implicitly thought of as white, American, and English speaking. Elaborations in the field of communication studies by David K. Berlo gradually erased these historical and cultural specifics of the model by identifying the sender/receiver model with biology, behaviourism, and the human sensorium. This lent the diagram a peculiar double-inflection characteristic of communications studies more widely, as at once a situated tool of power clearly aligned with particular infrastructures and operators, yet advertised as an unmarked universality that resolved the differences between biology, technology, and culture.

In the popularisation of information theory, the identification of neutral, unmarked technical terms with identity continued at the level of gender, which often assigned to 'senders' the non-innocent status of men imposing their will on impressionable female receivers. In a commentary that appeared in the republication of Shannon's article as the 1949 book *The Mathematical Theory of Communication*, Weaver explained the non-semantic basis of the theory in terms of the gendered division of labour in telegraphy: 'An engineering communication theory is just like a very proper and discreet girl accepting your telegram. She pays no attention to the meaning, whether it be sad, or joyous, or embarrassing. But she must be prepared to deal with all that come to her desk' (Weaver 1949: 116). In another work on the closely-related field of servomechanisms and control theory (fields where Shannon refined information theory during the war), Weaver wrote: 'The control art is an old one. With the broadest definition, it is a very ancient art; for one supposes that if Adam wished to control Eve's vocal output, he had simple mechanisms, such as a well-balanced club, with which he doubtless brought it down a goodly number of decibels' (Weaver quoted in White 2015: 2). In a widely circulated film sponsored by IBM, Charles and Ray Eames (1953) explored the problem of noise and redundancy through the discussion of the message 'I love you', embodied through still shots of what seem to be a man's lips and a woman's ear, of a man kissing a woman, and of a man whispering in a woman's ear. (In another scene, the same formula is transposed onto the buying and selling of stocks by telegraphy, as if to hint at the economic exigencies anchoring the schema.) Variously identifying men with sending and women with receiving (or conveying) messages, these popularising glosses hinted at the gendered conditions governing work inside the Bell System and its reinterpretation for widespread application across the sciences.

Early interpretations of information theory such as these disrupted the careful suspension of semantics enacted by Shannon, providing hints at the meaning-rich order of science, politics, and sociality that drew such distinctions. Far from eliminating messy cultural factors from the field of communication, the postwar boom in information theory shifted these factors to unmarked technical structures. In a move with profound implications for cultural and ideological critique, it embodied the values of the system in an impersonal infrastructure of production while shifting analytical focus to the circulation of unmarked data within this system. As information appeared depersonalised and desubjectivised, its regularity and order – and its potential critique – now shifted to another axis. Standing on the shoulders of actuarial adjustors and census takers, as well as their analytics and their instruments, information theory authorised the analyst to consider communication in terms of a new set of structural and statistical determinations: systems over statements, patterns over meaning, combinatorics over authorship, relay over articulation, conveyance over composition, reproduction over interpretation, infrastructures over individuals – and ultimately the valorisation of fidelity to an original message over critical and contested reception of that message. As political ideology, information theory reframed analysis in these technocratic terms – as if human actions, intentions, and encounters were incidental data in an ensemble of relations subtended by bits and codes. In so doing, it legitimated a new mode of expertise that rendered human action intelligible in terms of relay, exchange, codes, and statistics.

Works Cited

'Cablese'. 1928. *TIME* (March 12): 45.

American Telephone & Telegraph Company. 1908. 'One policy, one system, universal service'. *American Home and Gardens* (November): xii.

American Telephone & Telegraph Company. 1920. 'Our Many-Tongued Ancestors'. *The Survey* XLIII, no. 19 (March 6): 715.

Berlo, David K. 1960. *The Process of Communication: An Introduction to Theory and Practice*. New York: Holt, Rinehart and Wilson.

Bond, R. 1862. *The Handbook of the Telegraph, Being a Manual of Telegraphy, Telegraph Clerks' Remembrancer, and Guide to Candidates for Employment in the Telegraph Service*. London: Virtue Brothers & Co.

Carey, James W. 2009. 'Technology and Ideology: The Case of the Telegraph'. In *Communication as Culture: Essays on Media and Society*, 201–30. New York: Routledge.

Eames, Ray and Charles Eames. 1953. *A Communication Primer*. https://archive.org/details/communications_primer.

Hacking, Ian. 1971. 'Jacques Bernoulli's Art of Conjecturing'. *British Journal for the Philosophy of Science* 22: 209–29.

Hacking, Ian. 1982. 'Biopower and the Avalanche of Printed Numbers'. *Humanities in Society* 5: 279–95.

Hacking, Ian. 1990. *The Taming of Chance*. Cambridge: Cambridge University Press.

Hall, Stuart. 1989. 'Ideology and Communications Theory'. In *Rethinking Communication*, vol. 1, edited by Brenda Dervin, Lawrence Grossberg, Barbara J. O'Keefe, and Ellen Wartella, 40–52. London: SAGE.

Hartley, Ralph V. 1928. 'Transmission of Information'. *Bell System Technical Journal* 7: 535–63.

Hookway, Branden. 2014. *Interface*. Cambridge, MA: MIT Press.

Link, David. 2006. 'Chains to the West: Markov's Theory of Connected Events and Its Transmission to Western Europe'. *Science in Context* 19: 561–89.

Markov, A.A. 2006. 'An Example of Statistical Investigation of the Text *Eugene Onegin* Concerning the Connection of Samples in Chains'. *Science in Context* 19: 591–600.

Mattmüller, Martin. 2014. 'The Difficult Birth of Stochastics: Jacob Bernoulli's *Ars Conjectandi* (1713)'. *Historia Mathematica* 41: 277–90.

Nyquist, Harry. 1924. 'Certain Factors Affecting Telegraphy Speed'. *Bell System Technical Journal* no. 3: 324–46.

Peirce, John R. [ca. 1957]. 'What Good is Information Theory to Engineers?' Unpublished paper, Box 2, Folder 3, Claude E. Shannon Papers, Library of Congress, Washington, DC, USA.

Schmitz, H. Walter. 2018. '"Aber die Frage ist gerade, ob es nicht im Wesen der Sache liegt, daß es auch in der Wissenschaft Mode gibt.": Claude E. Shannons Diagramm eines allgemeinen Kommunikationssystems und seine Rezeption in Sprach- und Kommuikationswissenschaft'. Edited by Gerda Haßler and Angelika Rüter. *Beiträge zur Geschichte der Sprachwissenschaft* 28: 95–154.

Schramm, Wilbur. 1954. 'How Communication Works'. In *The Process and Effects of Mass Communication*, edited by Wilbur Schramm, 3–26. Urbana: University of Illinois Press.

Shannon, Claude E. [ca. 1954]. 'Information Theory', unpublished lecture, p. 1, ca. 1954. Speeches & Writings, Box 6, Folder 8. Claude Elwood Shannon Papers, Library of Congress, Washington, DC.

Shannon, Claude E. 1945. 'A Mathematical Theory of Cryptography'. *Bell Laboratories Memorandum* 45–110–92, (September 1), 10. The British Library.

Shannon, Claude E. 1948. 'A Mathematical Theory of Communication'. *Bell Systems Technical Journal*, 27: 379–423, 623–56.

Shannon, Claude E. 1949. 'The Mathematical Theory of Communication' in Claude E. Shannon and Warren Weaver, *The Mathematical Theory of Communication*, 3–93. Urbana: University of Illinois Press.

Shannon, Claude E. 1972. 'Information Theory'. *Encyclopedia Britannica*, 14th edn. 12: 246B-247.

Shannon, Claude E. 2004. 'The Redundancy of English'. In *Cybernetics: The Macy Conferences 1946–1953*, edited by Claus Pias, 248–72. Berlin: Diaphanes.

Shannon, Claude E. and Warren Weaver. 1949. *The Mathematical Theory of Communication*. Urbana: University of Illinois Press.

Weaver, Warren. 1949. 'Recent Contributions to the Mathematical Theory of Communication'. In Claude E. Shannon and Warren Weaver, *The Mathematical Theory of Communication*, 94–117. Urbana: University of Illinois Press.

Weber, Samuel. 1976. 'Saussure and the Apparition of Language: The Critical Perspective'. *MLN* 91: 913–38.

White, Kenneth Allan, Jr. 2015. 'Libidinal Engineers: Three Studies in Cybernetics and Its Discontents'. Unpublished Ph.D. dissertation, Stanford University, Stanford.

Part II: Interfacing Media

4

GUIding the Overwrite: Resurfacing Lexicality in the Xerox PARC Alto

Louisa Shen

> Computing is normally done by writing certain
> symbols on paper.
>
> – A.M. Turing

Computation is a scriptorial process, and the computer is a scripting machine. Its earliest modern instantiation – COLOSSUS at Bletchley Park – decoded Lorenz, a German cipher itself encoded by machine processes. Post-war, the transformation of boxy electro-mechanical apparatuses and massive mainframes into ultrathin mobile devices began to obscure the intimate entanglement between lexicality and computation. The compression of the physical chassis of the machine came hand-in-hand with a move away from alphanumeric and towards pictorial forms of input and output. Since the careful assembly of the war-time cryptographic machine, computation has become synonymous with digital imagery and networked interfaces. For the ordinary user, encounters with the computer are overwhelmingly graphical, the lexical partly enveloped in and partly effaced by the pictorial. The computational image invokes its own distinctive aesthetic world. Vilém Flusser remarked in 1973, coincidentally the same year in which the first graphical user interface was prototyped on the Alto at Xerox PARC in California, that 'written lines, although appearing even more frequently than before, are becoming less important than surfaces to the mass of people' (Flusser 2002: 22). The planar techno-image could be apprehended instantly, and as such pushed us away from the timeliness or diachronicity of procedural line-by-line reading, the very unfolding of which constituted a sense of history. At a moment when 'screen time' has emerged as a troubling distortion of common visual and cognitive experience, close attention might be paid to the period when we began to lose sight of the linear, alphanumeric nature of the machine. In recalling the broader narrative of the development of the graphical user interface (GUI), it becomes possible to chart the changing relationality between symbolic man and symbolic machine, even as the historical work is gently overwritten by the very nature of the scripting machines themselves, process engines undertaking a constant re-writing of their instantiation.

The arrival of computational graphicality is a familiar story, although contemporary accounts tend to overlook the material preconditions – the changes to hardware – that made such a transition possible (see, for instance, Pratschke 2015). Two entangled genealogies should be traced – firstly, a chronicle of the changing collection of physical input and output (I/O) devices attached to computational engines and latterly, a history of the kinds of programming that such devices permitted. The common starting point for this task must be a prior recognition that all computational I/O devices are visual in some way; mathematics must be represented by some form of notation inscribed or imprinted upon a material ground, with lexical symbols relying on the eye for interpretation just as much as pictorial images. Steven Connor (2016: 18–19) has suggested that every machine might be seen 'as a kind of writing' on the basis of its procedural action, and since the embryonic stages of the computer's twentieth-century development, scripting has formed the backbone of the computer's physical apparatus. The keyboard has been a mainstay of programming and processing, as has paper (albeit with varying degrees of importance as memory and display components have evolved). Alan Turing's conception of computing relied, of course, on the possibility of a 'very long' portion of paper tape (Turing 1936: 251). Paper's fixity made it the wrong medium for the kind of responsive and reversible graphical instruction that subsequent engineers thought the computer might take, and it would be the arrival of the electrical display monitor that set the ground for favouring the pictorial. Once the material basis for graphicality was in place, the implementation of the GUI deliberately blinded the user to the core scriptorial and procedural logic of the machine, necessitating strategies for guiding the user as s/he navigated the new visual landscape. Much of this guidance, ironically, came in written form, a less-pictorial explication of the computer's new guise. Examining the paratexts of the Alto in particular, we begin to reconstruct the way in which the early GUI sought to translate human intentionality in two directions – from programmer to user and from user to programmer – as both sides sought to exploit the machine's capabilities even while the limits and fragilities of the system were increasingly hidden from view. Early graphicality emerges as a mythologising of the machine, where it sought to present the computer as a tool without bounds, fit for application to any task or problem that might demand execution or remedy.

Towards the Interface

The binary computer has always been alphanumeric, but it has not always had an interface. That term did not arrive in the computational sense until the mid-1960s, when it was first used to denote a component used for data conversion between digital and analogue processors. Although some form of informatic conversion – specifically alphanumeric encoding and transcription – has always been the lifeblood of computing, no single, unified mechanism for I/O existed in the immediate post-war years. The computer's operation was spread across a number of separate fittings that variously fed, indicated, or translated its core processing activity. Paper tape or card was the medium of choice on which binary yes/no (Y/N) logic and written commands could be represented as punched holes. The encoding of these bits of paper was partially electrified. Commands were typed on teletypes, electrical typewriters that transmitted mechanical depression of the keys into pulse signals and vice versa. Flagship models included the Friden Flexowriter, produced under IBM's banner since the 1930s and used originally to drive typesetting for printing presses. Instructions typed at the keyboard would be expressed as a pattern of holes by the teletype's own in-built paper tape punches. These tapes were then fed into the computer, which articulated its own status as it was executing these instructions by means of a series of control panels affixed with indicator lights and meters. These panels of toggle switches and console lights were the primary means by which the computer made visible its performance and status, including any hardware errors (Sutherland 2012: 84). Once the program was executed, feeding in a slip of computer-generated output (punched paper) back into the teletype's reader had the eerie inverse effect of depressing the keys at the keyboard as it autonomously decoded and 'typed out' the pattern into letter-and-number print-outs. Paper would in part come to be replaced by reels of magnetic tape, before the popularisation of magnetic core memory invented in the 1950s. Approaching the computer, the operator saw no cohesive interface, and met with a motley collection of so-called 'peripherals'.

Glimpses of more integrated mechanisms for interacting with the computer were seen in the 1960s, but a consolidated interface would not emerge for at least another decade. Consolidation would eventually see the two twinned acts of input and output, programming and use, effected through *one type* of terminal. The adoption of the cathode ray tube (CRT) screen and light pen (a stylus that was a precursor to the mouse) alongside the keyboard and physical control panel consoles would, in hindsight, turn out to be a key pre-requisite for the shift to graphical display. As early as 1948, the use of two mirrored cathode ray tubes to store and display data in a simple dot matrix had been implemented as part of the development of the University of Manchester's SSEM, the first stored program computer. Other experimental uses of the electrified screen followed, including in the Zephyr computer at the University of Arizona and the Whirlwind I computers developed at MIT that were installed as part of the Cold War SAGE missile defence program (Smith 2016: 75–80). Whirlwind I could produce vector graphics displayed on a round radar CRT screen in the form of live maps of the American seaboard, constantly updated with information on the enemy's movements. Draughting was not foreign to the world of computing; some of the very first commercial programs released to the likes of Boeing and other industrial design firms were computer-aided design packages, made for the express purpose of drawing, and often driving *xy* plotters (often large table-sized contraptions with mechanical arms that held pens over paper) that could physically draw a copy of the design. Pictoriality was native to computation predominantly as an output, but these increasingly pictorial innovations did not assail the fundamental linear inheritance of transcription in the programming world. *Writing* code remained the province of the teletype and paper. A 1964 IBM System360 catalogue sold teletypes, punch card readers, and magnetic tapes alongside video terminals, the latter advertised predominantly as passive displays for output (Goldstein 1964: 6–10). Ivan Sutherland's *Sketchpad* (1963), the first program to split the screen and enable direct drawing on the display surface using a light pen, was still written in machine code on the TX-2, an experimental model that took two Lincoln Lab writers accommodating paper tape (Sutherland 1963: 169). Alan C. Kay's 1969 design of FLEX, an experimental 'personal computing' set-up that presented orthographic views of shapes and objects on-screen, still relied on an admix of CRT display, tablet and stylus, QWERTY keyboard, and 'five-fingered keyboard' (akin to the mouse) as I/O devices (Kay 1969: n.p.). The tablet and stylus allowed display parameters to be altered, thereby dynamically changing the user's perspective. Graphicality was not yet conceived as a means of *accessing* the computer beyond the surface-level manipulation of imagery during highly-bracketed instances of specialist use.

As the decade wore on, expert programming and lay operation drifted imperceptibly to rely solely on the screen, abolishing the extra mediation of paper and the host of apparatuses designed to handle it. It has proved difficult to trace the precise moment when instructing the computer shifted entirely to the on-screen command-line, and perhaps the record of such a moment might not exist. A clear, documented case for preferring the screen as a consolidated interface was made in a 1972 technical paper that described a new text-editing program developed for use with cathode ray tubes. The CRT's advantage of speed in data retrieval and modification and capacity for reversing what was typed to correct mistakes meant that '[t]he foremost application of the CRD [cathode ray display] editing system is, of course, to the preparation and testing of programs' (Irons and Djorup 1972: 19–20). The other primary function of this on-screen editing was as a 'delightful aid to the preparation of letters or reports' (20). The immediacy of rendering in the screen made it particularly suited to scripts that required iteration, revision, and versioning – the 'great advantage' being 'that revisions of some magnitude are easily introduced and immediately available to anyone with access to a console' (20). Together with the stable constant of the unassuming keyboard, the screen was now being asserted as a viable alternative to paper for *lexical* input and output at any level, be it specialist programming or general use. The earlier tendency to adopt the CRT console and light pen input as specialist devices only for drawing, cartography, or computer-aided design had faded. The operator was becoming habituated more and more to an integrated terminal for instructing the computer that was peripheral in name only.

Two intertwined strands of computational metamorphosis were now in play. Alongside the change in interface equipment, a tendency was growing to mask the procedural nature of the machine. Screeds of paper tape had produced a material substantiation of code. The paper and plastic ribbons had demonstrated a kind of endless continuity, visual proof of an unfolding process of inscription. Unbroken lengths of paper perforated with holes down the sides, much like celluloid film, passed through the electromechanical paper machines to receive their imprint of ink or row of perforations. Paul Allen, co-founder of Microsoft, later recalled incessant scripting of the Teletype Model ASR-33 attached to a GE-635 Mainframe in the late 1960s:

> [T]o [the keyboard's] left sat the punch, which spewed a continuous stream of inch-wide, eight-column paper tape. Each character was defined by the configuration of holes punched out among the eight channels. (An inch length of tape held ten characters; a small program might run two or three feet.) In front of the punch, a paper-tape reader translated your programs and sent them to the GE computer. The Teletype made a terrific racket, a mix of low humming, the Gatling gun of the paper-tape punch, and the *ka-chacko-whack* of the printer keys. [...] But though it was noisy and slow, a dumb remote terminal with no display screen or lowercase letters, the ASR-33 was also state-of-the-art. (Allen 2011: 27–8)

Linearity and lexicality were given material form, made loud and clear in the execution of code. Tape in particular had the advantage over decks of cards in that they could be spooled and could not be accidentally shuffled out of sequence (Hazel 2017: 8). Transferring computation to the screen imposed its own problem of boundedness. Lines of code could be written equally well on screen, but no supplemental surface area could be added simply by loading in a new roll of paper. Display units such as the IBM 2260 allowed only for shifting the displayed text up or down one line at a time (IBM 1968: 5–9). Scrolling subsequently became *de rigueur* in many text editing programs designed for the screen after the mid-1970s, although paging was a more unusual feature (Datapro 1976). The screen did seem to provide certain affordances of compactness, marking the very start of the semi-conductor revolution and the release of consumer models to the general public. Up until then, the bulk of paper and magnetic strips and the equipment for housing and interpreting them prevented the computer from migrating out of specialist labs. Prohibitive costs of memory and processing also restricted access to researchers funded by industry or government. Use was further constrained by the difficulty of learning often highly terse, highly cryptic programming instructions, and graphicality was seen as a means to a much more intuitive, approachable computer, that a child might be able to grasp on its own. Kay's imaginative manifesto that envisioned 'personal, portable information manipulators for children' where they might even 'write programs for their own ends' (Kay 1972) was the vision that the Alto engineers looked to realise (this device was dubbed the 'Dynabook' and recognisable as a tablet today).

By the beginning of the 1970s, graphicality on screen was well-established, but it did not serve as any systemic means of initiating or running a range of programs on the computer. The pictures and icons that were drawn were still overwhelmingly outputs. Douglas Engelbart at Stanford Research Institute demonstrated a more sophisticated exemplar of visually manipulating data through the oN-Line System (an early interactive computer prototype) in 1968, where a grocery list typed up could be re-ordered by 'drag and drop' and associated with the shops in which the items were available on a visual map of an ideal route (Engelbart 1968). (The arrival of the mouse as a replacement for the light pen meant that the screen was now visually unobstructed, but it also broke the natural relationship of hand-eye coordination in draughtsmanship, where the gaze held the hand and the marks it was making on paper in a single line of sight.) If the NLS 'proto-interface' seemed entirely intuitive under Engelbart's guidance, it was an illusion stemming from the effortlessness of expertise; Engelbart was a specialist running his own program. The lack of signposting on the blank screen – there were no lines or symbols to indicate buttons or demarcate areas or objects to focus on or navigate to – meant that any user without prior embedded knowledge of existing functionalities and how to invoke them would not be able to operate the NLS. The Alto would address some of these deficiencies, for many of the engineers working on it had old ties to Engelbart's projects, and the inheritance of influence would see the personal computer offer much the same capacity to marry and meld words and pictures.

Translating the linearity of paper tape and the command-line to an electric form burned in the phosphors of the screen had demanded improved memory and processing power to drive the display, but the magnitude of the change from lexical to pictorial representation would require extra computational resources. Butler Lampson's 1972 internal memo outlined the requirements for developing such a machine; on the user's side, the centrepiece of the set-up would comprise a '901 line TV monitor whose display surface is almost exactly the size of this page'. It would be 'oriented vertically', and 'driven from a bit map in the memory' requiring 32 kilobyte RAM capacity to fill (Lampson 1972: 1). Distributed personal computing needed significant resources to mimic the paper it was replacing – where it was envisioned that the Alto would have between 48–64K in RAM in total, at least half would be given over to rendering the screen. No real substitute for magnetic tape for core memory had as yet been found, but the I/O hardware was being redesigned into a purely electronic form. The team's willingness to reroute hardware capacity to 'bit map' the screen was the firmest commitment to the instantiation of a visual 'skin'. Bitmapping was a technique of allocating each point on the screen to a dedicated place in memory controlled independently by the processor. The ability to turn individual dots on and off in the matrix meant more sophisticated iconography could be generated. First encounters with this turn towards an illustrative approach, where icons stood for commands that no longer had to be typed out, is the next matter we might treat, through (perhaps somewhat speculative) archaeological reconstruction.

Icons as Illusions

Unlike the NLS showcase, which was recorded and 'televised' through an early form of video-conferencing, little footage exists of Alto demos in the 1970s. Extant television advertisements provide only a dressed-up and over-simplified portrayal of the Alto's capabilities, with the OS heavily anthropomorphised as an intelligent personal assistant (Xerox PARC 1972). Any attempt to recreate a more accurate phenomenology of the first systematically-graphical OS, replete with its own suite of programs, must rely instead on other sources. In ideal circumstances, all histories of computing and human-computer interaction might be written with recourse to an original machine, still operational and having all its peripheral hardware components intact. Such exemplars do exist – the Seattle-based Living Computer Museum completed a contemporary restoration in 2016 – but the inherent technical challenges in restoration and preservation mean these objects emerge as an increasingly rare and fragile resource. Jussi Parikka has described the revival of these 'old media' forms as a kind of remediating, resurfacing, and re-adaption of the original machine to '[find] an afterlife in new contexts, new hands, new screens and machines' (Parikka 2012: 3). Emulators (such as the ContrAlto) or simulators (such as the SALTO) might be used to replicate the experience of the GUI on a contemporary machine running a contemporary OS. Although their immediate value is to allow the media archaeologist to experience a sense of the original interface, they remain imperfect versions of the original. These programs stand as re-articulations of the original OS – a translation of Alto's native BCPL language (later superseded by the MESA, SmallTalk, and Lisp languages) into a current programming language (C#), with the programs running on a different 'life-support' environment (Unix, Windows, or OS X) to the one that Alto offered (Executive). (The first object-oriented programming language Smalltalk, the first object-oriented programming language designed to be particularly supportive of the presentation of GUIs, was written by Kay at Xerox PARC in the early 1970s.) To extend the metaphor, whereas the original machine sings as an Alto, the emulator hums as a ContrAlto. Indeed, depending on the configuration of the contemporary environment, the emulator may or may not be successfully supported (this author's inexpert attempt at running the ContrAlto program failed consistently until she installed a critical upgrade to her OS). In the face of more technical barriers to historical excavation, the normative methods of *textual* scholarship suggest another fruitful avenue of enquiry into the replacement of lexicality with pictoriality.

For as the machines went into commercial production (over two thousand units were made across the lifespan of the Alto I and Alto II) the engineers found they had to steer the uninitiated novice through the ostensibly intuitive graphical user interface. Much of this guidance took the form of 'paper' documentation that surrounded the machine – the notes, memoranda, briefings, and jottings that arose throughout the process of the computer's creation. These paratexts can uncover both the intended design and final implementation of a particular apparatus. The 1972 internal Xerox design notes for the Alto, though, remain unhelpfully quiet on interface specifications. Entry number 10, sub-headed 'Display' and 'Keyboard and Mouse', states rather baldly that they were 'To be written' (Lampson 1973: 11). Turning to the Alto's help guides that explain the interface and tools made available to the uninitiated user – technical writing of a different kind – gets the media historian closer to the first experiences of systematic computational graphicality, for the content more fully discloses the contours and dynamics of the engagement with the machine.

Technical guides operate as a kind of circuit breaker in the hermeneutic circle that is computational literacy. Help manuals describe ideal use scenarios – the expected behaviour of the machine when the user is operating it correctly. These documents offer a kind of userly verification and reassurance, describing both the anticipated pathways of the user's instruction of the machine to execute commands and the correct response of this unit to such instruction. Compiled by the engineers in many cases, they constantly re-state the texts, messages, and commands that appear on screen, in a replay of the OS on paper. These documents are thus also iterated alongside the very software they support; the release of a new version of the OS necessitates a parallel release of a new version of the guide, updated with the relevant changes. In this kind of meta-articulation of machine performance and operation, we have a written source that cleaves close to the original user experience affected by the original machines. In the case of the Alto, only reference documentation detailing code syntax (essentially a long list of commands with little context) was published for the 1973 prototype model, catering largely for a consumer base of expert programmers. The 1979 commercial model came bundled with fuller documentation designed for the lay user, albeit the guide was flagged as 'intentionally incomplete'. (No document can ever fully capture all the permutations of procedure and usage scenarios possible within a single program or OS.) We might glean from its reading the effect an insertion of pictoriality had on our relationship and encounter with the scriptorial machine.

It would be a mistake – an anachronism reaching back from our current graphical condition – to assume that a more pictorial approach to using the screen was immediately more natural or intuitive. In the *Alto User's Handbook*, literal explication was given at length of each of the icons and display areas. The customisable appearance of Laurel, the Alto's email messaging client, introduced the new concept of resizing:

> Laurel maintains four regions on the display screen. From top to bottom they are: the *table-of-contents region*, the *message display region*, the *composition region*, and the *feedback region*. [...] You can adjust the boundaries of the three major regions using the small squares at the upper-right hand corner of the two lowers menus. Point the cursor at the desired box, then press down and hold YELLOW. By moving the mouse up or down, you drag the box with you to a new position on the screen. When you release the mouse button, the menu will move to the new position, and the contents of the adjacent regions will be adjusted accordingly. (Xerox PARC 1979: 67–8)

No convention had yet been established for the allocation of screen space to different computational functions; the user was interpreting a foreign roadmap of sorts and the engineers did not assume that how to manipulate the appearance of the demarcated regions would be self-evident. Every step was made explicit in detail. Each delineated area represented a visual corral in which a different function might be applied to the things inside. The preponderance of planar space, symbols, and colours (usually indicative of the status of some pending, progressing, or complete action) distanced the user from the deeper scriptorial condition of the computer and fostered an experience of the machine as a space for manipulating items and objects, not logical sequences and processes based on true/false statements. Even in text-based programmes like the editor Bravo, words themselves became things that the user could point at and click to move them to a different demarcated area of the screen. It was possible to 'mov[e] the cursor into the *line bar*', whereupon the cursor would change into an arrow pointer as a visual indication of a shift from lexical composition to object manipulation. Clicking the red mouse button selected the 'entire line pointed to by the cursor'. Next, typing in the command 'Normalize' would send the selection to the top of the screen (Xerox PARC 1979: 52). These manipulations are recognisable today in their contemporary form as highlighting, cutting, and pasting. The user's conception of the computer at the start of the 1980s was on the threshold of becoming ideogrammic, with a 'proto-writing' of pictorial icons and cues standing in for lexical commands in a kind of short-circuiting of the unfolding of procedurality, *non verbis sed rebus*.

Many commands still had to be typed – technological change is seldom seismic and often fitful – but the new 'buttons' often truncated the process of scripting into single key stroke or mouse click. Pressing the 'carriage return' (enter) key remained a core mechanism for confirming or denying the user's intentions or carrying out the user's instructions, but other interactions with the computer now took place in an arena where icons could be selected and manipulated without any foregrounding of the command for moving the object. The guide appears at its most elaborate when the writerly quality of the machine was not immediately obvious to the user, especially for actions that involved the destructive dimension of committing information to disk. When the scriptorial element was masked by the GUI, the voice of the engineer-tutor implied that the user had little sense of how the machine actually ran, or of the implications of this hidden process for the task at hand. Writing or drawing on screen did not correspond to the computer writing to disk – no mirroring function existed, and this was a point of vulnerability in operating the machine that the handbook was quick to call to the forefront of the user's mind:

> The first thing you must understand before trying to illustrate a large document (i.e. a document with more than half a dozen illustrated pages) is that Markup consumes large quantities of disk space. As a rule of thumb, you should make sure there are at least 100 free pages on your disk for every illustrated page of the document. [...] The reason for all this caution is that Markup cannot be relied upon to recover gracefully if it runs out of disk space, unless it runs out after you have 'quit'. [...] [It] is still possible for you to spend three hours illustrating twenty pages, and then run out of disk space while working on the twenty-first, leaving you with no means of recovering your lost work. (Xerox PARC 1979: 94)

In the rush to graphicality, the operator was taking at face value the screen's mimicry of paper, where the latter by its very material nature provided instant, lasting commitment of hand-drawn marks. It was not necessary to think about having 'spare pages' in traditional draughting. The computer as an independent, scriptorial 'writer' that had a long history of processing work in small batches was recalled only as a *limitation* of the system, at the point of its failure. The starkest example of graphicality as a visual disavowal of the machine's constraints is evident in the explication of the Draw illustration program. Largely pictorial in its presentation, the limits of the software's capacity were only outlined as part of instructions on how to use the command-line, which could be used to tweak Draw's basic parameters 'under the hood'. The maximum number of lines and curves that any picture that Draw could support was in the vicinity of 200, a boundary that the 'paint brush' tool icon had no way to signal. These hard constraints revealed the computer to be a 'dumb machine', still ill-suited to accommodating the unspoken conventions and habits of 'analogue man'. The new interface was not 'intuitive'; demonstrably it failed to share all the cognitive assumptions and expectations a user might have when putting pen to paper, the latter's 'flexibility' making it the material the engineers sought to emulate (Thacker et. al. 1979: 15–16). Icons represented capabilities – distinct tools at the disposal of the user – but said nothing of how these rules could and could not be applied. The GUI disguised the computer as a metaphorical machine when it was strictly a literal one. Habituation to a particular *techne* impressed into the tool user an inertia of action and praxis that would be difficult to overcome. The originary form of the ancient tablet and stylus and the ingrained will to mark ideograms and diagrams meant that the newest scripting technology sought to approximate the qualities of the oldest processes of writing, without recourse to the same palimpsestic properties and material affordances of clay or paper which offered a direct causality between action and impression.

The computer broke this simple act of mark-making by asserting an indirect, complex mediality between the writer and the material grounds at his disposal, where this intermediary position translated one action into another. The nature of the interface was such that it did not give the user free rein to work as he pleased; instead the computer pushed back and prescribed a pre-determined series of options and pathways that the user must take. (Deviation from these steps was liable to create errors.) The set of possible conditions and the permitted permutations that could arise was laid out by the machine itself. On start-up, the Executive (equivalent to 'Windows Explorer' in a contemporary Microsoft system) would 'tell you at the top of the screen what it thinks the state of its world is', before it could receive any instructions. In Bravo's system window, the first two lines respectively '[told] you what you can do next' and 'what you just did, and whether anything went wrong doing it' (Xerox PARC 1979: 33). These kinds of reiterations of the machine's operational state – a kind of self-monitoring and self-articulation – were the basis of both the machine's self-scripting and its scripting of the user; that is, the user had to follow a script when he engaged with the machine. Occasionally, this requirement was baldly stated – 'You may type "?" at any point to obtain a brief explanation of what you are expected to type in next' (Xerox PARC 1979: 16). Eben Moglen, programming language specialist at IBM in the 1970s, would later characterise the basic premise of the command-line with the remark that 'What we were doing with computers was making languages that were better than natural languages for procedural thought' (Moglen and Worthington 2000). In linear interfaces, such procedurality was obvious. For Moglen, the pictorial turn in the user interface was atavistic:

> What I saw in the Xerox PARC technology was the caveman interface, you point and you grunt. A massive winding down, regressing away from language, in order to address the technological nervousness of the user. [...] Xerox PARC technology's primary advantage was that it allowed users to address computers in a pre-linguistic way. [...] I have nothing against a windowing environment, but it's a windowing environment which is network transparent and based around the fact that inside very window there's some dialogue to have with some linguistic entity. (Moglen and Worthington 2000)

A discursive split had been introduced into the computer with the arrival of the image as a portal of systemic access; it was being forced to articulate itself in a language that was untrue to itself. Graphicality, understood this way, was nothing short of a misrepresentation of the machine and its parameters.

Unmasking the Machine

If the Alto was the first prototype of the GUI, its ongoing reliance on these lexical formulations within a system designed to abolish the linearity of scripting with a 'WYSIWYG' ('what you see is what you get') exposed the illusory nature of graphicality. The lexical interface instantiated a mutual programming between man and machine; the effect of the graphical interface was such that the user was less and less aware of being disciplined. A sense of choice and possibility prevailed when all the tools in a programme were visually laid out before the user. The program Draw was exemplary of this phenomenon of surfeit; stylised brushes, selection pointers, transformation icons, text tools, copying buttons, and eraser options were all annotated in the guide, with examples of the diagrammatic effects these tools could achieve. The entire section showcased Draw capabilities, for all the illustrations were created using the program (Xerox PARC 1979: 98). Appendix C provided further samples of illustrated work, emphasising the versatility and endless combinations of the smorgasbord of tools. Selecting from *a menu* was precisely the format that foregrounded a sense of choice while backgrounding the limited, constrained repertoire of actual possibilities. It suggested the user might deploy this set of functions in any way or order, as she saw fit. Pictorial 'skins' emerge as a sleight of hand, establishing multiplicity of choice as a shorthand for an illusory freedom to manipulate the tool in idiosyncratic or unforeseen ways. The appearance of too much possibility meant it was easy to become misguided – the introduction in the *Handbook* posted a loud disclaimer: 'You will find that things are a lot clearer if you try to *learn by doing*. This is especially true when you are learning to use any of the services which use the display' (Xerox PARC 1979: 2). Pictoriality emphasised and provided a shortcut to praxis in a way that a lexicality – even in the form of a paratextual guide – did not. Giving the user the full gamut of options was too overwhelming, and the guidance tried to compensate for this confusion by using a smaller font to list 'non-essential' details about use. After listing lengthy and detailed typesetting measurements for formatting the page in the WYSIWYG document editor, Bravo, the section concluded with a dismissal of the task's whole premise – 'Of course, if you get disgusted, you can always type DEL to cancel the whole thing' (Xerox PARC 1979: 43). Pictoriality surfaced many commands at once; lexicality unfurled them one by one. The inherent paradox or tension in these two forms of presentation was that the former hid while the latter exposed the machine's rigid sequentiality and prescriptiveness, leaving the user to imagine a machine that operated intuitively – that is, laterally, associatively, and spontaneously.

For what the front of graphicality represented was an insistence or 'design philosophy' that the lay user might be given both the permission and wherewithal to modify the machine's base scriptorial process, without understanding the risks inherent in the task. Efforts to carefully manage the delicate and sensitive process of writing to disk, especially when the action was non-reversible and would cause the overwriting of existing data, were pronounced in the GUI. Reiterating the on-screen prompts, the manual inserted an extra level of insurance to the user at the moment of greatest danger. The user's intentions came under interrogation, a scrutiny designed to force the user to question and deliberate his own course of action, and one that betrayed a deeper concern that this novice might drive the machine towards a catastrophic end out of ignorance, achieving not the desired manipulation of data but some irrecoverable erasure of information instead. The CopyDisk function carried a double-barrelled query:

> You should now go through the following dialogue:
> *Copy from: [Banjo]DPoCR   *the digit zero, not the letter O*
> Copy to: DPoCR
> Copying onto DPo will destroy its old contents.
> Are you sure this is what you want to do? [Confirm] Yes
> Are you still sure? [Confirm] Yes

If 'all went well' from this point in, an identical copy would be produced on disk (Xerox PARC 1979: 27). The Alto's user prompts – which can be characterised as instances of the machine 'speaking back' to the user – sought to contain the threat of irreversible data or systemic erasure. These messages did not yet appear in the now-familiar graphical form of the 'dialog box', but the lack of cosmetic coverage had the effect of reinforcing the sense of inscription, as one line of query popped up after the other, the user each time having to type in their confirmation. Questioning the user's intent became the pre-emptive 'speech act' by which the programmer, anticipating certain wants or needs on the part of his imagined audience, confirmed a set course of irrevocable action. Programming emerged as an imaginative act that postulated both users and the tasks they wished to accomplish, and which laid out a semi-reversible procedure for doing so in a way the binary machine could interpret and execute, despite the user being only partially privy to the possible steps and corresponding outcomes established in that procedure. When those outcomes involved modifications to the very status of the machine itself, pictoriality was no longer an adequate form of instructing the user. System-critical functions defaulted back to the lexical, even as graphicality lent an overall sense of approachability and shaped the expressive style of the 'customer-facing' shell.

The repetitious verbosity of the GUI prompts and reassuring explanation of the implications of the user's actions on the system contrasted starkly with the messaging produced in industry-standard command-line releases prevalent at the time. The explications betrayed the engineer's anxiety that the user's operation of the *graphical* machine might translate poorly into actually achieving the outcome he wanted. The terms of the exegesis mattered. When the machine was experienced in *lexical* terms, it was assumed that the intended task would be easily accomplished for it required significant forethought regarding each step of the implementation. The Unix operating system serves as an illustration. Developed contemporaneously (1969 –71) with transition to a consolidated hardware interface and partly under the pretext of developing a word processing program for AT&T's patent typists, it was written firstly on the screen-less GE-645 mainframe and subsequently the equally screen-less PDP-7 at Bell Labs (Toomey 2011). The OS was an environment coded in the language C that omitted to prompt the user when she was deleting a file and provided little signal of whether a command was being carried out after the execution key was pressed (Norman 1981: 142). One of Unix's descendants, IBM's version of MS-DOS, IBM-DOS 1.0 released in January 1982, carried particularly curt demands: 'Abort edit? [Y/N]' and 'Terminate batch job? [Y/N]' were commonplace (IBM 1982: 2–29, 3–15). (Contorting the second verb into a noun only makes parsing the question's meaning more difficult.) Terseness had its place – it required far less processing and memory resource to support, for command-line interfaces did not need the screen to be bitmapped – and thus brevity conserved resources. Yet the constricting of the dialogic channel and the paring back of more effusive contextual information communicated a particular kind of abrupt impatience with the user at large. Curt guidance meant that the computer could be experienced as an impenetrable black box. An article of 1986 in the *Guardian* entitled 'Why Software is User-Hostile' made explicit the problem:

> [A] misconception is confusing use with conciseness. While it is true, for example, that UNIX is a paradise for the expert programmer, it is also true that it is a pain to those who do not have the time to invest in mastering it. Programmers choose

> conciseness because they spend many hours a day behind a
> computer doing the same job many times over. Conciseness is
> efficient. However, the situation is just the reverse for casual
> users. Heavily abbreviated notation results in disappointment.
> (Hekmatpour 1986: 24)

The repetitiousness of the programmer's job is revealing – computation itself is a re-iterative process, in coding-speak it is full of loops, recursions, routine, and versions. It is not a coincidence that the technical language of programming is full of words relating to articulation: call, query, confirm, dialogue. These repeats are the re-written mechanisms that the lay user wants to forget behind the veil of the GUI, in a kind of Bartleby-esque retreat from the work of scrivening. The preference not to engage with the transcriptive and prescriptive nature of the computer created an ironic tension in the use of words to represent the machine – when code lines were hidden, more words were sometimes needed to explicate the steps in the process. If a picture paints a thousand words, the GUI became a way to compress that explication into icons, which themselves were not always semantically obvious. The symbol of scissors did not denote the action 'cut' but rather the act of 'drawing a dotted line' in Alto, an ambiguous miscommunication or description of the capabilities of an otherwise black-and-white binary machine (Xerox Parc 1979: 104).

Opening up the scripting machine in such an obfuscated way to non-experts introduced a significant element of unpredictability in usage, with the veneer of pictoriality masking exactly where the system might have gone wrong. Righting the machine required the resurfacing of the lexical. Alto's recovery mechanisms were entirely alphanumeric. Backups and fail safes were built by scriptorial means, compiled as logs or transcripts. Each log consisted of the machine re-articulating to itself each action it performed, meta-writing into a plain-text file its every move. If some mistake occurred, these documents could be used as the basis for retracing the user's actions to reconstruct the work that she was generating with the computer. In Bravo, 'replay[ing] the transcript up to the error' would reproduce the document up to the point of the malfunction (Xerox PARC 1979: 54). A similar means could be exploited in Markup using its 'scratch file', a temporary version of the modifications implemented but still to be committed to stable hard disk memory. When a program that did not offer a command-line form encountered problems, the troubleshooting suggestions in the handbook were tentative and hesitant, asserting only probable diagnostics and solutions. The 'symptoms of trouble' might well come from 'disk incompatibility', in which case the hardware would need to be 'realigned'; or if the problem was operational in nature, the user might try to start up the repair program Scavenger, but 'if that doesn't work', it could well be an ethernet connection issue. Scavenger itself may or may not 'succeed in making your disk healthy', and 'if things are still in bad shape', the user might want to reinstall the OS, and 'if this doesn't work, there is one more step to try', which would be to resort to the File Transfer Protocol (FTP) to fetch a new OS file (Xerox PARC 1979: 9). When a programme – specifically the FTP – ran entirely on command-line prompts, the statements of potential problems were entirely unequivocal. Command-line errors 'fall into three groups: syntax errors, file errors, and connection errors'. Errors are either fatal or non-fatal (Xerox PARC 1979: 137–8). Alphanumeric notation was not an antidote to unexpected errors (the machine itself was perfectly capable of garbling its own output as it ran its own transcription processes), but the command-line made apparent the step at which the code stopped or broke. Computational clarity and certainty improved when the linear procedurality of the code being executed *could be seen*.

Graphicality thus offered visibility of a different order, a different way of seeing the machine that largely bypassed its scriptorial ontology. Commands previously threaded into a linear, linguistic corpus that prescribed proper articulation using the correct grammar were rendered in an isolated ideographic form, a keyword picked out of the support structures of the wider syntax. The scripting process – the writing-out of every step as it was being executed on screen so rapidly that each new line continued to push the scroll of text upwards – was submerged. The pictorial turn in the interface cut both ways – it offered both exposure and obfuscation of the computer's utility, exposure of what tasks it could do and obfuscation of how it did those tasks. The lexical interface provided the inverse. The disappearance from view of the read/write process at the heart of the machine came only after the post-war consolidation of print and punch equipment into the electrical screen, and presented to the user the computer as a set of simplified, pre-determined options accessed through an interface – a *system* of images presenting the tool as-it-is rather than the tool that might-be-made. For the lay user, the computer as a machine for tooling – for designing tools – was forgotten. The instrumentality of the computer – the sense that it is an object on which we might be able to write and compose original programs – retreats. Instead, the GUI seemed to promise the abolition of the learning curve in our encounter with the computer. The child's electronic tablet with its stylus arguably emerged as the absolute expression of this technological fantasy in the 1970s, where the complex machine might be taken up effortlessly, a proverbial pre-linguistic blank slate. The interposition of graphicality actually meant that the GUI itself became a kind of pidgin grammar to be learnt. Command-lines demanded more fluency in 'computer speak', while the GUI required far less. The mediality of the interface emerged out of Alto as a problem of literacy, which is to say that interfaces arise when reciprocal unintelligibility or illegibility of some form between man and machine exists. (The use of medial*ity* rather than mediat*ion* here emphasizes the in-betweenness as a state, which seems to be the condition of the GUI, rather than as an action, which is the prerogative of the user and programmer.) The user of a tool need not know how it works in order to use it, but the guidance system that must be in place to compensate for this lack of proper command has to satisfy at once the machine's own forms and the procedures of operation and the preferences of the user. When this translational mechanism knits together into a veil that affords only glimpses of the machine's real face, it becomes itself an obfuscatory symbology we need to learn to decipher.

Works Cited

Allen, Paul. 2011. *Idea Man: A Memoir*. London: Penguin.

Connor, Steven. 2016. 'How to Do Things with Writing Machines'. In *Writing, Medium, Machine: Modern Technographies*, edited by Sean Pryor and David Trotter, 18–34. London: Open Humanities Press.

Datapro Research Corporation. 1976. *Alphanumeric Display Terminals – Basic Characteristics*. Delran: Datapro Research Corporation.

Engelbart, Douglas et. al. 1968. 'A Research Centre for Augmenting Human Intellect'. Stanford Research Institute. https://web.stanford.edu/dept/SUL/library/extra4/sloan/mousesite/1968Demo.html

Flusser, Vilém. 2002. *Writings*, edited by Andreas Ströhl, translated by Erik Esel. Minneapolis: University of Minnesota Press.

Goldstein, Gordon D. ed. 1964. *Digital Computer Newsletter* 16, no. 4. Washington, DC: Office of Naval Research.

Hekmatpour, Sharam. 1986. 'Why Your Software is User-Hostile'. *The Guardian*, October 30, 1986: 24.

IBM. 1968. *Operator Manual: IBM 2260 Display Station, IBM 2848 Display Control, IBM 1053 Printer*. New York: IBM Corporation.

IBM. 1982. *Disk Operating System*. First revised edition. Boca Raton, FL: IBM Corporation.

Irons, Edgar T. and Frans M. Djorup. 1972. 'A CRT Editing System'. *Communications of the ACM* 15: 16–20.

Kay, Alan C. 1969. 'The Reactive Engine'. Unpublished PhD dissertation, University of Utah.

Kay, Alan C. 1972. 'A Personal Computer for Children of All Ages'. *Proceedings of the ACM Annual Conference* 1: n. p.

Lampson, Butler. 1972. 'Why Alto'. Xerox PARC Inter-Office Memorandum. http://www.bwlampson.site/38a-WhyAlto/Acrobat.pdf

Lampson, Butler. 1973. 'Design Notes for Alto Operating System'. Xerox PARC Inter-Office Memorandum. http://www.bwlampson.site/38b-AltoOSNotes/38b-AltoOSNotes.pdf

Moglen, Eben and Jay Worthington. 2000–2001. 'The Encryption Wars: An Interview with Eben Moglen'. *Cabinet* 1. http://www.cabinetmagazine. org/issues/1/i_moglen_1.php

Norman, Donald A. 1981. 'The Trouble with UNIX'. *Datamation* 27: 139–50.

Parikka, Jussi. 2012. *What is Media Archaeology?* Cambridge: Polity.

Pratschke, Margarete. 2015. 'Interacting with Images – Towards a History of the Digital Image: The Case of Graphical User Interfaces'. In *The Technical Image: A History of Styles in Scientific Imagery*, edited by Horst Bredekamp, Vera Dünkel, and Birgit Schneider, 48–57. Chicago: University of Chicago Press.

Smith, Alvy Ray. 2016. 'The Dawn of Digital Light'. *IEEE Annals of the History of Computing* 38: 74–91.

Sutherland, Ivan. 1963. 'Sketchpad, A Man-Machine Graphical Communication System'. Unpublished PhD dissertation., MIT. https:// dspace.mit.edu/handle/1721.1/14979

Sutherland, Ivan. 2012. 'The TX-2 Computer and Sketchpad'. *Lincoln Laboratory Journal* 19: 82–4.

Thacker, C.P., E.M. McCreight, B.W. Lampson, R.F. Sproull, and D.R. Boggs. 1979. *Alto: A Personal Computer*. Palo Alto, CA: Xerox Corporation.

Toomey, Warren. 2011. 'The Strange Birth and Long Life of Unix'. *IEEE Spectrum*. https://spectrum.ieee.org/tech-history/cyberspace/ the-strange-birth-and-long-life-of-unix

Turing, A.M. 1936. 'On Computable Numbers, With an Application to the Entscheidungsproblem'. *Proceedings of the London Mathematical Society* 2: 230–65.

Xerox PARC. 1972. 'Office Alto Commercial'. *Computer History Museum*, published online April 20, 2012. https://www.youtube.com/ watch?v=Mozgj2p7Ww4

Xerox PARC. 1979. *Alto User's Handbook*. Palo Alto: Xerox Corporation.

5

The Performative Function of Hope: An Archaeology of LambdaMOO

Caroline Bassett

In our time history aspires to the condition of archaeology, to the intrinsic description of the monument.

(Foucault 1972: 7)

Optimism and pessimism are forms of fatalism [...] authentic hope [...] needs to be underpinned by reason. In this it resembles love.

(Eagleton 2015: 3)

In the early 1990s the explosive growth of the internet, and its translation into more public realms, produced new forms of digitally mediated life; this was the time of 'virtual community', 'cyber-subjectivity', and of 'life on-line'. All of these terms circulated widely, crossing between nascent internet studies, techno-cultural (and sub-cultural) milieus, and Silicon Valley circuits. Life on-line, in particular, was used to invoke or designate a social practice, a mode of computer-mediated communication, and sometimes a fantasy construction that was nonetheless operational; a subject and a world – something *paracosmic*. Emerging out of gaming, but abandoning rule-based play for informal social interaction, multiple sites engaging in experimentation with virtual subjectivity and virtual life sprung up. One of them was LambdaMOO, an Object Oriented Multi User Domain, accessed through the telnet protocol, which became a habitat and a site of experimentation for performing the 'self' and doing 'gender'. (MOOs are multi user domains using object-oriented programming techniques to organise databases of objects. MOOs allow users to programme in ways that change the server space [virtual site] for all users; see, for example, Curtis 1992.) One of many experimental sites that were at once 'spaces off' and 'spaces on' – databases that were at once fictions and/or laboratories, Lambda was influential in techno-cultural circles (see, for example, Turkle 1997). It was owned by Xerox PARC and run by one of its employees as an experiment in computer mediated communication. It is questions about mediation – about a multiply articulated relationship, between language and code, places on-screen and off, bodies and virtual bodies – that arise through a study of Lambda, that are taken up here. My starting point is that it is not only 'computers' that mediate, but also always language; what is at issue here then might be described, following Gabrillo and Zetter's introduction to this collection, in terms of the stakes of a 'mutual determination'.

Lambda was (code and) text-based but had a 'real' imaginary geography; hallways, rooms, palaces or caves were mapped. It organised public and private talk channels – for shouting, whispering, and public debate, for instance, and supported code-enabled actions such as 'dancing' or 'eating' together (Curtis and Nichols 1993). It also enabled the self-conscious production and on-going editing of the self, valorizing fluidity, self-invention, and experimentation. LambdaMOO inhabitants were invited to check their flesh bodies and 'warranted' identities 'into the closet' on arrival; not so much coming out, as coming *in* to a new world (Stone 1995: 40). Once there, they might describe themselves (via the command, '@describe me as') as they wished, and through this production in language and code, *perform* their chosen identity to others. It was thus through multiple and re-iterated performances of the self, undertaken in contexts in which, to invoke Derrida (1990), the performative utterance felt the 'force' of a particular kind of law – the law pertaining to the distancing of flesh bodies and the intimacy of coded texts that was the virtual condition – that Lambda, articulating code and natural language, flesh and immaterial bodies, came together as a virtual community (Rheingold 2000).

For some, Lambda instantiated what cyber-activist John Perry Barlow encapsulated in the libertarian *Declaration of Independence* – where he defined cyberspace as 'a world that is both everywhere and nowhere, but it is not where bodies live' (Barlow 1996). On the other hand Lambda was obsessed with identity and with the creation of imaginary or virtual bodies; and was – for a time – notorious for the gender-switching practices of its inhabitants, many of whom exploited the possibilities virtual space offered to release themselves from the constraints of normative bodily conformation (Bassett 1997); Lambda provided multiple gender identities, including various options for radically non-binary identifications – 'spivak' and 'neuter' amongst them.

Even in the 1990s, when being on-line was a non-mainstream affair, LambdaMOO was a fragment, a tiny *avant-garde* space, against which stood the 'well lit' and cultivated gardens of AOL and others, with their millions of members. It was however a fragment in which fierce hope was invested by some, being for a time a locus for techno-feminist interventions, both in net activist and academic circles. (My own virtual ethnography of LambdaMOO is recorded in Bassett 1997.) Seen as a cauldron for new forms of identity construction and performance, its subjects constructed or materialised in discourse and code, it seemed to offer possibilities to queer forms of sex and gender essentialism founded in immutable or stubborn flesh. It thus resonated with the feminist politics of critical gender performativity inspired by Judith Butler's Foucauldian analysis of the political technology of the subject in *Gender Trouble* (1990), and her treatment of iteration as a mode of identity production which relied on Derrida's reading of Austin, and 'doing things with words' in *Bodies that Matter* (Derrida 1974; Austin 1975). Lambda moreover was part of a more general 1990s revival of various strands of an explicitly technophile feminism, which had been largely eclipsed since the late 1960s. These differed in their readings of technological determination – ontological accounts were in tension with media sociological constructivism, for instance – but shared a belief that the 'technology gender relation' could be transformed.

In this chapter the focus is not on what Lambda became – it still exists today in a truncated form – but rather on its early days, and the activist engagements that were part of them, and on how these are remembered as part of that 1990s internet constellation that is now being widely historicised. Specifically, I am interested in something often lost in emerging histories of the internet; namely a form of hope for the future which found its justification in the potential for disruption cyberspace opened up, but was also aware of the precariousness of the moment; those engaged in hopeful activities often understood them as constituting a tactical response to contingent possibilities (to put it in Hakim Bey's terms [1991], and/or De Certeau's [1984: especially 102–18], such operations exploited what was only ever a 'rented' space). Against hope a different sensibility or belief about how the internet future might 'play out', here defined as a mode of technological optimism, *is* widely acknowledged as having been present in the early net. Why then, but also *how* – did this come to dominate later accounts of Lambda and the early (feminist) politics of the net, and how does it inform judgements that say the early cyber-feminists simply 'got it wrong' about the digital and its potential? This not least because they were said to have misunderstood the degree to which, despite speaking 'in code' as well as 'in language', they could not escape processes of 'articulation' – defined here both in terms of a material interface and via Laurence Grossberg's cultural theoretic definition, as that which 'links this practice to that effect, this text to that meaning, this meaning to that reality, this experience to those politics' (Grossberg 1992: 54).

What follows might be a missing persons story; it asks what happened to LambdaMOO's insouciant gender-burning inhabitants and their hopes, and it asks if – *despite their apparently being proved wrong about the future by the future itself* – their sense of cyberspace as an opening might be re-found. In other words, can there be a way of 'doing time' (or doing history) that enables elements apparently dealt with in dominant historical accounts of the early internet to regain their potency today? This is a question that has a peculiar piquancy for cyber-feminism given the gender politics of the (supposedly) 'post-digital' era.

The story is traced out at various scales and through different registers; LambdaMOO itself, and its memorialisation, is further considered. This is undertaken partly by way of a critical adoption of media archaeology, and through an engagement with Walter Benjamin's work on time and technology, both as it has been read by Terry Eagleton (2015) in the latter's critique of progress, and as it contributes to media archaeological treatments of technical media (see, for example, Parikka's 'Introduction' to Ernst 2013). Eagleton's own elaboration of hope and optimism as entailing different relationships to grand narratives of (neo-liberal) Progress, is also key here, not least because it resonates with a body of critical techno-cultural thinking exploring specifically media-technological progress and its reduction to a matter of growth. Finally, there is Judith Butler, whose feminist critique of essentialist forms of thinking gender in the 1990s, and development of a politics of gender performativity inspired by Foucault's understanding of a discourse that materialises the subject (Butler 1990, 1993), comes (back) to inform this account.

Non-progressivist Forms of Hope?

In a work attacking the easy embrace of 'the doctrine of progress', Eagleton identifies two distinct forms of future orientation currently circulating (2015: 33). Future optimism, defined as a simple belief in progress as that which will be delivered by markets, is seen as more or less linear. It appears to be based on reason (on 'reasonable' or 'inevitable' market logics), but (like pessimism) in reality amounts to a 'form of fatalism'; what will be delivered will be delivered. This may sound not only fatalistic, but frankly eschatological (certainly if it is *we* who will be delivered), but it is recognised here that future optimism increasingly takes a technological rather than theological form. As evidence Eagleton invokes scientist Steven Pinker, and the *Rational Optimist* author Matt Ridley – who understands technological progress simply as Progress – and notes *inter alia* that for the Ridley the 'liberation of women' can be attributed to 'labour saving electrical machinery' (Ridley, cited in Eagleton 2015: 15).

In contrast to optimism as an orientation underpinned by a commitment to/belief in an ever accelerating but largely unexamined progression, there is hope. Hope is designated as more uncertain, but by virtue of that, potentially more radical in its ambitions and its sense of where the future might lead, than optimism. Eagleton's account of hope – and what it may open up in the future – leans heavily on Benjamin's insistence on the unfinished nature of the past. In the *Theses on the Philosophy of History* (Benjamin 1992, 2006), the latter famously argues that, as Eagleton puts it, 'the meaning of the past lies in the keeping of the present' (Eagleton 2015: 32). If the histories of the dispossessed are lost, this is because they lack 'succession' – we might say they are not well kept, or have no keepers, in the present. This formulation at once recognises history's violence and raises the possibility that consignment can be contested. For Benjamin, as Eagleton puts it, 'the past […] is curiously mutable' – and this in turn suggests that what happens 'at the core of time' may be at least as important, or rather *more* important, than what happens at its end, or as its end. As Eagleton reads Benjamin contestation of history given by the present is possible and may be (should be) pursued; to 'strive to keep the past unfinished' amounts not only to 'choosing to read [the past] in certain ways' but is undertaken 'by virtue of our actions' (Eagleton 2015: 32).

The demand emerging here, as I read it, is that 'we' – we who would wish to be critical time keepers perhaps – should find ways to 'short-circuit time' (Eagleton 2015: 29). This kind of short-circuiting, may pertain not only to what has already been consigned to the past (the lost hopes for technological change in LambdaMOO perhaps) but may also relate to the future and how it is predicted as 'coming about' (and viewed in this way it is clear that the stakes scale up; from the instance of Lambda and the lost temporal orientations articulated by its feminist inhabitants to more general questions about digital technologies and their capacity to open or close various kinds of futures). Hope is important here because it can provide an active orientation towards an as-yet-un-given future; the latter is itself no longer understood as simply the next step 'forward' in the chain (the as-yet-unrevealed *end* of the development chain), but as something that may be reached, or *reached for*, or made, in new ways. What is called for, what needs to be actively theorised – or made operational – is thus what Eagleton terms a 'non-progressivist form of hope' (Eagleton 2015: 31). This would be a form of hope, here defined against technological optimism's adherence to unexamined progress, that would not be based on the 'given', particularly on the given limits or horizons of a particular social system, but that rather attends the possible. And perhaps it needs to do more than bloodlessly 'attend'; Eagleton himself invokes Paul Ricoeur, another philosopher of time, who followed Kierkegaard in arguing for that '*passion* for the possible' (Eagleton 2015: 48) that founded hope.

Eagleton's critique of Progress, and of optimism as a belief in Progress that produces an orientation towards the future made myopic by the given-ness of the present (the givens of the market producing the endless repetition of the commodity form; see Eagleton 2015: 34), shares much with a body of extant work spanning digital media, cultural theory, and critical software studies. This has questioned teleological accounts of media technological progress, particularly those conjoining ontological essentialism (technological determination as that which determines future deliveries) with a belief in progress as growth. An example is my own work on digital silence (Bassett 2013), or Matt Fuller's argument against accepting that what the market produces as software is the only way software could be (Fuller 2008). Others have shown that giant social media platforms are not the inevitable outcome of the early virtual spaces, that web 2.0 (a 'pattern book' for commercial exploitation; see Bassett 2008) did not inevitably follow the early net. By the same logic 1990s cyber-feminism did not *need* to lead to 'Lean In' style digital post-feminism as a dominant cultural logic (albeit one which is contested; for instance by Foster 2016). These critiques of teleologically informed optimalist internet development stories span analyses of the current moment and its theorisation (in critical software studies), and work disputing 'standard' media histories of digital media coming from media archaeology where issues of (historical and technical) progress are rehearsed specifically in relation to media technologies.

The distinctions between hope and optimism elaborated here can be useful at multiple levels. They provide an analytic lens to understand such orientations as they may have existed 'in the wild' or at a certain moment (e.g. in Lambda as an early internet formation); they may be deployed to question the ways the late internet (and some late internet feminism) has *judged* the earlier formation and the feminist ambitions that circulated within it. Finally, they may produce insight into historical methods and their capacity (or desire) to re-wire or *short* the circuits that have laid down particular events or technological formations or temporal orientations as of their time, finished with, curtailed.

Cyberfeminist Ambition?

Cyber-feminism's assessment of the potential of the early internet took diverse forms. It was argued by some feminists that the internet (or virtual space) had dealt a death blow to essentialism; the performative production of the subject had moved from theory and discourse to the real. Parallels can be drawn between this and discourses claiming that hypertext constituted 'deconstruction delivered' extant in literary hypertext circles around the same time (notably via Landow 1991). Working more or less along these lines Allucquère Rosanne Stone argued that you could 'wear identity like a garment' in cyberspace, and discard it as easily (Stone 1991: 109). Others argued cyberspace itself *was* female, and in a sense revealed what technology always had been in essence (see, for example, Plant 1998).

Others again were more tentative – amongst them many LambdaMOO feminists, who were also excited by the flexibility of virtuality, but were nonetheless often – and explicitly – more hopeful than optimistic in their orientation towards/expectations of the digital future. On the one hand Lambda *was* a world in which the slipping of the normative knot joining sex with gender could be contemplated in new ways. Moreover, whilst it was, patently, a constructed world, a play of surfaces, a thin film of writing (see de Certeau 1984: xxi on the thin film of writing that becomes 'a play of spaces'; cited in Bassett 1997: 539), a few lines of code, a populated database, it supported a surprisingly 'real' sense of place, in which its inhabitants made and remade bodies that did not directly cite or iterate sex-gender norms since they were not directly 'warranted' by the flesh of their 'owners'. This was highly suggestive. But, as Butler's own arguments would suggest (and these were influential at the time) slippage was partial. Normativizing discourse continued to intervene in the iterated performances Lambda enabled, not least because these were enabled in bodies made in language as well as in code. This was a queer space perhaps, but it was not 'free' from gendered histories, or normative constraints that were elsewhere policed by flesh embodied in more standard ways. Rather, producing conditions in which the naturalisation of sex-gender binaries could be revealed *as a naturalisation*, rather than *as natural*, Lambda could be seen as a laboratory for exploring *possible* new forms of life and sociality. It produced gender trouble, that could be played with, claimed, used to hope with. (It shared with Sadie Plant, whose work was a manifesto as much as an analysis; see Plant 1998.) Hope as an active orientation – but one that was not aligned to a belief in inevitable technological progress, but rather to disruption and queering – might be said to set this strand of feminist thinking, or this form of feminist inhabitation apart. There were those simply living in cyberspace and those also theorizing it, or rather finding within it a place for doing theory. It also distinguishes this position from that held by feminists for whom cyberspace or the virtual world was, by virtue of its ontology, already a form of feminist utopia; a utopia *delivered*.

Lambda Calculated

The celebratory engagements with identity play Lambda entertained were brought up short when -- in an echo of what is now drearily familiar – it was hacked by an 'evil' resident who turned inhabitants into sock puppets forced to act out his will and his desires. After the 'rape in cyberspace' (as it was described in *Village Voice;* Dibbell 1993). Lambda's unorganised free-wheeling 'society' became more self-conscious, a corporate responsibility was felt; the heterotopia became something else (Curtis and Nichols 1993). There were also broader shifts as the early net era drew to an end. The World Wide Web changed the ways in which intersection was organised, interaction built, and platforms produced. Later Web 2.0 valorised the cultivation of harvested gardens where the produce, the fruits of interactions between named, located, and increasingly finely sliced individuals, demanded not anonymity and slippage, but precision and anchoring. The self was not to slip away into the nets but on the contrary was to be held more tightly within networks that were increasingly controlled, so becoming the locus of series of deliverable and delivered desires. LambdaMOO did not fit well with this new order.

Today Lambda tends to be recalled (when at all) as an experiment in transforming social subjectivity that turned out to have been a dead end. The early cyber-feminism, with which it was bound up, has also been criticised; for being over-optimistic about what digital technology could do, for having inflated ideas about the disruptive potential of virtuality/virtual life, for believing in a virtual/real-world split (an ontology of the virtual) that could renew a Cartesian division between flesh/mind in the first place, and (worst of all perhaps) for having *desired* such a division. These judgements inform ways in which Glitch feminism or Everyday Sexism activism read early net feminism as 'unrealistic', while Web 2.0 style *post*-feminism, with its consumer-orientated sense of a 'realist' feminist politics whose boundaries are set by the possibilities given in the immediate present – the era of burgeoning platform monopoly – represents an explicit rejection of all of Lambda's wild hope. Clearly these strands of feminism/post-feminism are very different, but the common charge laid today against the feminists of the 1990 by many of those operating today is that their project failed. In particular gender trouble of the kind celebrated in LambdaMOO is now widely viewed as evidence of an earlier naivety; about what digital technology itself could usher *in* (for instance radically new forms of queered identity and collective community), and about what virtual worlds could keep *out* (for instance normative social relations and discriminations).

It is striking how far these judgements rely for their authority on what has come about 'in the end'. Thus these early experiments tend to be viewed as – at best – pale shadows of the more material, substantial, realistic, *progressed* engagements now afforded through pervasive technology, the Internet of Things, and machine learning. Moreover this reliance is not based only on the presumption of technological, but also human, progression; the discourse of digital nativity, after all, is a discourse that, presuming the inevitable advancement of the digital self, also presumes that those who follow 'know better' or *are* better able to judge than those who came before. (Ontologically naïve perhaps – although it is interesting to note that Lambda itself was a born digital world.)

The present, now 'knowing better' about digital culture and gender issues, thus corrects the hopes of the past for a radical future for gender relations in a technological society (which might remain potent, or which might be easily understood to obtrude into the present as an unfinished project), by translating hope into (misplaced) optimism, said to be based on an over-reaching confidence that the digital technology of the time could be a delivery vehicle for a sex-gender revolution that can now been seen to have exhausted itself. The technological world we have emerged into is proffered as proof of this; we didn't get here from there and so the rational kernel which founds hope as hope (and distinguishes it from unmoored dreaming) is thus retrospectively determined as always already having been absent. The dynamic discerned operating around Lambda isn't exceptional; there is much else from the early internet years that has been, or is being over-written or *corrected* in a similar way in popular and academic histories; a dominant tale of 'early' and 'mistaken' investment in 'the virtual' as a distinct sphere takes this form for instance. An investigation of correctionism as it operates more broadly within techno-feminism and/as wave theory would also seem to be necessary – although this is not pursued further here.

A Medium Theory of Correction and Succession

In the following sections of this chapter, correctionism *is* used to explore and perhaps define a particular way of doing revisionist history, a way in which the politics of 'succession' may operate in times of ubiquitous technical media which complicate presence and absence, continuity and rupture, and which make different claims on the future. This entails an engagement with media archaeology, explored for its potential to engage with and contest particular forms of correctionism.

And here some obvious connections can be pointed out. We have already noted how Eagleton, engaging with Benjamin's messianic sense of time, is inspired by the latter's demand for a radical historiography to generate a call for hope as a politics of future time. Media archaeology draws heavily on Benjamin, and in particular takes up his demand to develop a history 'from the middle'. Indeed in its attempt to grapple with the complex non-linear temporalities of computational forms it takes at least as much from the Benjaminian tradition as it does from the Foucauldian requirement that history 'aspires to the condition of archaeology, to the intrinsic description of the monument' (Foucault 1972: xi–xxiv), from which it takes its name.

With these connections in mind I now circle back to the question of why certain histories are lost, going first to the blunt response from Walter Benjamin to this question, which is that history is written by the victors. What is written out are the costs to the losers and – we might add – their future hopes. In the *Theses on History,* a meditation on the politics of time, this is directly related to the violent storm of 'Progress' which leaves in its wake the wreckage of what it has destroyed in its rush onwards. Elsewhere in Benjamin's writings, however, it is made clear that media technological developments are not simply part of this storm, or at one with its simple trajectory. Notably, in *The Work of Art in the Age of Mechanical Reproduction* (1992), which explores the technological aesthetics of new media as a medium politics, Benjamin counters the violence of Progress with the dynamite of cinema. The 'dynamite' of the tenth of a second, he famously argues, may enable new forms of engagement and action that offer an escape from a world and a time that had us trapped, so that we may 'calmly and adventurously go travelling' in the ruins of a world re-made. This escape is not only spatial but temporal; film, stripping away the aura given by what has been stored up and held through time in earlier cultural forms, opens the way to consider a continuous re-making, and a more open production or engagement, perhaps with the past and the future as well with the given environment (those offices, factories, metropolitan streets which had us 'locked up'). *The Work of Art* thus points to ways in which the workings of succession might be disrupted by the hybrid temporalities and materials of a world re-organised through the advent of a powerful new technical media system; in this case film and photography.

If what emerges here is an account of how older media technologies intervene directly in (re)making human experience in time and space, and an outline of how the new forms of complex experience they enable might offer ways to contest a given succession, or to confound the hard lines of a linear history, then at issue today are the still more complex and layered temporalities that pervasive computational media systems produce.

Succession questions take on a peculiar complexity when explored in relation to these systems, with their capacity to hold and release modes of experience previously laid down in uneven ways, to join previously disparate spheres whilst simultaneously introducing fragmentation. On the one hand multiple clock times and speeds produce simultaneous but divergent temporalities, on the other boundaries between the past and present are re-drawn; thus pervasive networks mean we increasingly live in the present and in the archive, while predictive technologies seek to pull the future into this new kind of 'now'. In this situation continuous modulation and revision become a new mode through which matters of succession are negotiated, and forms of consignment characterised not by absolute presence or absence, appearance or disappearance, but by complex emerging arrangements. Emulation offers an example for thinking through how this might operate, bringing back to life technical elements that constituted earlier systems but often leaving behind the social contexts in which they became operational. The result may be a cultural practice based on nostalgia, aesthetic revivalism, or inauguration. But it is also useful to consider the potential pitfalls of emulation as an (archaeological) methodology for cultural study; since in emulation a formal architecture may be revived, but what animated it, and/ or gave it its political character may be transformed, understood in new ways, or thought to be as 'quaint' as the code that drives them now appears. This may be the basis for a mode of correction relevant to net histories in general; only too often in relation to accounts of the 1990s net, that passion for the possible (going back to Riceour for a moment), a passion that drove its radical elements, is hollowed out, while old code remains available in decontextualised or recontextualised forms.

Medium disruption of temporal and spatial givens is a core theme in media archaeological writing; variously explored as a proposition, taken as a given starting point, and/or constituting the basis of an injunction to switch the locus of cultural inquiry from representation, the symbolic, and/or narrative accounting, to the operations of technology. And its demand to recognise temporal complexity, or to acknowledge the hybridity of those assemblages that give us time, is useful. A strong version of the media archaeological is evidenced in the work of Wolfgang Ernst, who builds an archaeology in conditions of media saturation by inserting (Kittler's) material into (Foucault's) document; for Ernst it is the machine that is to be monumentalised in the work of doing history. Ernst's work can open the way to re-thinking succession itself as not only a matter of what is *told*, or received as a tale, but of what is *held, stored, belayed*, through various technical arrangements. For Ernst this turn is absolute; his point is to challenge directly what he terms standard media history and its tendency to work 'in the narrative mode'. (Ernst 2013: 56 recognises that this is not straightforward. He notes that that the cultural burden of 'giving sense to data through narrative structures is not easy to overcome'.) The charge is that narrative approaches dissolve the intractable and non-linear operations of heterogeneous materials in order to produce linear texts, when it is precisely these new operations that have to be foregrounded – because they now give us our time.

Media archaeology provokes a re-assessment of the digital's capacity to transform what might be termed the workings of succession, now a matter of storage media and its operations. It does however tend to produce its own closures – and here Ernst's contribution is useful as a limit case. For the latter, technical time now determines events, but the priority this accords to the purely technical (over the symbolic or perhaps over writing itself) threatens to produce a new kind of reduction: to give us a history determined solely by the formal and technical conditions of the say-able. Jussi Parikka rightly notes that Ernst's bid to offer 'insight into the *a priori* of writing' is in danger of 'mythologizing the machine as completely outside other temporalities' (Parikka, as quoted in Ernst 2013: 10); for instance those given by the material of our bodies, or those produced through the symbolic, both key elements within a socio-technical assemblage. This kind of fetishisation (as Chun 2011 has put it in relation to software) isn't confined to Ernst's admittedly polemical analysis; Lisa Gitelman (2007) points to deleterious effects of such a prioritisation in general critique of technicist approaches, and while Ernst's position is stronger than many others writing in this vein, it does connect with a widely held tendency in the media archaeological retrieval project to valorise the material and in doing so to divide it from the actions of the symbolic; from narrative and discourse, and from those materials through which this is *articulated*. A necessary adjunct then, to media archeology's important demand to attend to the materials and the temporalities they provide, is to explore this in relation to – *and as a relation with* – what is held in writing.

Going Back to LambdaMOO

These questions concerning technical media and time and its relation to writing bear directly on LambdaMOO and on the project not only to re-find, but re-operationalise, cyber-feminist hopes that have been subject to correction in historical accounts. It allows us to re-approach LambdaMOO and the feminist projects it hosted – and indeed to grapple with performativity and its disruptive or unfinished business as a digital politic.

First then, a media-archaeologically *oriented* investigation of LambdaMOO can avoid binding it into that linear trajectory that reads early MUDS and MOOs in general as precursors of later social media platforms, and/or that binds it into a general history of the rise of the internet as unproblematically a matter of progression. Moreover it invites reconsideration of what LambdaMOO was, and what it did, as a media apparatus. Exploring only what was said there (about gender or anything else) is only half the story; there is also the question of how this was articulated, in code as well as language, and how as a consequence it interfaced with other productions (of the gendered self). Stuart Hall said of articulation that it was a form of connection that could make 'a unity of two different elements' – but added that this was so only 'under certain conditions' (Hall, cited in Grossberg 1996: 141).

The issue arising therefore – and here we need more than the media archaeological, and also need to reach beyond Hall's comments on discourse – concerns *what* kind of apparatus we are talking about here; what kind of 'conditions' it provided? We have noted that the media archaeological demand that attention be paid to materials is both its strength – and, where this demand becomes exclusive, its weakness. LambdaMOO *was* an object in code, but it was *also* made in language. Digging in the ruins, starting in the middle, blasting back into being an apparatus now dismantled, isn't enough if that apparatus is always already presumed to be constituted *in essence*, or determined only, by its strictly technical features. This isn't a pious argument about the need to think about the operations of ideology at the level of the symbolic (as if any technical apparatus did not also and already bear the scars of the ideological operations that co-constituted it in the form it has come to take), but a practical one. The disruptive potential the cyber-feminists played with came not through code alone, and not even because the language or discourse of sex/gender was released from its constraining supports in fleshed bodies, by its translation into code. What was potentially disruptive about Lambda was that it afforded a new *disposition* of code, bodies, flesh, and language. It thus provided a new *matrix* out of which, or through which, gender could be performed. That is, Lambda's feminism, at once a contestation in code, and a delirium in language, found its force precisely in engaging with that new entanglement *between* the symbolic and the material that virtual space produced. You could say it operationalised the techno-feminist Donna Haraway's (more or less contemporary) injunction to use the resources of code and the resources of imagination to *turn* language. Haraway indeed defined cyborg politics as: 'the struggle for language and the struggle against perfect communication, against the one code that translates all meaning perfectly, the central dogma of phallogocentrism' (Haraway 1991: 176).

Lambda's feminists worked through digital technology to 'struggle for language', to queer the 'passion of the signifier' (Lacan 1977), the 'one code' that resounds in language, that is the relation of speech, and that constitutes, in so far as speech is phallogocentric, the law of the father. Their hope therefore can be (re)found and (re)assessed as cradled in, perhaps as articulated as, that relationship *between* the material and the discursive.

To take language's performativity seriously, as LambdaMOO's injuncts us to do, suggests the need to re-think what may signify and what may act. Performativity queers media-archaeological hierarchies; the material first and the representation later, the technology first and the interpretation after the act; a mode of organisation that makes it blind to some of what it explores, notably those aspects media history that are concerned tightly with questions of intention as well with action or operation. We need the narrative and the machine. Ernst's version of media archaeology – in so far as it is a form of critical archaeology that *replaces* discourse with code or material can't get us to LambdaMOO's feminists' orientations, to let us feel the force of their actions, because it has abandoned half of what *made* that world; and I stress, not what represented it, but what *made* it.

You might say that while media archaeology can disrupt optimism as an orientation that is only interested in the past as the delivery mechanism for the present, and that it is therefore useful, it is hard to for it to handle hope. In LambdaMOO the disruptive potential celebrated by feminism emerges between language and code, the material and the symbolic, as a new relation. When it misses this, media archaeology itself is in danger of naming hope as false and technology as destining; a history 'from the middle' that oddly enough always has an end.

A Tentative Conclusion

One reason the new net pragmatists dislike old net politics so much might be the latter's refusal to accept the 'normal' or 'sober' measure of what might constitute a reasonable demand, or a reasonable thing to hope for. LambdaMOO's gender insurrection has been consigned to history as a failure. To re-find its potency as a hopeful moment of genuine promise has meant both taking it seriously as a medium, and contesting what constituted it as a technological system; it is this that might enable us to 'correct the correction', to contest the way in which 'old' Lambda has been consigned to the archive in a way that means the hopeful cyber-feminist politics it entertained are now viewed as outdated – and as always having been hopeless or mistaken.

I have suggested here that *distinctions* between the temporal promises contained in hope and those in optimism – as orientations towards the future – can be deployed to develop a critique of teleologically informed, optimalist internet history. Specifically, to develop a critique of the ways the late internet (and some late internet feminism) has judged early-feminist ambitions and hopes as mis-placed, and has corrected them. I conclude that digital correctionism is the adjustment technique of the victors to protect a version of digital history – and more to the point a version of the coming future – that sees its development only in terms of technological advancement and only within the grounds of the market. It is that vision which is written against here. Finally, a comment on why any of this matters; after all, Lambda, as noted, was a tiny shard. Media archaeology might respond that the non-obvious itself can open new doors simply by virtue of not being mainstream. My own reasons are threefold. First, the feminist demands arising around Lambda, are, as shown, both modest and utterly impiously grand – and not yet met. Second, because this kind of delete (critical hope) and insert (market optimism) process, which I have identified as a mode of correction, is deployed widely as a means through which technological/computational history is sanitised by the successors.

The third reason that it matters to re-find past hope in digital techno-cultures is that, as Eagleton reminds us, hope itself may act; that indeed is a key way in which he distinguishes hope for the future from confident optimism about the next steps within a system that closes down real possibility for social change. As Eagleton (2015: 84) notes (and he has often been far from Butler but here they are oddly close), hope is 'performative as well as optative' – and is in that way tangled up with desire but also based on reason.

The radical demand in hope indeed is that it at once breaks the current horizon of what is presumed to be possible, but also acts to make new kinds of possibility. It is in this sense I think that we can re-assess the usefulness of Lambda's hopefulness as a putative force to act in the present. Hope as an orientation for the future is ambitious because it sees further than the view that the tightly controlled, pre-corralled technological optimism of the market provides. If what is re-found may again be performative, beginning to produce that which it again can name, then I think it is worth attempting to bring the feminist moment of hope back into salience, to act and operate in internet politics today.

In particular, LambdaMOO's feminist moment might be used to disrupt contemporary digital-social formations; the digital, the post-digital, the age of platforms, behaviourism, accountability. Perhaps it can contribute to unsettling some of the assumptions informing both feminist politics of glitch and the 'everyday sexism' movement as a movement that responds to mediated life. Thinking about this kind of early cyber-feminist attempt to confound by exploiting digital technology, that which resounds in language as a relation of speech, that which echoes and is part of a relation of power and dominance, a final question that returns here is *what might a feminist media archaeology really look like? And what would it look like if it applied its own new method to itself?*

Works Cited

Austin, J.L. 1975. *How to Do Things with Words*. Oxford: Clarendon Press.

Barlow, John Perry. 1996. 'A Declaration of the Independence of Cyberspace'. February 8. https://www.eff.org/cyberspace-independence.

Bassett, Caroline. 1997. 'Virtually Gendered, Life in an On-line World.' In *The SubCultures Reader*, edited by Sarah Thornton and Ken Gelder, 537–50. London: Routledge.

Bassett, Caroline. 2008. 'New Maps for Old?: The Cultural Stakes of "2.0"'. *FCJ-088* 13. http://thirteen.fibreculturejournal.org/fcj-088-new-maps-for-old-the-cultural-stakes-of-2-0/.

Bassett, Caroline. 2013. 'Silence, Delirium, Lies?' *First Monday* 18 (3–4), March. http://firstmonday.org/ojs/index.php/fm/article/view/4617/3420.

Benjamin, Walter. 1992. *Illuminations*. London: Fontana.

Benjamin, Walter. 2006. 'On the Concept of History.' In *Selected Writings, 4: 1938–1940*. London: Harvard University Press.

Bey, Hakim. 1991. *The Temporary Autonomous Zone*. London: Autonomedia.

Butler, Judith. 1990. *Gender Trouble: Feminism and the Subversion of Identity*. London: Routledge.

Butler, Judith. 1993. *Bodies That Matter: On the Discursive Limits of Sex*. New York: Routledge.

Chun, Wendy Hui Kyong. 2011. *Programmed Visions: Software and Memory*. London: MIT Press.

Curtis, Pavel. 1992. 'Mudding: Social Phenomena in Text-Based Virtual Realities.' In *Proceedings of the 1992 Conference on Directions and Implications of Advanced Computing*, Berkeley, May 1992.

Curtis, Pavel and David A. Nichols. 1993. 'MUDs Grow Up: Social Virtual Reality in the Real World.' Report published by Xerox PARC, January 19. Proceedings of Compcon '94, 193–200. https://ieeexplore.ieee.org/document/282924.

De Certeau, Michel. 1984. *The Practice of Everyday Life*, translated by Steven Rendall. California: University of California Press.

Derrida, Jacques. 1974. *Of Grammatology*, translated by Gayatri Chakravorty Spivak. Baltimore: Johns Hopkins University Press.

Derrida, Jacques. 1988. 'Signature, Event, Context.' In *Limited Inc*, translated by Samuel Weber and Jeffrey Mehlman. Evanston, Il: Northwestern University Press.

Derrida, Jacques. 1990. 'Force of Law: The "Mystical Foundation of Authority"'. *Cardozo Law Review* 919, translated by Mary Quaintance.

Dibbell, Julian. 1993. 'A Rape in Cyberspace: How an Evil Clown, a Haitian Trickster Spirit, Two Wizards, and a Cast of Dozens Turned a Database into a Society'. In *The Village Voice*, December 23.

Eagleton, Terry. 2015. *Hope Without Optimism*. New Haven: Yale University Press.

Ernst, Wolfgang. 2013. *Digital Memory and the Archive*. Minnesota: Minnesota University Press.

Foster, Dawn. 2016. *Lean Out*. London: Repeater.

Foucault, Michel. 1972. *The Archaeology of Knowledge*. New York: Pantheon Books.

Fuller, Matt. 2008. *Software Studies: A Lexicon*. Cambridge, MA: MIT Press.

Gitelman, Lisa. 2007. *Always Already New: Media, History and the Data of Culture*. Cambridge, MA: MIT Press.

Grossberg, Laurence. 1992. *We Gotta Get Out of This Place: Popular Conservatism and Postmodern Culture*. New York: Routledge.

Grossberg, Laurence. 1996. 'On Postmodernism and Articulation: An Interview with Stuart Hall'. In *Stuart Hall: Critical Dialogues in Cultural Studies*, edited by David Morley and Kuan-Hsing Chen, 131–50. London: Routledge.

Haraway, Donna. 1991. *Simians, Cyborgs and Women*. London: Routledge.

Lacan, Jacques. 1977. 'The Signification of the Phallus'. In *Écrits: A Selection*, translated by Alan Sheridan, 281–91. London: Routledge.

Landow, George. 1991. *HyperText: The Convergence of Contemporary Critical Theory and Technology*. Baltimore: The Johns Hopkins University Press.

Plant, Sadie. 1998. *Zeros and Ones*. London: Fourth Estate.

Rheingold, Howard. 2000. *The Virtual Community: Homesteading on the Electronic Frontier*. London: MIT Press.

Stone, Allucquère Rosanne. 1991. 'Will the Real Body Please Stand Up'. In *Cyberspace: First Steps*, edited by Michael Benedict, 81–118. London: MIT Press.

Stone, Allucquère Rosanne. 1995. *The War of Desire and Technology*. London: MIT Press.

Turkle, Sherry. 1997. *Life on the Screen: Identity in the Age of the Internet*. New York: Touchstone Press.

6

At the Edge of the Audible:
Auscultating Non-Auditory Geographies

EMMA McCORMICK-GOODHART

The world does not presuppose itself: it is only
coextensive to its extension as world, to the spacing of its
places between which its resonances reverberate.

– Jean-Luc Nancy

Resonance calls into question the notion that the nature
of things resides in their essence and that this essence can
be exhausted by a sign, a discourse, a logos. An account
of something such as resonance must therefore situate
itself in a kind of echo chamber with other things – signs,
discourses, institutions, and practices.

– Veit Erlmann

Can we try to de-suppose the sophisticated wetware and media of our senses,
which lead us to perceive as if by magic? In the passages that follow, there
are two dynamics at play: the *from within* of hearing, and the *from without* of
space. I propose to trace how vibration becomes apprehensible as sound,
via the transductive technology of our sense of hearing, before musing on
its purported absence, as in deafness, where a 'sounding' sense of hearing
is often substituted for by the inscriptive technography of sign language
within heightened, mediatised environments known as DeafSpace. The aim,
ultimately, is to prompt our reconsideration of concepts of *sonic literacy*, and
even *sound as such*.

I. Interlude: Mute Archaeoacoustics

The shell operates at once as mouth, damp and resonant grotto,
and doppelänger ear – an eerie object becoming (never entirely) a
disenchanted scientific thing.

(Helmreich 2012)

The ear-snail, we are its shell, resonant bodies. The shell is a
telephone reaching the scale of the earth. Which is noise, the sea or
the snails, or the sea moving through the snails? The aggregate, the
multiple, noise can be described but not defined.

(Ahmed 2016)

In 1962, winemaker archaeologist Georges Bérard unearthed a Neolithic human skull (fig. 6.1), dating to the third millennium B.C., while excavating a megalithic chamber tomb at Roque d'Aille in Southwest France. Nested in the chamber's lowest, and hence oldest, stratigraphic layer, analysis revealed it to have undergone cremation though at a temperature too low to induce cellular

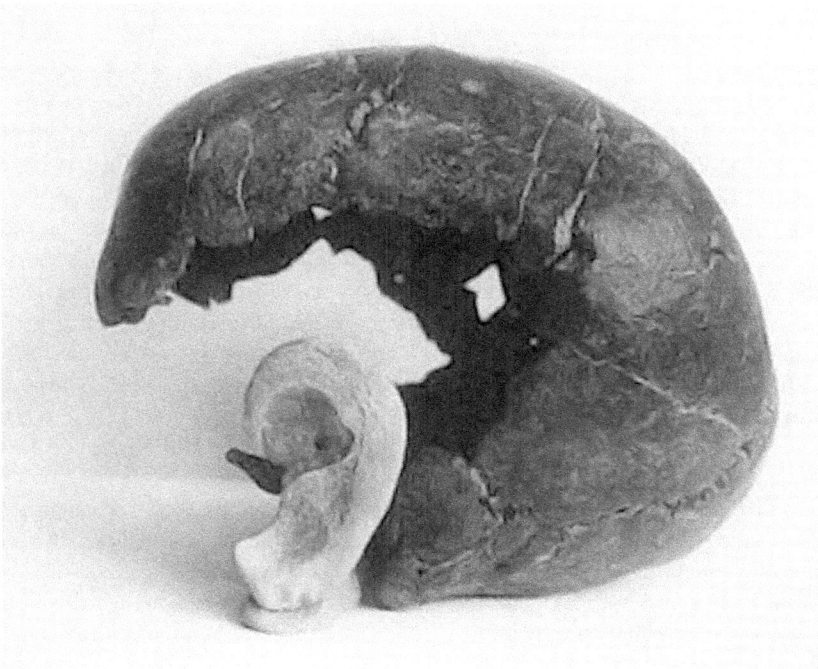

Figure 6.1: Neolithic skull with a prosthetic seashell ear. Photo by Gustaf Sobin.

decomposition, such that, remarkably, its *prosthetic seashell 'ear'* remained visibly intact.

Etymology gives us some clue as to the anatomical intricacies of the human inner ear's labyrinthine spiral shape and fluid-filled environment. The inner ear was named the 'cochlea' by anatomist Gabriello Fallopio in the mid-sixteenth century in reference to Latin *cochlea* for 'snail shell' and Greek *kokhlias* for 'spiral' (also related to 'mussel, conch') – a morphological likeness, which suggests that the very mechanisms of hearing itself, at least in their *otological*, or ear-based, dimension, are materially entangled with the figure of the spiral and water. While scientists have surmised that cochleate coiling took place to preserve space within the skull, evolutionary biologist Lynn Margulis holds that the human senses were infolded from a once freely swimming spiral-shaped bacterium called spirochete, meaning that 'hearing, as a biologically enabled capacity, is itself enabled by chimerical compounds' (Helmreich 2016: 160).

Paleopathologists determined that the Neolithic skull (fig. 6.1), identified as belonging to a young female, had been opened with a rough flint and surgically implanted with a seashell, of the genus *spondylus gaederopus*, which had been carved to replicate an earlobe and concave outer whorl of skin, known as the *pinna*. This elaborate 'open brain' procedure, inscribing a nine centimetre-long scar into the skull in its wake, would likely indicate that the shell's purpose was not purely ornamental, but instead to serve as a functional conduit for vibration.

Featured in poet Gustaf Sobin's book *Luminous Debris*, which sets out to listen to nominally 'mute artefacts', the author muses at the possible 'extrasensory' or 'extrasocial functions' that this Neolithic female might have performed within her community. Did she possess 'the ability to hear what others couldn't?' (Sobin 1999: 51–5). What evidence might these now inaudible frequencies have left – what 'sonorous' *tracings*? As one of the world's earliest known prostheses, or artificial body parts, to have been discovered, is it possible that this skull figures as the world's first 'cyborg' of a prehuman, rather than posthuman, order? The first to inhabit cyborg – even chimerical, multispecies – sound after requisite passage through a mollusc-made shell interface, a former exoskeleton? A beacon of 'deaf futurism', millennia before disability studies scholar Mara Mills's coinage of the term in relation to advocacy movements for cochlear implantation (Friedner and Helmreich 2012)?

The field of archaeoacoustics, otherwise known as aural or acoustic archaeology, has largely emerged as a sub-discipline of archaeology in the decades since this skull was found. It studies sound in archaeological contexts, often to test and map sites for their capacity to produce resonance through ritual reenactments, thereby inquiring into how sites might have been selected or technologised to augment oral and aural transmission. Never technically a participant in archaeoacoustic proceedings, the skull nonetheless sustains

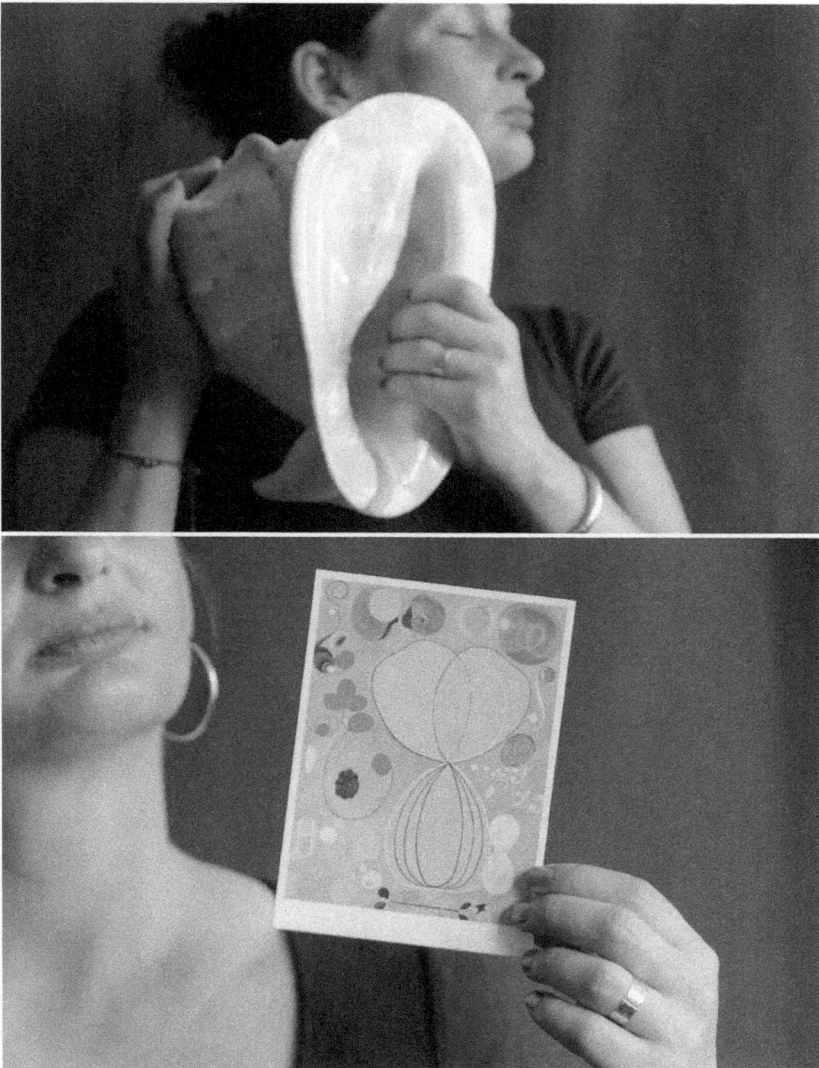

Figure 6.2: 'Conchology' and 'Cilia/Hilma Af Klint', from Emma McCormick-Goodhart, *Sounding in Sign*, 2016. Digital inkjet prints.

an 'implicit sonicity', in media theorist Wolfgang Ernst's phrasing (2016), through its implanted prosthetic ear, as well as a direct relation to the sonic – for it signals towards a 'deep time' of hearing via its attendant counterpart conditions of hearing loss, or aural impairment. I offer this specimen as an *episteme* of *imaginary media*, a fictive hearing aid and biosemiotic device with which we might auscultate and 'sound' mute matter in order to *think hearing*

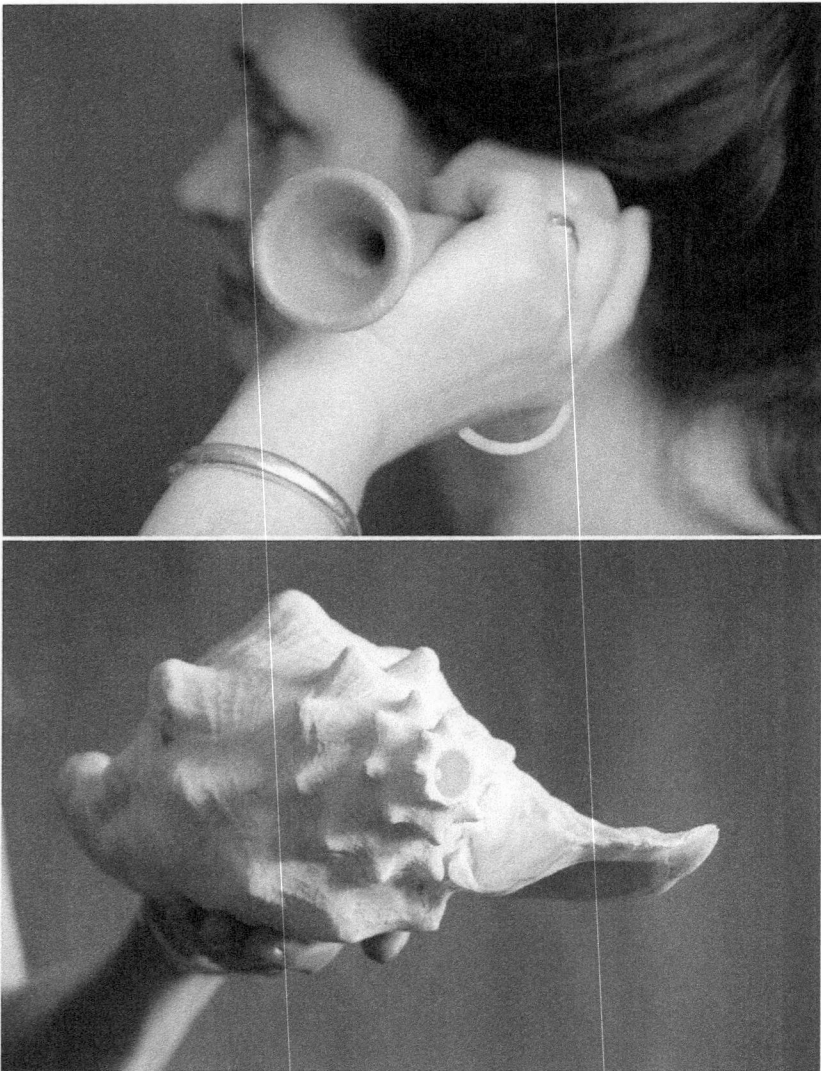

Figure 6.3: 'Stethoscope' and 'Shell Prosthesis', from Emma McCormick-Goodhart, *Sounding in Sign*, 2016. Digital inkjet prints.

beyond audition: across millennia, materials, scales and species. What would it mean to *image* a material history of hearing and hearing loss, or conversely, to push towards *hearing material histories themselves*, auscultating and unsedimenting 'natural history' by ear, rather than by eye? Can we 'hear through' materials, as John Cage provokes of us in *Silence*; can we hear through our hearing thereof?

II. Introduction

To talk about hearing in material terms is to acknowledge the fact,
as Bruno Latour insists, that the material world always comes to
us in cognisable forms.

(Erlmann 2014)

In the ensuing passages, I investigate material histories of oral and aural culture by conceptually re*sounding* – or auscultating – a range of media archaeological artefacts, premodern prostheses, spatial instantiations and etymologies. An attempt will be made to expand the logic of the prosthesis, normally body-bound, to include architectural space, yet in an *anarchitectural* spirit – in playful borrowing of artist Gordon Matta-Clark's term – where architecture extends beyond built space into actively composed modular, social and sensed *milieus*. Transiting between and across the scales of cells, cilia and spaces, I pay particular attention to the physiological passages in humans and other species that convert vibration into interpretable sound, as biosemiotically significant ones, alongside alternative modes of sensory perception, such as those practiced by deaf culture, which, contrary to popular misconception, is *not* immune to sound, but only infers it differently. Deaf geographies and 'Deaf space' encompass protocols of visual and vibrational amplification that enable spatial conditions for communicating in ways other than through spoken language. In the interest of formulating 'auditory geographies' not premised on the acoustic propagation of voice, I explore these conditions as *other than sonic* social settings – as spaces of substitutive sensory realities and assemblages.

This paper originates, in part, from a conjunction – an intradisciplinary provocation – articulated by anthropologist Michele Friedner and Stefan Helmreich in their 2012 essay 'Sound Studies Meet Deaf Studies'. Here, Friedner and Helmreich make a convincing case that scholars of auditory culture should join with those in Deaf studies to make active their respectively ingrained *sonocentric* and *oculocentric* biases. By *inhabiting* communicative interstices, the authors envision an unfolding of the 'common and uncommon senses of the world' through ontological cross-examination and methodological exchange. Divergences might lead to contiguities and novel modes of interarticulatedness that mix sign language and speech, Deaf and hearing constituencies to the extent that, as Jacques Derrida writes, 'a new situation for speech, of its subordination within a structure in which it will no longer be the archon' might be engendered (Derrida 1997: 6–7). 'Hearing, deafness, and seeing operate as ideal types, which downplays continuums between and multiplicities of sensory capabilities', and indeed, Friedner and Helmreich write, 'far from being peripheral, sound also penetrates deaf worlds' commonly, albeit falsely, presumed to be silent (Friedner and

Helmreich 2012: 75). In fact, Deaf worlds, as *other than sonic* lifeworlds, might instead produce a variety of exploratory hearing knowledges, where 'audition' is supplanted by other means and modes of *reading with* the sensible world.

Pertinently, in *Sonic Warfare: Sound, Affect and the Ecology of Fear*, Steve Goodman locates 'sonic potentials', or the potentials of sonic culture, at the interstices of sound, vibration and the 'physiologically and culturally inaudible' – a category that he terms 'unsound' to connote that which is *'not-yet-audible'* (Goodman 2010: xvi). Goodman's theoretical framework and conceptual scaffolding for a *'(sub)politics of frequency'* outlines an 'ontology of vibrational force', which serves to remind us that the limited spectrum of human audibility is but 'a fold on the vibratory continuum of matter' (9). His vibratory cosmology generates room for a *multi-species ecology of audition* across all strata of matter, wherein hearing is understood always already as a differential *threshold condition* boundaried by heterogenous points of entry and exit. (Granted, thinking nonhuman hearing cannot be approached except through binaural points of human audition, for it will always remain an *anthroposonic* project [Barcelos 2016: 72]).

Like Goodman, I seek to *think hearing*, both corporeal and not, as a threshold condition and genre of spatial practice through the realms of sound, as well as inaudible frequencies in excess of the so-called sonic, in that unsound (or vibration) is always a precondition for sound's occurrence. In its physical passage as wave energy through space, sound is constitutive of spatiality, just as spatial configurations inscribe and shape sound, synchronously, as it migrates and mutates: they are, in other words, coauthors of commensurate phenomena. With this in mind, I will interarticulate sound's capacity to generate such a *sense of space* alongside alternative modes of audition, which help to extend the notion of hearing beyond the audible, in material, rather than immaterial, terms; for perception, at the biochemical level, *is* a material process. In tandem, DeafSpace and Deaf geography, as an emergent design movement and field, respectively, may open new understandings of media and materials (without subscribing to object-oriented ontology or new materialist doctrine) in terms of their capacity for signification – wherein materials and spaces must serve as substitute organs of hearing. (I maintain an insistence on the audiological throughout, for the orientational capacity of audible sound – however this is registered – comprises the phenomenon in question and at stake in this paper.)

Tangoing with Stefan Helmreich's logic, the notion of 'sounding' (and that sound and unsound may be sounded), when deployed as a verb in both conceptual and technical operations, will transit throughout as an analytical concept linked to the *audile technique* and medical listening practice known as *auscultation* (from Latin *auscultare* 'to listen attentively to'). In his book, *Sounding the Limits: Essays in the Anthropology of Biology and Beyond*, Helmreich introduces sounding as a method for mapping born of oceanography, for it probes untransduced underwater phenomena and frequencies into legible

Figure 6.4: Emma McCormick-Goodhart, stills from *Sounding in Sign*, 2016. HD silent video interpreted in American Sign Language by Louise Stern.

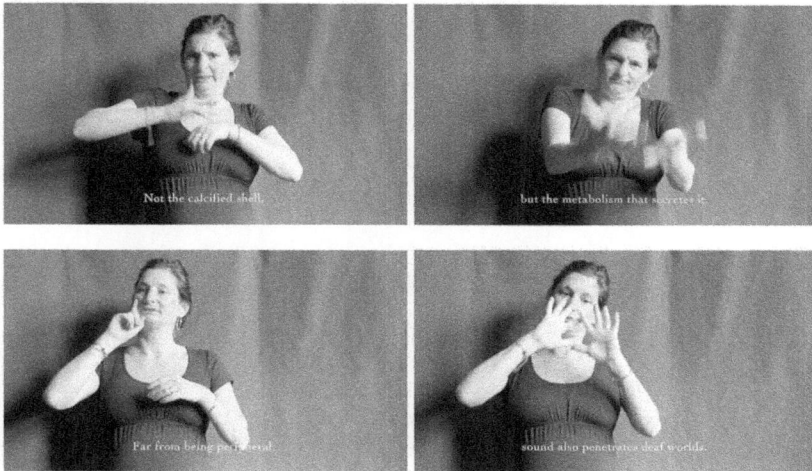

Figure 6.5: Emma McCormick-Goodhart, stills from *Sounding in Sign*, 2016. HD silent video interpreted in American Sign Language by Louise Stern.

formats, using prostheses, or mediatic extensions at various scales, to take its fathomings. This paper attempts to perform the watery etymology of sounding traced by Helmreich:

> To sound something is to ascertain its depths, as, for example, when oceanographers sound the ocean floor. This sense, of sound as fathoming, has etymological moorings in the Old English *sund*,

'sea'. The sense of 'to sound' as 'to emit an audible tone' reaches back to Old English *swinn*, 'melody' (and from there to Old English *swan*, the 'sounding' bird). (Helmreich 2016: x)

The idea is that sounding, understood in its capacity as an agile, operative verb – a conceptual mechanism for measuring imperceptible unheards – can find speculative application within the variegated material phenomena that comprise and produce sound itself. To sound sound's occurrence may help elicit how, and through what media, we come to hear at all.

III. Biosemiotics: Sounding Transduction as a Form of Physiologic

Without the organ of hearing with its vital endowments, there would be no such thing as sound in the world, but merely vibrations.

(Johannes Müller, quoted in Sterne 2003: 11)

If we hear sounds with our ears, with what organ do we hear what is going on inside the organ of hearing? What organ does the ear use to overhear itself?

(Connor 2011)

The being of sensation is not the flesh but the compound of nonhuman forces of the cosmos, of man's nonhuman becomings, and of the ambiguous house that exchanges and adjusts them, makes them whirl around like winds. Flesh is only the developer which disappears in what it develops: the compound of sensation.

(Deleuze and Guattari 1994: 183)

Biosemiotics emerged as a field of analysis during the first half of the twentieth century through the work of Estonian zoologist Jakob von Uexküll. Located at the crossing of 'evolutionary thinking in biology with the humanistic enterprise of semiotics' (Tomlinson 2016: 142), Uexküll formulated a theory of *Umwelt* while studying particularities in the physiology and environments of invertebrates. In Uexküll's cosmos, every organism occupies an *Umwelt*. These connote the lived *milieus*, or lifeworlds, of organisms, which Uexküll conceives as existing separately for every organism in every species. Feminist philosopher of evolution Elizabeth Grosz situates his investigations as the 'earliest attempt to develop a phenomenology or a biosemiology of animal life' (Grosz 2008: 40).

In Uexküll's formulation, organisms cannot be regarded except in relation to their lived experiences within a given environment, always authored by an organism's organs – and only ever as complex as the organs that comprise it. Such environments co-evolve separate 'sense-bubbles, monads composed of co-extensive overlapping beings' (Grosz 2008: 41), which echo Deleuze and Guattari's (1987: 10) infamous example of '*aparallel evolution*' in the orchid and the wasp in *A Thousand Plateaus*. Uexhüll ventures so far as to consider *Umwelten* to be 'musical counterpoints, that are only given outside, to which the organism is itself a brilliant and inventive response' (Grosz 2008: 41). In this way, *Umwelt* aids us in *sounding* an organism through differential sets of attunement, consisting of 'carriers of significance' and 'marks', to the milieu that it occupies, forging a kind of 'musical symphony' (Grosz 2008: 44) not unlike how different parts of the cochlea, or human inner ear, are tuned to respond to certain frequencies. Every organism becomes an enviro-organism, at once constituted by and constitutive of the sum of its relation to a milieu.

Fast forward, and in musicologist Gary Tomlinson's conception, biosemiotics becomes a crucial analytic for conceptualising the emergence of *musicking* (or music-making) and affect – rather than language and symbolic cognition – across a 'deep-historical axis'. From biosemiological perspectives, musicking must include the *prehuman*, as well as the nonhuman and posthuman, in order to arrive at a broader, intergenerational 'communicative stream in the biosphere that encounters much more than the human alone'. A '*parahuman* stream', he theorises, moves us towards a 'more far-reaching semiosis, a nonsymbolic making of signs that embraces but exceeds the human' (Tomlinson 2016: 144). Tomlinson elucidates how biosemioticians have built upon Charles Sanders Peirce's framework of the sign and its emphasis on the '*process* of signification'. For Peirce, signification takes place not solely as the relation of sign to object (*secondness*), but also, and most importantly, as *a relation to this relation* (*thirdness*), which Peirce terms an 'interpretant' (Tomlinson 2016: 146). In biosemiotics, the interpretant stands for an aspect of an organism's active and lived experience: the result of an '*attending* to stimuli', and to 'a relation external to itself, the fold or wrinkle that constructs a relation to a relation and thereby draws bits of information into a semiotic process' (147).

Such configurations, in terms of their capacity to engender semiotic relations of *thirdness* – or of relations to relations – between things, substances and lifeworlds, resonate with polymath philosopher Michel Serres's writing on the self-constitutive capacities of noise, sound and the physiological process of audition: 'We are surrounded by noise. And this noise is inextinguishable. It is outside – it is the world itself – and it is inside, produced by our living body' (Serres 1982: 126). Enmeshing information theory with the laws of thermodynamics, in Serres's formulation, hearing commutes mechanical waves (external input) into electrical input (internal output) in a movement from '"hard" form into "soft" information' for *incorporation* as sensory data in the body – a procedure known as *transduction*, wherein vibration is metamorphosed into sound (Connor 1999). Serres conceives of this process of hearing architectonically, as a threshold space and 'black box':

> Take a black box. To its left, or before it, there is the world. To its right, or after it, travelling along certain circuits, there is what we call information. The energy of things goes in: disturbances of the air, shocks and vibrations, heat, alcohol or ether salts, photons […] Information comes out, and even meaning. We do not always know where this box is located, nor how it alters what flows through it […]; it remains closed to us. However, we can say with certainty that beyond this threshold, both of ignorance and perception, energies are exchanged, on their usual scale, at the levels of the world, the group and cellular biochemistry; and that on the other side of this same threshold information appears: signals, figures, languages, meaning. Before the box, the hard; after it, the soft. (Serres 2008: 129)

Yet, as Serres posits above, the mechanisms that comprise the event of *transduction* itself remain obscured from us, ironically, as the very sensing agents in question. We cannot *overhear* biochemical conversion – the intracellular machinations that enable the *organised* perception of sensory information – as it occurs. Peter Sloterdijk encapsulates this paradox in his assertion that 'no listener can believe himself to be standing at the edge of the audible' (Sloterdijk quoted in van Maas 2003: 10). I hold, however, that *we can* speak of auditory reception in material and informatic, rather than immaterial or phenomenological, terms.

Indeed, for 'sound' to occur at the level of cognitive perception, whereby sensory information is organised and interpreted, vibrational input in the form of mechanical waves, or oscillations of matter, must metamorphose via conversions into biochemical signals that register as sound. That these conversions take place imperceptibly instantiates 'unheard' forms of Elizabeth Grosz's 'cosmological imponderables' (Grosz 2008: 23). Nothing is *audibly* sonic, nothing is audible at all, prior to the *transduction* of vibrations into nerve impulses that might then be processed by the brain as *sensory data*. As such, all sound is embodied, incorporated and inhabited phenomena collectively transduced; it might even be possible to think of sound as a *biological imaginary*, 'half anatomy and half imagination' (Connor 2011: 15), especially in instances where sound is perceived without auditory stimulus, i.e. through tinnitus, otoacoustic emission and auditory hallucination.

Sound necessarily denotes *the production of sound itself* by a sensing agent (whether biological or technical) – and sound, forged in biosemiological terms in relation to another relation, is the *interpretant*. Audition, in other words, is semiotic, resting 'between the orders of the material and the informatic' (Connor 2011: 15). But what if the cochleate event of transduction functions 'improperly', or not at all? What bearing would Serres's architectonic conceptualisation of the process of audition exert on untransduced vibrations *in excess* of sound's 'black box'; or of sounds unheard by human ears or assistive listening technologies, as in the case of deafness?

Broadly speaking, deafness is defined from biomedical perspectives as aural impairment, wherein vibration is not transduced into audible sound – sound, in such instances, does not write itself from the 'inside' of hearing. It remains, however, that there are multiple ways to inhabit noise 'from without', via deafness and alternatives modes of audition, which activate Sloterdijk's proverbial 'edge of the audible'. In studying the vast spectrum of conditions collectively labelled as 'deafness', it is crucial not to oppose sound to deafness, frequently (if incorrectly) framed as a silent condition, even if John Cage's praxis of listening closely to the internal noisescapes made by bodies in anechoic chambers teaches us otherwise: that there is no such state as pure silence. Friedner and Helmreich's 'Sound Studies Meet Deaf Studies' is once more helpful in this respect, for it outlines possible 'zones of productive articulation' between Sound studies and Deaf studies. In particular, they call for further explanation of how sound, especially low frequency vibration and infrasound, is inferred by Deaf persons, circumscribing it within Goodman's framework for a 'politics of frequency'.

In that deafness provokes differently attuned relations to the sonic, 'audition' can occur through vibro-tactile measures, a myriad of composite sensory modalities or prostheses, including sign language, that assist listening by serving as substitute organs of auscultation. As Serres writes, 'each time an organ – or function – is liberated from an old duty, it invents' (Serres 2008: 344). Thus, to sound or auscultate deafness in terms of its very relation to vibration, resonance and space may open new terrains – or better, milieus – of *sonance* or *sonant otherness*. No longer ear-bound or ear-limited, in deafness, the entire body becomes ecologised in fully 'corporeal hearing'. Skin, too, becomes additionally significant as medium for haptic transduction. If Goodman locates 'sonic potentials' at the interstices of sound, vibration, and the physiologically inaudible, what spaces or milieus can deafness, when framed as a practice of para-audition, open towards *inaudible* auditory cultures?

In the next section, I analyse the stethoscope as a device for sounding body pathology. Notable for the ways in which its use decentred and disturbed the primacy of patient speech towards an attending to non-vocal vibration and sound, the device made vibration and sound meaningful in their own right, as key communicants of bodily conditions. I also draw upon the link that media theorist Jonathan Sterne makes to disability, for I argue that to practise being *hard-of-hearing* via prostheses that render 'inaudible sonorities' (Ikoniadou 2014: 24) audible, can help produce, at least conceptually, new modes of *sounding hearing* in terms of material and semiotic relations. The aim is to transition thereafter into conceptualising Deaf space, and DeafSpace more formally, as a mechanism for 'hearing through' materials.

IV. The Stethoscope: Sensorial Triangulation

> *Place your hand on the body of a cello, Rousseau said. Can you not tell whether the sound is low or high, whether it comes from the A string or the C string, just by the vibrations? 'Let the senses be trained in these differences. I have no doubt that with time one could become sensitive enough to be able to hear an entire melody with the fingers'.*

> (Lane 1988: 83)

René-Théophile-Hyacinthe Laennec's invention of the monaural stethoscope in 1816, and its accompanying 'audile techniques' known as *mediate auscultation*, led to a paradigmatic shift in the biosemiotics of clinical diagnosis. In replacing *immediate auscultation*, wherein a doctor would place his ear directly upon a patient's chest, and other finger-based techniques for percussing the body to attain haptic data, the addition of the stethoscope at once prostheticised and technologised medical listening and sensory perception. The linguistic content of the patient's speaking voice was no longer equivalently significant, nor as accurate or 'telling', as the purely sonic content of various internal body parts. In generating a novel 'acoustic enclosure' between doctor and patient – a telephone line direct to the body – in which 'speaking patients with mute bodies gave way to speaking patients with sounding bodies' (Sterne 2003: 117), the stethoscope pushed its users to migrate their praxes from narrative oral to multilayered aural. Henceforth, both vibration and sound were ascribed new authority in terms of their capacity for non-verbal signification, reverberating, thus, with Michel Chion's assertion that 'every sound, if listened to long enough, becomes a voice. The sounds speak' (Chion quoted in Dolar 2011: 134).

In *The Birth of the Clinic*, Michel Foucault traces how the stethoscope served to *spatialise bodies* through the doctor's reception of a patient's internal soundscape. That vibration and sound, as opposed to speech, became meaningful as signifiers in their own right meant that the 'complexity of spatial data' contained in a body was rendered, for the first time in modern medicine, *three-dimensional*. Now that sight was no longer an adequate probe by itself, doctors began to 'touch, tap, listen' in order to *hear through* and sound below skin's envelope (Foucault 2003: 200–02). By extending the 'anatomo-clinician's gaze […] a gaze that touches, hears, and, moreover, not by essence or necessity, sees', the use of a device for auscultation helped 'bring to the surface that which is layered in depth' (200–02). It cultivated a newly 'plurisensorial structure' and 'sensorial triangulation', cross-modal in essence, among and between hearing, seeing, and touching.

But could it be that Laennec's stethoscope's most radical innovation was in its delivery of a 'functional disability' to hearing doctors, and that such a 'functional disability' could actually serve to *enable* the practice of clinical diagnosis? Jonathan Sterne frames Laennec's stethoscope as a direct descendant of the ear trumpet, an early analogue hearing aid, in that the stethoscope's principal function served to assist listening:

> Mediate auscultation endowed its practitioners with a functional disability. The unaided ear was not enough [...] now doctors – whose hearing was ostensibly healthy – could augment their auditory abilities. (Sterne 2003: 106)

Laennec, too, described the stethoscope as a hearing aid, writing that it 'adds to the naked ear and the sounds of the patient's body its own acoustic properties, which aid in the detection of certain physical properties in the patient' (Laennec quoted in Sterne 2003: 107). Augmenting techniques of 'detection' through vibration and sound, it signalled a shift in the semiotics of clinical diagnosis – and at a biosemiological level, too. In the logic of biosemiotics, a doctor arrives at Peirce's 'interpretant' – medical knowledge and information, in this case – by attending aurally to the triangulated *relation* (through sound) *of a relation* to his or her patient.

When conceived as a medical hearing aid descended, at least in Sterne's logic, from the ear trumpet, the stethoscope forcibly converts hearing doctors into ones *hard-of-hearing*, thereby supplanting negative notions of aural impairment with those of enablement. As a spatialised, triangulated 'acoustic enclosure', it might be further analogised to 'Deaf space', that is, *other-than-auditory geographies* not premised on the production and reception of spoken language. I will unfold this analogy in the following section, for I want to expand the normal limits of auricular, or ear-based, prostheses and hearing aids, in order to *sound hearing* into further categories that include architectural space and body techniques. It is my suspicion that such *spatial prostheses*, when conceived as (earless) para-hearing things in themselves – or substitute organs of hearing and *remote sensing* – might enable different kinds of social, sensory and mediatic assemblages as material carriers of information. To what extent can we attenuate anatomical structures and physiologies into spaces, or to think *physiographically*? Can we disinvaginate Lynn Margulis' theory of once infolded senses, displacing *cilia* onto walls?

V. Prosthetic Architecture: Sign Worlds in Deaf Space

> *sip,*
> from our sonorous jars, our verb
> tipped, in-
>
> audible.
> [...]
> oscillum
> quavers.   the air's
> curtain
>
> *runs taut.*
>   (Sobin 1995)

> *Only two* speaking people *were given the rare privilege of*
> *attending this foreign / strange feast* [...] *lacking in the speech of*
> *mimique, pariah of the society present, obliged to fall back on a*
> *pencil as a means of conversing with the heroes of the feast* [...]
> Poor thing, *said those happiest in that moment,* he can't make
> himself understood.

> (*The Deaf-Mute Banquet* 1834)

In his essay, 'Sound and the Pathos of the Air', Steven Connor evokes sound, inclusive of vibration, as constitutive of and inseparable from its propagation in space, as a form of space or spacing. 'Air is the body of sound, in the sense that it is the occasion, medium or theatre of sound', he states, 'but sound is equally the body of air – air gathered into form, given itinerary, intensity and intent' (Connor 2007). Some centuries earlier, Vitruvius, writing on acoustics in 'Book V' of his treatise *De Architectura* (1486), stipulates that 'particular pains must also be taken that the site be not a "deaf" one, but one through which the voice can range with greatest clearness. This can be brought about if a site is selected where there is no obstruction due to echo' (Vitruvius 1914: 138). The Ancient Greeks compounded this criterion by employing acoustic vases, strategically positioned throughout open-air amphitheatres, as an analogue technology of amplification whereby actors' voices would be conducted at sufficient volumes to all corners of the audience.

By presuming that all humans are hearing subjects, such *phonocentric* or *audist* criteria for establishing *auditory geographies* becomes troubled, however, by a category known as *Deaf space* (variants include DeafSpace) – spaces whose designs are not premised on the propagation of voice, but which might be read as forms of spatial prostheses via orientations that substitute for the perception of sound. Deaf space augments early Deaf educator and activist Georges Veditz's assertion that Deaf people are 'first, last, and all the time the people of the eye' (quoted in Friedner and Helmreich 2012: 73) by denoting a primarily *visual production of space* that imbricates gatherings of sign language users.

As a nascent object of inquiry within Deaf studies, architecture and design, Deaf space inscribes itself within Deaf geographies, a hybrid sub-discipline of Deaf studies and geography that investigates 'what and where Deaf social geographies emerge', as well as 'what happens when Deaf spaces meet hearing-world spaces and begin to describe, explore and/or regulate each other' (Gulliver n.d.). Mike Gulliver, a (hearing) Deaf geographies scholar and one of its key proponents, differentiates Deaf space from problematic definitions of a '"Deaf" community or spaces "for deaf people"', in that Deaf space is *a space produced by deaf people themselves*, yet not as 'an antagonistic response to the spaces of the hearing world', and which maintains the 'same validity' as hearing world equivalents (Gulliver n.d.). (Gulliver's doctoral thesis, cited above, studied Deaf-Mute Banquets in nineteenth century Paris, gatherings conceived as incarnations of a Deaf nation.)

In its most articulated and formal manifestations, Deaf space mobilises protocols of visual and vibrational amplification for establishing spatial conditions that are conducive to communication other than through speech. 'DeafSpace' was formulated as a design movement in manifesto form following a set of workshops led by Hansel Bauman, with both Deaf and hearing architects and researchers, at Gallaudet University in Washington, D.C. – the largest Deaf liberal arts university in the world. It provides a methodological framework for composing milieus within architectural space, often in pedagogical venues, and its five (seemingly general) principles include: 1.) *space and proximity*, emphasising flexible configurations to not impede upper-body movement in sign language; 2.) *sensory reach*, where surfaces become legible as carriers of information; 3.) *mobility and proximity*, in order to enable the continuation of signed conversation while in transit; 4.) *light and colour*, largely to prevent eye strain for signers; and 5.) *acoustics*, to maintain acoustically neutral spaces that do not interfere with hearing aid and cochlear implant users.

A technique for inscribing information into and around materials, DeafSpace would seem to expand notions of embodiment and 'sensory reach', where buildings' surfaces must convey and transmit spatial information not through sound, but viscerally, as through vibration or what Goodman calls 'bass materialism'. It pushes hearing in the media ecological direction of tactility and haptic architecture, and away from its merely aural dimension. Within this expanded logic of the prosthesis, even sign language – in serving as a substitute for spoken language, a body technique for communication – might also be considered a prosthetic device for the production and composition of *other than sonic space*.

Figure 6.6: Emma McCormick-Goodhart, *This Antithesis*, 2016. Choreographic silent lecture commissioned by Nahmad Projects, London, as part of *I am NOT tino sehgal*, curated by Francesco Bonami. Performers Deepa Shastri and Louise Stern voice, in British Sign Language and American Sign Language, respectively, on loop, the artist's critique of Tino Sehgal's phonocentricity. Photo by Benedict Johnson.

In his essay, 'Space, Time and Gesture: Gestural Expression, Sensual Aesthetics and Crisis in Contemporary Spatial Paradigms', Deaf architect Jeffrey Mansfield situates sign language as a spatiotemporal body technique that 'cannot be perceived without the body'. Indeed, that sign languages are 'not so much "read" or "seen" as they are *lived-in* from the inside', implies the extent to which sign language is an *inhabited*, rather than verbalised, articulation; a form of being and self-presence that produces, in neurologist Oliver Sacks's mind, an entirely '*linguistic use of space*' (Sacks 1989), and parallels certain Deaf constituencies' identification as a linguistic minority, not a disabled community.

Elaborating the (bio)semiotics of sign language as a spatial practice of the 'body-that-is-deaf', Mansfield highlights its potential for subversive spatialities, *jouissance* and layered 'morphological movements'. The possibility for queering signs in sign language, largely through pre-signs and classifiers conveyed via the mouth, voice, and face can 'betray' taxonomies of 'linguistic time and space' to the extent that signing might resist signification as such. It arises in opposition to efforts to codify a manual alphabet during the Enlightenment. 'The gestural excess of sign language', Mansfield writes, 'inevitably spills out of its assigned spaces [...] producing a contemporary space of symptomatic *fullness*' (Mansfield 2014: 127).

Figure 6.7: Emma McCormick-Goodhart, *This Antithesis*, 2016. Choreographic silent lecture commissioned by Nahmad Projects, London, as part of *I am NOT tino sehgal*, curated by Francesco Bonami. Performers Deepa Shastri and Louise Stern voice, in British Sign Language and American Sign Language, respectively, on loop, the artist's critique of Tino Sehgal's phonocentricity. Photo by Benedict Johnson.

I suggest that DeafSpace, and Deaf space more generally, might be articulated as an infrastructure of *sign-space*, not sound-space – a genre of space that operates in keeping with Steven Connor's notion of chorality, connoting acts of joint vocalisation or speech, usually in public spaces, which 'does not require language, and where it does not, it may seem to be more than usually choreographic, or impregnated with space and gesture [...] There is [...] a kind of chorology (the study of spatial distribution and limit) in every chorality' (Connor 2016: 10). Deaf space might be read biosemiologically, too, at Serres's material-informatic intersection of the "hard" and the "soft", as a *spatial projection* of the physiological process of transduction. Made up of material-informatic relations in space through webs of surfaces and sign language, Deaf spaces cultivate and write milieus out of differently transductive attunements.

VI. Conclusion

> *A vibratory nexus exceeds and precedes the distinction between subject and object, constituting a mesh of relation in which discreet entities prehend each other's vibrations.*

(Goodman 2010: 82)

How to characterise the move from the proverbial 'black box' of hearing into sounded body pathology, which establishes sound as significant by augmenting doctors' 'functional disabilities', and finally, into evanescent forms of Deaf geographies and Deaf space? I argue that to pay attention to the physiological mechanisms, processual nature and divergent material histories of hearing itself as biosemiotically significant 'signals', alongside alternate modes of audition, reminds us that sound is the product of *transduction*, rather than always already given; and that vibration, more often than not, exists *in excess of sound*, as unheard frequencies beyond the limited spectrum of human audibility.

As an architectonic and spatial prosthesis, Deaf space composes conditions to enable non-spoken communication, such that sign language becomes a mode for the active production of space and spatial knowledge – leading, perhaps, to auditory emancipation and new forms of sociality, spatiality and articulation between differently abled constituencies.

Can we think, like Jacques Rancière, of a *sensory commons*, in terms of that which is *not held in common*? If hearing is contested matter, often public practice, a fault line and 'sound barrier' when flatly dichotomised as Deaf or hearing, Deaf space functions as a modular technology of assembly. To explore deafness and the variety of non-sonic knowledges it imparts, as a spatial condition, linguistic, compositional and proto-architectural practice, may open new geographies within auditory culture, ones not phonocentric, which re-sensitise us to hearing always already as a threshold condition. In this, Deleuze's provocation that 'all consciousness is a matter of threshold' (Deleuze 2006: 101), echoes Uëxkull's vision wherein we, as sensing agents variously abled, actively tune ourselves towards musicking our lived milieus. Those attendant thresholds of sonicity remain contingent, whether arriving via the *from within* of hearing, or alternatively, via the *from without* of material environments. Inhabited as inscriptive spaces of inferentiality, the latter become double, incidentally, as ones of media ecological inquiry.

Works Cited

Agamben, Giorgio. 2004. *The Open: Man and Animal*, translated by Kevin Attell. Stanford: Stanford University Press.

Ahmed, Nabil. 2016. 'Sounding Chaos'. *Rapture 03*. Oslo: OCA/Verksted.

Barcelos, Lendl. 2016. 'The Nuclear Sonic: Listening to Millenial Matter'. In *Aesthetics After Finitude*, edited by Amy Ireland, Baylee Brits, and Prudence Gibson, 71–88. Melbourne: re.press.

Bauman, H-Dirksen L. and Joseph J. Murray, editors. 2014. *Deaf Gain: Raising the Stakes for Human Diversity*. Minneapolis: University of Minnesota Press.

Bonnet, François. 2016. *The Order of Sounds: A Sonorous Archipelago*, translated by Robin Mackay. Falmouth: Urbanomic.

Callon, Michel. 1986. 'Some Elements of a Sociology of Translation: Domestication of the Scallops and the Fishermen of St Brieuc Bay'. In *Power, Action and Belief: A New Sociology of Knowledge?*, edited by J. Law, 196–233. London: Routledge.

Connor, Steven. 1999. 'Michel Serres's Five Senses'. http://www.stevenconnor.com/5senses.htm.

Connor, Steven. 2004. 'Building Breathing Space'. http://www.stevenconnor.com/bbs/.

Connor, Steven. 2007. 'Sound and the Pathos of the Air'. http://stevenconnor.com/pathos.html.

Connor, Steven. 2011. 'Auscultations'. *Sound Effects: An Interdisciplinary Journal of Sound and Sound Experience* 1: 5–18.

Connor, Steven. 2016. 'Choralities'. *Twentieth-Century Music*, 13: 3–23.

Daston, Lorraine J., editor. 2007. *Things That Talk: Object Lessons from Art and Science*. New York: Zone Books.

Deleuze, Gilles, and Félix Guattari. 1994. *What Is Philosophy?*, translated by Hugh Tomlinson and Graham Burchell. New York: Columbia University Press.

Deleuze, Gilles. 2006. *The Fold: Leibniz and the Baroque*, translated by Tom Conley. London: Continuum.

Deleuze, Gilles and Félix Guattari. 1987. *A Thousand Plateaus: Capitalism and Schizophrenia*, translated by Brian Massumi. Minneapolis: University of Minnesota Press.

Derrida, Jacques. 1997. *Of Grammatology*, translated by Gayatri Chakravorty Spivak. Baltimore: Johns Hopkins University Press.

Dolar, Mladen. 2006. *A Voice and Nothing More*. Cambridge, MA: MIT Press.

Dolar, Mladen. 2011. 'The Burrow of Sound'. *differences: A Journal of Feminist Cultural Studies* 22: 112–39.

Erlmann, Veit. 2014. *Reason and Resonance: A History of Modern Aurality*. Cambridge, MA: Zone Books.

Ernst, Wolfgang. 2016. *Sonic Time Machines: Explicit Sound, Sirenic Voices, and Implicit Sonicity*. Amsterdam: Amsterdam University Press.

Foucault, Michel. 2003. *The Birth of the Clinic: An Archaeology of Medical Perception*, translated by A. M. Sheridan. London: Routledge.

Friedner, Michele and Stefan Helmreich. 2012. 'Sound Studies Meets Deaf Studies'. *The Senses & Society* 7: 72–86.

Goodman, Steve. 2010. *Sonic Warfare: Sound, Affect, and the Ecology of Fear*. Cambridge, MA: MIT Press.

Grosz, Elizabeth. 2008. *Chaos, Territory, Art: Deleuze and the Reframing of the Earth*. New York: Columbia University Press.

Gulliver, Mike. [n.d.]. 'DEAF space'. *MIKE GULLIVER: Deaf geographies and other worlds*. https://mikegulliver.com/research/.

Gulliver, Mike. 2005. 'Deafscapes: The Landscape and heritage of the Deaf world'. A paper presented at the Forum UNESCO Conference, Newcastle University, April 2005.

The Deaf-Mute Banquet: 122nd Anniversary of the birth of Abbé de l'Epée, translated by Mike Gulliver. Transcript from the banquet held in Paris, November 1834.

Helmreich, Stefan. 2016. *Sounding the Limits of Life: Essays in the Anthropology of Vibration and Beyond*. Princeton: Princeton University Press.

Ikoniadou, Eleni. 2014. *The Rhythmic Event: Art, Media, and the Sonic*. Cambridge, MA: MIT Press.

LaBelle, Brandon. 2014. *Lexicon of the Mouth: Poetics and Politics of Voice and the Oral Imaginary*. London: Continuum.

Lane, Harlan. 1988. *When the Mind Hears: A History of the Deaf*. London: Penguin.

Latour, Bruno, and Peter Weibel, editors. 2005. *Making Things Public: Atmospheres of Democracy*. Cambridge: ZKM/Center for Art and Media in Karlsruhe.

Mansfield, Jeffrey. 2014. 'Space, Time and Gesture: Gestural Expression, Sensual Aesthetics and Crisis in Contemporary Spatial Paradigms'. *Tacet #03 – From Sound Space*, 121–126. Paris: Les presses du réel.

Martin, Reinhold. 1998. 'The Organizational Complex: Cybernetics, Space, Discourse'. *Assemblage* 37: 102–27.

Mills, Mara. 2011. 'On Disability and Cybernetics: Helen Keller, Norbert Wiener, and the Hearing Glove'. *differences: A Journal of Feminist Cultural Studies* 22: 74–111.

Parikka, Jussi. 2011. 'Media Ecologies and Imaginary Media: Transversal Expansions, Contractions, and Foldings'. *The Fibreculture Journal* 17: 34–50.

Rasmussen, Steen Eiler. 1959. *Experiencing Architecture*. Cambridge, MA: MIT Press.

Ronell, Avital. 1989. *The Telephone Book: Technology, Schizophrenia, Electric Speech*. Lincoln: University of Nebraska Press.

Sacks, Oliver. 2009. *Seeing Voices*. London: Picador.

Serres, Michel. 1982. *The Parasite*, translated by Lawrence R. Schehr. Baltimore: Johns Hopkins University Press.

Serres, Michel. 2008. *The Five Senses: A Philosophy of Mingled Bodies*, translated by Peter Cowley and Margaret Sankey. London: Continuum.

Serres, Michel. 2011. *Variations on the Body*, translated by Randolph Burks. Minneapolis: Univocal.

Serres, Michel. 2012. *Biogea*, translated by Randolph Burks. Minneapolis: Univocal.

Shaviro, Steven. 2015. *Discognition*. London: Repeater.

Sobin, Gustaf. 1995. *By the Bias of Sound: Selected Poems, 1971–1994*. Jersey City: Talisman House.

Sobin, Gustaf. 1999. *Luminous Debris: Reflecting on Vestige in Provence and Languedoc*. Berkeley: University of California Press.

Sterne, Jonathan. 2003. *The Audible Past: Cultural Origins of Sound Reproduction*. Durham: Duke University Press.

Stone, Rob. 2015. *Auditions: Architecture and Aurality*. Cambridge, MA: MIT Press.

Tomlinson, Gary. 2015. *A Million Years of Music: The Emergence of Human Modernity*. New York: Zone Books.

Tomlinson, Gary. 2016. 'Sign, Affect, and Musicking before the Human'. *boundary 2*: 143–72.

Van Maas, Sander, editor. 2015. *Thresholds of Listening: Sound, Technics, Space.* New York: Fordham University Press.

Vitruvius. 1914. *The Ten Books on Architecture,* translated by Morris Hicky Morgan. New York: Dover Publications.

Part III: Situating Media

7

Play it Again: Remediation, the Archive, and Ted Berrigan's 'Telegram to Jack Kerouac'

RENÉE A. FARRAR

In 1968, John Giorno created *Dial-a-Poem*, a phone-based service, which allowed individuals to call 'Giorno Poetry Systems' and listen to a randomly selected contemporary poet recite his or her work. Through several staged iterations of this telephonic artwork – envision ten rotary phones in an otherwise empty room at the Museum of Modern Art (MoMA) in New York City – this exhibit connected over a quarter of a million people with recordings of contemporary poets via a rudimentary answering system. One of these featured poets, Ted Berrigan, recited his composition 'Telegram to Jack Kerouac' for a later iteration of this instalment: 'Bye-Bye, Jack. / See you soon' (Berrigan 2005: 235). In two spoken lines, Berrigan invokes an array of media: the dots and dashes of the telegram, the cyclical nature of recorded, spoken word, and the immediacy of the telephone are juxtaposed with the deliberate and slow choices wrought out by pen and paper.

The difficulties of sorting through the media that converge in Berrigan's performance parallel a collective struggle that our contemporary age faces as it revisits, reconstructs, and accesses older media, especially recorded sound, through digitised recordings. In 2012, MoMA crafted a web-based interface through which a new generation might connect with the artists featured in *Dial-a-Poem*. While the technological developments which made this exhibit possible deserve praise, its curation also emphasised the difficulties the archive faces as it strives to cultivate historically-informed experiences that can be accessed by geographically-distant users.

Scrutinising the historical devices upon which and for which moments were recorded is an essential element of media-based study. However, contemporary digital practice frequently omits critical information about the material from the archival shelf, making it exceedingly difficult for users to trace the origins of the remediated product. Researchers depend on the integrity of the entries that archivists supply, but insufficient content risks reducing the comprehensiveness of future access to historically-significant apparatuses. Simply preserving sound is not enough.

What remains at the crux of this issue is the question of archival integrity. Contemporary electronics archive sound as physical signals in the analogue or through sampling in the digital. This process, in many ways, preserves the essence of an entry. However, when accessing recordings on digital interfaces, the archival process becomes problematic for media archaeologists, for whom scrutinising the underlying technological apparatus is as essential as the preserved data itself. Traditionally, the responsibility for tracing the genesis of an entry has remained in the hands of the researcher. Media archaeologists must, according to Foucault (quoted in Parikka 2012: 18), engage with a medium by considering its 'conditions of existence', but this task is made exceedingly difficult as those very conditions face deletion while remote, seemingly-infinite access is demanded and remains *en vogue*.

Physical distance masks the chronology and evolution of technological apparatuses. Renowned digital artist Erkki Kurenniemi writes,

> [The computer's] major effects on the arts will be the separation of art from material and the separation of art from man [...] These processes of separation are different from those caused by earlier inventions in computing. The printing press, film, audio records, and electric communication caused the separation of art from time and the separation of art from location. (Kurenniemi 2015: 97)

Earlier media captured data by conserving in the analogue, distancing the audience from the event, both in a temporal and physical sense. However, the process still bound the user to material, historical objects. However, Kurenniemi predicts in the digital age a 'separation of art from man'. This gap alienates the user from the artist's intended mode of conveyance, seriously threatening the user's ability to experience a work on the device for which it was intended. Further, this dissociation all but eliminates the possibility of tracing a recording's device history. To prevent this erasure during remediation into the digital, the archive must adopt and employ a more substantial role in preserving the media-archaeological evolution of its entries, in spite of the daunting scope of this task. Failure to revise archival methodology places the lineage of entries composed on older media at risk, severing ties with the artist's original conception and effectively rendering the remediation inauthentic and inaccurate.

The practical nature of students and scholars in a global community is a demand for access to distant materials, but it is from this demand that a problem of archival inadequacy derives. Writing about the challenges the British art institution Tate faces in advancing its own archive to meet this demand, Sue Breakell states: 'Archivists find that researchers not only come with ideas of what they hope to find but also cannot accept that it is not there. There is an expectation of completeness. But, in reality just as much as in theory, the archive by its very nature is characterized by gaps' (Breakell 2008: 6). In both its material and digital forms, the archive cannot achieve the level of inclusiveness expected by its users. Even in the physical realm, an archive cannot be wholly inclusive. Damage occurs and documents are lost, before inclusion or while being used. In these items' translation to the digital, machines often choose what and how these physical objects are preserved, even under the oversight of a careful archivist. In this new medium, elements of the original must be excluded, as the 'most important' elements are included. As Matt Serlectic, former executive of Virgin Records, states, 'to get the content to people, you have to play by their rules' (Levine 2007: 4). If the people want volume, then volume is what will be supplied. But as quantity becomes the focus of the archive, the quality certainly suffers.

In attempting to supply a breadth of materials to the user, rather than depth, the archive risks the integrity of its entries. Of course an archive must, at the most basic levels, be able to 'organize and store' media (Kieckhefer 2018: 1). And, of course, what sounds like a simple task for a discrete entity becomes convoluted as the 'dialectic between storage and retrieval complicates the objectives of an archive' (1). This task becomes increasingly difficult, because as items are archived in the digital, some elements of the original necessarily become censored out. In 1937, the British archivist and archival theorist Hilary Jenkinson asserted that individual entries 'themselves state no opinion, voice no conjecture; they are simply written memorials, authenticated by the fact of their official preservation, of events which actually occurred and of which they themselves formed a part' (Jenkinson 1937: 4). By placing the responsibility wholly on the individual record, Jenkinson discards the archivist's role in the preservation process. Although he wrote *A Manual of Archive Administration* in 1922, before digital remediation, his definition indicates how individuals often expect their interaction with remediated material to occur: the expectation that a record presents and represents itself and nothing else. However, machines' algorithms and archivists' choices, especially in digitisation, significantly influence the cultivation of the record. The value added or lost due to the process of archiving via remediation cannot be written off as negligible.

At the most basic level, remediation is the process of taking something that exists in old media and refashioning it in new media. As Jay David Bolter and Richard Grusin put it in *Remediation: Understanding New Media*, remediation is 'the representation of one medium in another' (Bolter and Grusin 2000: 45). In the digital age, we are no strangers to this concept. Shakespeare's first folios, Picasso's miniature maquettes, and Nirvana's iconic concerts are all accessible through the digital realm that remediates them. Accessing remediated works through the digital does not, of course, imply an exact replication of the work. We certainly accept that a 3D image of a sculpture is not the object itself. We acknowledge that scrutinising a digitised copy of a frontispiece differs from doing so with the book in hand. However, sound recordings are often relegated to a category separate from those that require visual participation. When it comes to sound, the user understands that the remediated recordings differ from each other, but the analogue and digital replicas are often regarded as equivalent to or better than the original. Limited access to older media reinforces their reputations as inferior and insufficient. With this justification in mind, academics, students, and the general public alike are generally guilty of accepting and scrutinising digital forms, without interrogating the extent to which the machine influences the preservation of the entry.

Often, the digital audience is so grateful that technology allows access to these works, even in a diminished form, that it overlooks the transformation taking place. And, although the strength of the digital is its ability to remediate and allow access, its weakness occurs through this same process. Bolter and Grusin, again, state:

> Since the electronic version justifies itself by granting access to the older media, it wants to be transparent. The digital medium wants to erase itself, so that the viewer stands in the same relationship to the content as she would if she were confronting the original medium. Ideally, there should be no difference between the experience of seeing a painting in person and on the computer screen, but this is never so. (Bolter and Grusin 2000: 45)

The digital is unlike any other form of media, because it wants the audience to pretend that it plays no part in mediating. The remediation attempts to silence itself. It wants the viewer to feel as though engaging with material through the digital allows not only access, but perhaps even a *less* inhibited engagement with the material. The digital says, 'You can still see brush strokes, but in my platform you can zoom in to examine those brush strokes more closely than you could with the naked eye!' In the same moment that the digital provides access, it also makes no admission of its own involvement in how it reforms those original strokes and cuts.

As online resources provide access to works composed on and for increasingly distant, unfamiliar, and even obsolete media forms, the archive faces the overwhelming challenge of providing a robust experience meant to allow its users access, without sullying, sterilising, or contorting the experience. The digital promises access to older media, but the user must pay a price for this access. As music, language, or conversations undergo analogue-to-digital conversion (commonly referred to as 'sampling'), the aesthetics degrade, often without explanation. The impetus to ignore what is lost in representing older works that depend on older media emboldens the listener to assume that experiencing newer, 'identical' reincarnations of the work is an interchangeable form of participation. The analogue is often classified as no more authentic than the remediated, digitised, archived version, or at least no more relevant. For example, in his *Language of New Media*, Lev Manovich suggests that mourning the 'fixed amount of detail in a digital image' is wholly unnecessary. He contends that 'technology [has] already reached the point where a digital image could easily contain much more information than anyone would ever want' (Manovich 2001: 53). However, what is touted as a replica is anything but that. By dismissing what might be lost in remediation, especially the remediation of sound, as negligible, the audience is fooled into listening to a degraded, un-contextualised, and often irresponsible version of the work it had hoped to experience.

Some might contend that the differences between an original and remediated version are too insignificant to scrutinise when considering the content of sound recordings. However, the most eye-opening evidence supporting a necessary excavation of sound-based media comes through examining Berrigan's own remediation of his poem 'Telegram to Jack Kerouac'. The written poem demands that attention be paid to the medium in which it exists. Composed after the death of Jack Kerouac, Berrigan's poem takes the form of an unusual elegy. Although eerily sombre, his lament is terse, casual, and foreboding: 'Bye-bye Jack / See you soon' (Berrigan 2005: 237). The poem was first published in Ted Berrigan's *Sonnets*, but one cannot help wondering if its first iteration actually took the shape of a telegram. Telegrams signify urgency. They require a recipient. An operator translates meaningful words into dots and dashes, and another operator assembles them into language once again. Much like a telegram itself, Berrigan reassembles meaning as he tries to make sense of his friend's death, an event obviously out of his control, but finding structure through language. The form of a telegram mirrors the staccato of Berrigan's single-syllable words. The hard sonics of the first line ease into the second line's sibilance, mimicking the numbing and stifled sounds of grief that follow the jarring shock of unexpected news. This telegram, in particular, carries a message that, out of context, might sound eager or excited. A telegram for a dead man, instead of a postcard or a phone call, seems appropriate.

The invention of the telegraph brought with it an immutable connection to the dead. In 1837, when the Morse alphabet was first invented, assemblages hoping to contact the deceased almost immediately turned to this new medium to provide that connection (Kittler 1999: 12). A new dependence on the telegraph arose from a spiritual longing:

> Media, and media only, fulfill the 'high standards' which (according to Rudolf Arnheim) we expect from 'reproductions' since the invention of photography: 'They are not only supposed to resemble the object, but rather guarantee this resemblance by being, as it were, a product of the object in question, i.e., by being mechanically produced by it – just as the illuminated objects of reality imprint their image on the photographic layer',

or the frequency curves of noises inscribe their wavelike shapes
onto the phonographic plate. (Kittler 1999: 11)

No longer needing mere words to chronicle the dead and conjure up illusions
through text-based memories, individuals instead relied on media to reliably
resurrect the dead. Through this practical séance, a cultivation dependent on
media surmounted a connection once severed by death. Kittler takes this idea
further, explaining:

> Media always already provide the appearances of specters. For,
> according to Lacan, even the word 'corpse' is a euphemism in
> reference to the real. [...] The realm of the dead is as extensive
> as the storage and transmission capabilities of a given culture. As
> Klaus Theweleit noted, media are always flight apparatuses into
> the great beyond. In our mediascape, immortals have come to
> exist again. (Kittler 1999: 12)

When media provide a forum for the dead to materialise, again, they give
life to moments, ideas, and relationships that should have, for all intents and
purposes, vanished, except for our imaginations. As theorist Wolfgang Ernst
writes, 'Signal recording actually allows for addressing the dead as something
alive. The humanist desire to speak with the dead is the phantasma of a
rhetorical feedback channel between past and present' (Ernst 2015: 203).
In a new format, media gives agency to the 'spectre', but also to the user.
It provides a vehicle through which moments from the past can materialise
infinitely. Just as language hoped to account for the real, so do media, but the
act of preservation always carries risk.

When Ted Berrigan recorded 'Telegram', he changed the audience's
experience with it, because it was no longer nine words on paper. He gives
voice to his work, immortalising his own 'spectre', as he pays homage to
another. The transition from page to vinyl, then to magnetic tape for Giorno's
collection, necessitated a different performance and an altered artefact. It
became 79 words with noisy t's and s's punctuating the reading, making the
listening experience a bit abrasive, like its message. Berrigan narrates:

> My name is Ted Berrigan. When the beautiful, American writer
> Jack Kerouac died, not really so long ago, and a certain part of
> my life ended and another part began, I was too far away to go to
> him to the place, where he was going to be buried in the ground.
> And so, I wrote this telegram to send to him, where he lay in
> Lowell Massachusetts:

> 'Telegram
>   To Jack Kerouac

Bye-bye Jack
See you soon.'

Thank you. (Berrigan 2005)

Here, the beginning and the end lack clearly defined boundaries, when spoken. Forty-seven of the seventy-nine words make up a long, almost rambling, second sentence, which contrasts with the abbreviated nature of the poem itself. As ideas bleed from one into the next, it is difficult to discern where Berrigan's recitation begins and his narration ends. The flow remains uninterrupted, lending the recording a personal, confessional, and casual tone. Alongside the changes to content, the machines' presence makes itself known. What might have gone unnoticed becomes undeniably accentuated by the media itself. The listener cannot ignore the soft scratch of a needle on vinyl indicating that the first recorded iteration of this poem was not polished. Those noisy consonants allude to what must have been present (a booth, a microphone, and papers). In this instance, mediation exaggerates and even distorts the prosody of 'Telegram' in its reproduction, drawing the listener's attention where it might not have focused before.

Noise is an indispensable and, in many ways, desirable element of recorded sound. Recordings capture both intended and unintended noise. While the subject of the recording may be the event for which the recording took place, the ambient noises reveal much about the history of that recording. (This is what Paul DeMarinis describes as 'sound-multiplicity' [Parikka 2012: 92].) The scratching of a needle on vinyl, the puffs of air that punctuate the use of a microphone, or even the well-worn grooves on a record, shape not just what the user hears, but also give context by archiving details that were not intended for inclusion. Jussi Parikka, in *What is Media Archaeology?*, describes Claude Shannon's diagram from 1948, which first accounted for the planned presence of noise in a communication system. Parikka writes: 'Even though noise is seen as coming from the outside and invading the mediating powers of a communicative act, it still is diagrammed as an integral part of the system. Hence it is accorded a position within the diagrammatic framework instead of residing as pure noise outside the communication act' (Parikka 2012: 95).

Whenever an object is remediated, it inevitably differs from the original composition. With sound, the person facilitating the process of mediation via the program du jour has choices to make: assembly editing, sweetening, output levels, compressing, limiting, equalising, etc. Regardless of the jargon, with each of these choices, the promise of something gained accompanies the risk of something lost. The phrase 'lost in translation' exists for a reason, but the consequences of a machine conducting that translation intensifies the likelihood that something will be lost. In his *Rolling Stone* article 'The Death of High Fidelity', Robert Levine explains that 'MP3 reduces a CD audio file's size by as much as ninety percent, with an algorithm that eliminates sounds listeners are least likely to perceive – including extremes of high and low frequencies' (Levine 2007: 5). That is, in utilising a program intended to capture the content of one medium and convert it to be accessed in another, that program excludes elements of the original that it deems less perceptible, and therefore less necessary, to the recording itself. Levine goes further to explain that:

> Computer programs [...] make musicians sound unnaturally perfect. And today's listeners consume an increasing amount of music on MP3, which eliminates much of the data from the original CD file and can leave music sounding tinny or hollow. 'With all the technical innovation, music sounds worse', says Steely Dan's Donald Fagen, who has made what are considered some of the best-sounding records of all time. 'God is in the details. But there are no details anymore.' (Levine 2007: 1)

In attempting to preserve sound in a way that sounds 'perfect', unadulterated by excess noise or imperfections, the program achieves its goal. It produces a seemingly flawless, digital recording. However, that goal runs contrary to the goal of the archive. Rather than retaining the integrity of the original, which includes ambient noise and imperfections, the machine translation compromises the original recording during translation. An effective erasure of noise obscures clues about a device history, effectively divorcing the entry from its mediated past.

The digital renderings of Berrigan's reading do not necessarily exclude all of these elements; however, they do reinforce the distance between a digital user and the device for which the poem was intended. Berrigan performed and recorded 'Telegram' for a particular medium in a particular context: *Dial-a-Poem*. In that medium, the recording is in its most effective state. As a user connects with the poet, she waits not knowing what to expect. Like any personal phone call, unpredictability and spontaneity play a key role in bridging the gap between here and there. This element demands attention and participation, before the recording ever begins. From the outset of his recording, Berrigan provides context via an introduction and an explanation. As the user cups the receiver to her face, Berrigan briefly and thoroughly, explains the origin and object of his composition. Spoken softly, haltingly, and mournfully, it becomes impossible to dissociate the tone of Berrigan's performance from his poem. The intimate conveyance of honest admiration contrasts with the almost startling earnestness of his grief. It highlights the proximity of death, while anticipating the immortality promised by media. The contextual introduction contrasts with the marked brevity of the poem, further reinforcing the immediacy of this connection via telephone. Media intertwine and complicate the entire experience: in black and white, written words compose; in recorded perpetuity, the poet recites; perhaps never, Berrigan's telegram eulogises; with the touch of ten buttons, the phone connects; and in real time, the listener hears. The complexity of this performance is veiled by the incredible simplicity and intimacy of the telephone in the user's hand.

The issue with remediation is not the form that the work has taken, but that new media replace older media without acknowledgment or explanation. John Giorno, himself, writes that 'Poetry's basic nature is Mind. Then it takes many forms' (Whalen-Bridge and Storhoff 2009: 76). Although poetry can manifest in many forms, when the work is remediated, the work is now veiled and therefore more complex or more simplistic than its original incarnation. An insistence on medium specificity presents a challenge to the archivist compiling a digital collection. Anyone remotely familiar with media theory is familiar with Marshall McLuhan's concept that 'the medium is the message' (McLuhan 1994: 4). An artist never begins only with a blank canvas, or a poet with a blank page. Rather, the media influences the content, both in composition and in access. So, as the media of 'the message' changes, it shapes the form the content takes and the user's experience of that content. Bolter and Grusin point to problems with converging media, when they argue: 'Although each medium promises to reform its predecessors by offering a more immediate or authentic experience, the promise of reform inevitably leads us to become aware of the new medium as a medium' (Bolter and Grusin 2000: 19). That is to say, although the digital wants the user to feel uninhibited by its remediation, the experience is always inhibited. Regardless of its efforts to erase itself, the digital will always be detectable.

The remediation of sound into digital is particularly troubling. As new sound devices replace older systems, those older versions are often discarded and disregarded, even though they were the platforms for which a particular recording was intended. With the ease of access provided by the digital, the tendency is to avoid the trouble of finding older media. However, as Gotthold Ephraim Lessing recognised in 1766, old and new media are 'two equitable and friendly neighbours' (Lessing 1984: 91). Although remediation allows content to take different forms, it does not create exact replicas. For the average or distant user, accessing the essence of a recording in a new platform serves a valuable purpose: it provides a vehicle through which that user may be introduced to content, examine that content, and determine if pursuing an original for in-depth study has merit.

Returning to the *Dial-a-Poem* example elucidates the problematic nature of the digital archive as a substitute for hands-on, media-based, contextual interrogation of an entry. Ted Berrigan's poem 'Telegram' is accessible as spoken word via a digital file archived at *Ubuweb.com*. Berrigan originally performed this reading for its inclusion in the 1980s iteration of John Giorno's *Dial-A-Poem*, entitled *Sugar, Alcohol, and Meat*, originally started as an exhibit in the Architectural League of New York in 1968. Giorno's installation included six telephone lines that showcased thirteen poets and their poems via an answering system that played, when someone called the publicised number.

The Architectural League exhibit ran for five months, during which time it received over a million calls. The installation was briefly resurrected in Chicago, before being picked up by the Museum of Modern Art in 1970. In an interview, John Giorno speculates about the populations accessing this MoMA installation:

> One day a New York mother saw her 12-year-old son with two friends listening to the telephone and [giggling]. She grabbed the phone from them and what she heard freaked her out. This was when Dial-A-Poem was at The Architectural League of New York with worldwide media coverage, and *Junior Scholastic Magazine* had just done an article and listening to Dial-A-Poem was homework in New York City Public Schools. It was also at a time when I was putting out a lot of erotic poetry, like Jim Carroll's pornographic 'Basketball Diaries', so it became hip for the teenies to call. [...]
>
> Then we moved to The Museum of Modern Art, where one half the content of Dial-A-Poem was politically radical poetry at the time, with the war and repression and everything, we thought this was a good way for the Movement to reach people. [...]
>
> The newspaper, magazine, TV and radio coverage had the effect of making everyone want to call the Dial-A-Poem. We got up to the maximum limit of the equipment and stayed there. 60,000 calls a week and it was totally great. The busiest time was 9 AM to 5 PM, so one figured that all those people sitting at desks in New York office buildings spend a lot of time on the telephone, then the second busiest time was 8:30 PM to 11:30 PM was the after-dinner crowd, then the California calls and those tripping on acid or couldn't sleep 2 AM to 6 PM. So using an existing communications system we established a new poet-audience relationship. (Giorno 1972)

Dial-a-Poem began as an intimate, provocative affair. The telephone allowed a compression of time and space that directly connected the user on one end with the recording of a poet on the other. The new 'poet-audience' relationship re-envisioned how individuals might connect with authors and works, using personal devices like the telephone.

At the time, telephones were different than they are now. A phone was shared. In 1960, roughly 20 percent of households had no telephone available. Those that did have access were not necessarily telephones in the home, but might be at a neighbor's house or down the street (Bureau 2010). This differs greatly from the current situation. In 2017, 50.8% of United States households were wireless only, relying only on cell phones to make calls. 6.5% have just a landline, and 39.4% have both, leaving only 3.2% phone-free (Bureau 2010). Few remain without telephone access. Carolyn Marvin explains that 'the telephone was the first electric medium to enter the home and unsettle customary ways of dividing the private person and family from the more public setting of the community' (Marvin 1988: 6). This welcome intruder connected separated individuals by offering them an informal way of communicating in 'real time' with others outside of the home. This concept continues to develop further, as in many households each individual purchases a personal device, extending and individualising the reaches of telephonic communication.

More than the written word, which requires some formality and forethought to be coherent in composition, the telephone became a source of spontaneous, creative conversation. Joshua Meyrowitz writes, 'Without nonverbal cues, careful construction and rewriting are needed to capture the correct "feeling". Sarcasm, teasing and other nuances of meaning are easily lost in [print]. This is why even intimate love letters tend to have a "formal" quality, while [...] telephone conversations seem quite intimate and personal' (Meyrowitz 1985: 101). Meyrowitz's assertion that spoken word assumes a more personal and informal quality over written word elucidates the particular nature of the telephone and its influence on relationships. But, because the phone of the 1960s and 70s was shared, using a phone was often still a communal experience, even when the conversation was only meant for and heard by an individual. It was a moment carved out for individual experience in the presence of others.

Although the function of the telephone established it as coveted and essential in households, the design of the material object itself magnifies its character. Telephones are intimate, sensual objects, not only in use, but in composition. Long before the electric glow of the rigid cell phone, the receiver of the rotary phone stretched on its tightly coiled leash. That receiver cupped the face of its user, whispering (or shouting) directly in his ear, excluding others while drawing the listener in closely. McLuhan posits that the telephone 'unites voice and ear in an especially close way [...] so it is quite natural to kiss via phone' (McLuhan 1994: 266). Because of this uniquely personal way of listening and communicating, telephones focus the user's attention in a way unmatched by other media. They depend upon spontaneity and require active participation. Conversing in one location, while consumed with the content and context of a distant other, links time, space, individuals, and ideas in a way most media cannot hope to achieve. Unlike telegraphs or letters, the telephone was the first object to fully enter the home, controlled by users on both ends of the call and allowing for immediate access. It became a convenient and crucial object for relaying important information. But more importantly, it evolved into an indispensable and essential means of communicating.

    The digital archive discounts medium-specificity as inconsequential in order to justify remediation and access in this new configuration. Users often neglect or ignore the material through which original compositions were intended to be accessed. This is, in part, a function of convenience. The digital provides instant gratification. It removes much of the pomp and circumstance associated with visiting and accessing records in locations dedicated to that purpose. Competing multi-media platforms, like smartphones and computers, are the stage upon which today's archives must perform and compete. However, the most invasive of these objects, today's smartphone, actually undermines its ability to create intimacy with its capacity to offer several functions at once. If the telephone is an exercise in focus, the smartphone is an exercise in distraction. So, necessarily, as a user engages with archived material, it becomes one of the many competing demands on the digital system at any time. The entry is sullied in more ways than a machine's remediation. The experience itself lacks authenticity, because it is no longer conveyed through the medium for which it was composed. Rather than that sensual, sensory, focused experience, it is one of seven tabs open on a browser, blasted over speakers, while the user checks email.

    This gap between the medium for which a work was composed and the medium for which an object was remediated must be minimised in order to refine and understand the entry in a comprehensive sense. The scholar is ultimately responsible for excavating layers of forgotten or obsolete media. However, the work of unearthing what machines, both analogue and digital, attempt to make invisible is difficult and, in many cases, impossible. Because each new technology wants to provide access without hindering the user's access, remediations become almost untraceable for a piece newly entered into the digital archive. That an academic ought to know the genesis of a particular work might seem an obvious, implied task. It certainly seems like it should be easy to accomplish with the 'world at our fingertips'. However, returning to Berrigan's 'Telegram' as a practical example, proves that tracing the media archaeology of a performance in the digital archive remains a problematic venture.

    In the preservation of Giorno's *Dial-a-Poem*, each remediation alters the exhibit significantly. The first remediation's record sleeve fills in some gaps about the origin of 'Telegram'. It identifies a time of publication (1980) and assigns a few names, faces, and poems to other featured poets. However, the connection to the telephone is all but lost. In fact, this iteration never received a telephonic audience. Instead, the record plays music on a speaker. Unlike the individualised, private nature of the telephone's receiver, a speaker performs for many, not for one. The intimate connection of a solitary message spoken for one particular listener is dissociated from this incarnation. In this remediation as a record, the elements of predictability and accessibility are also altered. Should the listener choose to listen to Berrigan's performance, and only Berrigan's performance, there is neither obstacle nor the urgency of temporality. On demand, the *user* controls the content, not the artist. Furthermore, the listener remains anchored in time and space. That is, no longer does the telephone aid in transporting the caller, via a focused, participatory experience, with a remote recipient. The experience remains limited to the confines of the machine and locale.

When MoMA again remediated *Dial-a-Poem* in 2012, the curators attempted to educate both its digital and physical audience about the original objectives of the installation by maintaining the elements of unpredictability and remote accessibility. MoMA designed this newest iteration on two stages: a physical installation in the museum itself and a digital page accessible remotely on personal devices. The physical installation mirrored the set-up of Giorno's. Telephones lined the walls in a room that connected the listener to a performance from among Giorno's selections via a rotary-style telephone. The selection was random, and lacked user control, much like the original. Unfortunately, in a museum, the experience lacked much of the spontaneity and intimacy implied by accessing from a personal space, like the home. However, this staged experience attempted to carve out a moment for an individual, private connection to the poet on the original medium for which it was composed.

The digital iteration, which is still accessible, dedicates itself to creating a responsible, although still undeniably altered, version of *Dial-a-Poem*. The main page for the installation lists the authors and their featured works. However, these works are not accessible to the user by choice. Rather, the user clicks a 'play button', which randomly selects a performance. Although the poets and their poems are listed and give context, the user lacks control, much like the original. Further, this remediation also maintains the integrity of the original in that it remains accessible from a distance. In a personal space, the user chooses a moment to connect with a poet. What this iteration lacks, however, is a predetermined way in which the user finally accesses the content. While the audience must access the installation via the internet, it can listen via speakers, headphones, or the smart phone's earpiece. The audience listens to *Dial-a-Poem* in the same manner that it listens to a loved one, but the mode is personalised to their own listening preferences. This final choice is not one that would have existed for the first iteration of the installation; however, in many ways, it seems to reinforce the fact that MoMA curated the intimate nature of the process alongside the installation for an audience accessing data in our current, cultural moment.

Although the installation is admittedly different from Giorno's original, the MoMA curators thoughtfully crafted the exhibits to incorporate essential elements of the original installation's appeal. In the physical installation, it attempted to educate through the work's tactile experience. Online, it gives a brief history of the first iterations of the exhibit and how the content of that exhibition were accessed in Giorno's original installation. Both versions make a bold attempt at acknowledging their differences from the original experience, while trying to maintain those essential elements: physical distance, personal connection, and artist control. While these remediations are certainly responsible, they are the exception, not the rule. Most digital archives lack the time and resources to be able to construct or reconstruct such conscientiously composed records.

Both the boon to and bane of the digital is that any number of remediated versions exist, each claiming to be as authentic and transparent as the original. *UbuWeb* maintains an incredible digital archive of avant-garde poetry, boasting both the obscure and the celebrated. *UbuWeb*'s remediation of *Dial-a-Poem*, however, disappoints. It maintains the sound content of the original, but not much else. The experience differs greatly from Giorno's original collection or even the one carefully crafted by the MoMA. It is, simply, a collection built for access and not experience. In practice, the set-up mimics the record. Sara Boxer of the *New York Times* writes about accessing *Dial-A-Poem* in *UbuWeb*'s archive:

> Ah, you think to yourself, I can swallow this whole movement in a day. If you don't like a poem or, hey, you get the point already, just click on another selection.
>
> Click. Click. Click. You're in control, and there's the rub. You're not waiting on the telephone to see who in the world is going to whisper or shout in your ear. You're not looking nervously over your shoulder to see if your mother is going to walk in while you're listening.
>
> It's just you now, the gray zip of your QuickTime player and a whole lot of choices. You can listen through headphones or speakers. You can fold laundry while you're at it. You can make a poem repeat over and over. You're the consumer, and you know best. (Boxer 2005: 3)

Discrete recordings are accessible virtually anywhere (or at least anywhere an individual has Wi-Fi signal and a personal computing device). The performance can be public or private. It is on-demand. It is particular and certainly not random. And, although it is available in this digital archive, it lacks many of the elements that made it so appealing at its inception, elements the MoMA tried to incorporate. *UbuWeb* makes an effort to contextualise what the digital experience omits in remediation, but its contextualisation is buried and separated. The recordings exist, but the installation does not. This digital version isolates the content from the conceptual and material.

When Berrigan's work was remediated into the digital, it became a work out of time, place, and context. His carefully crafted spectre became distorted through seemingly transparent remediation, as the digital simplified, and in some ways sterilised, the performance. Rather than media converging, the digital replaced. Although this process is laden with media complexity, this additional layer problematises the exhibition, censoring the creation and inhibiting the user. Rather than archiving the entire experience, the user is left with the remnants of an algorithm's compressed version of Berrigan's recitation. And, while Berrigan's oral description remains in the *UbuWeb* version of his poem, the process deletes indispensable scaffolding thereby defiling the integrity of the entry. When the archive limited this entry to only sound, an author, and a title, it chronicled a corrupted copy in its annals. Although the tone, pauses, breaths, and language are captured by this remediation, *UbuWeb*'s attempt at replicating 'Telegram' in *Dial-a-Poem* fails. *UbuWeb* undeniably provides a breadth of access. However, it provides no acknowledgement of or education about the process of that archival remediation. It makes no effort to include inseparable elements of the instalment, like removing control and predictability. Rather, it senses the demands of the digital world and prioritises 'on-demand', one-dimensional content, instead of curating the entire experience. The original *Dial-a-Poem*'s appeal exists in its spontaneity and its demand for personal, sensual connection and attention. What remains on *UbuWeb* is only noise, and edited noise at that.

As we 'play it again', new media attempt to supersede old media, encouraging the reader to evaluate a work without considering the context of its first creation. Emboldened by unrestricted access and the promise of transparency, users tend to gloss over the necessity of engaging with older media in its original platform. It is certainly unrealistic to think that all eager individuals will have access to original exhibits and sound recordings. I know I could not even locate a record of *Sugar, Alcohol, & Meat* to listen to 'Telegram', as I researched this paper. I only interacted with the recording itself courtesy of *UbuWeb*. And, although I am grateful for this access, I remain troubled by the lack of transparency in the archive's methodology. What *Ubuweb* includes is not haphazardly selected, because certainly sound content is paramount. It is not the responsibility of the archive to ensure that the user has access to a rotary phone through which the experience might be reproduced as completely as the first instalment. Such demands would be unreasonable and unrealistic.

However, there currently exists an attitude in which the archivist and audience comfortably accept remediation in the digital as a replacement for the original, or as a 'good enough' substitute. As the demand for access to entries via digital archives expands, the resources of time, funding, space, and bandwidth will continue to be strained. In spite of these constraints, students, scholars, and users deserve a more responsible form of conservation, and this form includes the device history of an entry. If the current procedures do not change, then the archivists who hoped to chronicle these original compositions will actually contribute to their extinction.

Works Cited

Berrigan, Ted. 2005. *The Collected Poems of Ted Berrigan*, edited by Alice Notley, Anselm Berrigan, and Edmund Berrigan. Berkeley: University of California Press.

Bolter, Jay David and Grusin, Richard. 2000. *Remediation: Understanding New Media*. Cambridge, MA: MIT Press.

Boxer, Sarah. 2005. 'Dial-A-Poem Enters the Digital Age'. *New York Times*, April 30. https://www.nytimes.com/2005/04/30/arts/dialapoem-enters-the-internet-age.html.

Breakell, Sue. 2008. 'Perspectives: Negotiating the Archive'. *Tate Papers* 9. http://www.tate.org.uk/research/publications/tate-papers/09/perspectives-negotiating-the-archive.

Bureau, United States Census. 2010. *U.S. Census of Housing Telephones*. https://www.census.gov/hhes/www/housing/census/historic/phone.html.

Ernst, Wolfgang. 2015. 'E-Kurenniemics: Becoming Archive in Electronic Devices'. In *Writing and Unwriting (Media) Art History*, edited by Joasia Krysa and Jussi Parikka, 203–12. Cambridge, MA: MIT Press.

Giorno, John. 1972. *Dial-a-Poem Hype*. http://www.ubu.com/sound/dial.html.

Giorno, John. 1980. 'Telegram to Jack Kerouac,' recorded by Ted Berrigan. On *Sugar, Alcohol, & Meat* [vinyl]. http://www.ubu.com/sound/sam.html.

Jenkinson, Hilary. 1937. *A Manual of Archive Administration* (second edition). London: P. Lund, Humphries.

Kieckhefer, Daniel. 2018. 'Archive'. In *The Chicago School of Media Theory*, January 17. https://lucian.uchicago.edu/blogs/mediatheory/keywords/archive/.

Kittler, Friedrich. 1999. *Gramophone, Film, Typewriter*, translated by Geoffrey-Winthrop-Young and Michael Wutz. Stanford: Stanford University Press.

Kurenniemi, Erkki. 2015. 'Computer Eats Art'. In *Writing and Unwriting (Media) Art History*, edited by Joasia Krysa and Jussi Parikka, 97–105. Cambridge, MA: MIT Press.

Lessing, Gotthold Ephraim. 1984. *Laocoon: An Essay on the Limits of Painting and Poetry*, translated by Edward Allen McCormick. New York: Bobbs-Merrill Company.

Levine, Les. 2013. 'Remembrance'. In *The Architectural League of New York*. http://archleague.org/2013/03/remembrance-by-les-levine/.

Levine, Robert. 2007. 'The Death of High Fidelity'. In *Rolling Stone*, December 26. http://www.rollingstone.com/news/story/17777619/the_death_of_high_fidelity.

Manovich, Lev. 2001. *The Language of New Media*. Cambridge, MA: MIT Press.

Marvin, Carolyn. 1988. *When Old Technologies Were New: Thinking about Electric Communication in the Late Nineteenth Century.* New York: Oxford University Press.

McLuhan, Marshall. 1994. *Understanding Media: The Extensions of Man.* Cambridge, MA: MIT Press.

Meyrowitz, Joshua. 1985. *No Sense of Place: The Impact of Electronic Media on Social Behavior.* New York: Oxford University Press.

Parikka, Jussi. 2012. *What is Media Archaeology?* Cambridge: Polity Press.

Sugar, Alcohol, & Meat (The Dial-a-Poem Poets). 1980. *Discogs*. https://www.discogs.com/Various-Sugar-Alcohol-Meat-The-Dial-A-Poem-Poets/release/742260.

The Dial-a-Poem Poets. *Weird Retro*. http://www.weirdretro.org.uk/the-dial-a-poem-poets.html.

Whalen-Bridge, John and Gary Storhoff. 2009. *The Emergence of Buddhist American Literature.* Albany: SUNY Press.

8

Situating Google's Alphabet

Rebecca Ross

In 1964, communication theorist Marshall McLuhan (2001: 93), following on the heels of economist Harold Innis and setting the tone for future invocations of the so-called 'alphabet effect' by the Toronto School of Communication, claimed the superiority of Western civilisation on the basis of its development of a phonetic alphabet: 'The breaking up of every kind of experience into uniform units in order to produce faster action and change of form (applied knowledge) has been the secret of Western power over man and nature alike.' The Toronto School understood the defining characteristic of the alphabet to be its phoneticism. In contrast to pictographic (or even syllabic) writing systems, the phonetic alphabet dissociated the specific writing system from the language being transcribed and could therefore be used with any language regardless of fluency (Logan 1986: 20). In this instance, the definition of an alphabet as both a universally applicable (portable) and independent symbol system becomes directly intertwined with a colonial proposition.

A half-century later, one of the world's largest and most influential publicly traded corporations, Google, Inc., restructured itself as Alphabet, converting Google – the search engine – into a separate company to be held as a subsidiary of the newly formed Alphabet, Inc. In his letter explaining the transition to the public, Google co-founder Larry Page (Google 2015) wrote, 'We liked the name Alphabet because it means a collection of letters that represent language, one of humanity's most important innovations, and is the core of how we index with Google search!' This definition of the alphabet as 'letters that represent language' is characteristic of Google's oversimplifying approach to knowledge, making a subject appear better understood than it might be in practice with the confident flourish of an exclamation point. The web page containing Page's letter is itself decorated with brightly coloured children's ABC blocks.

The Toronto School and Google /Alphabet have approached their interest in communication from a different perspective, at different times in history, and with varying values and motivations, but they share a claim to the concept of an alphabet. On one level, the re-definition of Google as Alphabet in the context of Google's dominance as a tech giant seems irrelevant.

From the point of view of the US's security and exchange commission, re-structuring would have been identical financially and legally if another single-word moniker, such as 'elephant' or 'bubble', had been chosen instead. Indeed, much of the ensuing discussion in the mainstream, technology, and design presses focused on either the financial aspects or the accompanying change of logo and typeface. Once this chatter subsided, as was intended from the outset – 'we are not intending for this to be a big consumer brand with related products – the whole point is that Alphabet companies should have independence' (Google 2015) – the activities of Alphabet since 2015 have largely fallen out of view of all but certain elements of the finance sector. The company continues to trade as GOOG and GOOGL in stock markets; its presence online is lean, fulfilling the basic publishing requirements of a publicly traded corporation. It may however be precisely because Alphabet the holding corporation so far has faded into the background, that the question of the implications of the renaming for other notions of alphabet grows in importance.

The difficulty of reflecting actively on the concept of alphabet is balanced with its intuitive ubiquity. Most users of alphabets are immersed in their application to the extent that they more often relate to the world through them than with any well-considered or articulated concept of the alphabet in mind. Similar to the division of time into hours and minutes, it has become deeply embedded and naturalised in many cultures. In 1957 historian of printing and typography Stanley Morison (1972) delivered a significant series of lectures on the subject of the history and politics of western scripts at Oxford University. In 1985, linguist Geoffrey Sampson wrote an introduction to writing systems that he hoped would redress written language's status as, according to philosopher Jacques Derrida, 'the wandering outcast of linguistics' (quoted in Sampson 1985: 11). In contemporary scholarship, the alphabet remains quietly present at the periphery of a small number of academic fields and professions: sub-branches of linguistics, literature, graphic design, communications and media, printing, lettering, bibliography, computer programming (to name a few). Perhaps it is due to the extent to which academics use alphabets to transact that it has so infrequently been attended to by scholars as a far-reaching concept, nor would it be possible to do so comprehensively in a lifetime of work, let alone in the space of this short chapter. Google's renaming to Alphabet nevertheless gives pause and demands that we attempt to consider its implications for other alphabets and notions of alphabet or alphabetic-ness.

In 2004, communications scholar Paul Grosswiler (2004) carefully reverse-engineered the Toronto School's 'alphabet effect', tracing the term through a large corpus of associated literature and demonstrating a range of flaws in the notion that phonetic writing systems are inherently superior. For example, where the Toronto School identified the fact that phonetic writing systems can be used with unknown languages as a distinct advantage, Grosswiler countered by describing the commensurate value that a shared pictographic writing system offered to speakers of diverse spoken languages, such as in China. More recently, scholar of Chinese literature Lydia H. Liu (2015) has challenged histories of writing systems that attribute the colonial dominance of the Roman alphabet entirely to its phonetic characteristics. Rather than attempt to 'dispel' the alphabet effect, as Grosswiler suggests, it may be more productive to regard more clearly its colonialist definition and, indeed, evaluate the 'effects' that it has had despite, or perhaps as a function of, its compromised premise. What does it mean to define the alphabet in such exclusive terms? What does it do? It is on this basis that the present chapter considers the question of what it means for the world's largest actor in the domain of spatial data, not to mention one of the world's largest multinational corporations, to lay claim to, and indeed entangle its very identity with, the concept of alphabet. Building on this, it also speculates more broadly on relationships in the development of location as a medium and the role of situatedness in our understanding of media.

I.

The Toronto School's understanding of the phonetic alphabet as exceptional is based on the association of symbols with component sounds rather than the meaning of words or parts of words:

> The phonetic alphabet is a unique system of writing in which a small number of letters or visual signs (twenty-two to forty) are used to represent the basic sounds or phonemes of a spoken language. The letters are used to code the sounds of each word phonetically. (Logan 1986: 19)

On more or less this basis, McLuhan (2001: 88) in *Understanding Media* described the alphabet as a transposition of the sonic into the visual, 'an eye for an ear'. The relatively small number of visual symbols that compose a phonetic alphabet was understood to facilitate the 'breaking up of every kind of experience into uniform units' (93). The fact that these symbols are concurrently entirely separate from, and extensions of, the human ear was identified by the Toronto School as a point of origin for western thought.

Like McLuhan, working decades later in the twentieth century and on the other side of the Atlantic, media theorist Vilém Flusser, in his essay *Does Writing Have a Future?*, also referred to the phonetic alphabet as the basis for a series of extended arguments about communication. In the broadest terms, both McLuhan and Flusser invoked its invention as productive of a phase of human existence presently approaching an end. Both were also engaged with, to use McLuhan's term, 'an intensification and extension of the visual function' (2001: 91), and to use Flusser's, the coming of 'technical images' (2011b).

However, where for McLuhan the alphabet is an assertion of the visual, for Flusser writing exists in productive tension with images, which he equates to numbers for their shared semiotic irreducibility. As references to phonemes, Flusser understood letters in relation to sound and music. In order to become meaningful, letters require a subjective process of interpretation, whereas numbers, which Flusser (2011a: 24) associated with images and science, are inherently meaningful and do not depend on interpretation: 'Letters are about a discourse, numbers about content'.

While both Flusser and McLuhan share a sense of numbers as associated with the immediate, they are less of an emphasis for McLuhan than they are for Flusser and are understood differently in relation to writing. McLuhan (2001: 119) understood numbers as a 'shadow' of writing, wielding 'a separate life and intensity' from letters yet developing over the long-term in concert 'with the growth of literacy'. With reference to the association between numerical digits and human fingers, McLuhan (2001: 116) explicitly framed numbers as an extension of the human sense of touch: 'Just as writing is an extension and separation of our most neutral and objective sense, the sense of sight, number is an extension and separation of our most intimate and interrelating activity, our sense of touch'.

Where to a certain extent Flusser shared McLuhan's understanding of vision as 'neutral and objective', he departed from McLuhan in his analysis of numbers as continuous with images. This analysis is complicated by McLuhan's readings of certain mid-twentieth century works of art and music as well as Flusser's (2011b: 12, 33–5) somewhat rigid distinction between 'traditional pictures' and 'technical images'. Nor do their divergent thoughts on letters and numbers put into question their shared sense of an impending broad reconfiguration of human existence. However, the variations between their understandings of alphabet are nevertheless worth tracing for their distinct implications concerning the way in which they envision the future role of humans relative to their media.

Where the Toronto School argued that the phonetic alphabet produces western culture, Flusser (2011a: 7) argued that, in tension with images/ numbers, 'the gesture of writing produces historical consciousness'. Unlike images, which are 'scenes', writing and reading are 'processes' which engage human faculties (2011a: 39). In this sense, an alphabet serves as a counterpoint, or medium of 'resistance' to images/numbers (Poster 2010: 9). Flusser understood alphanumeric texts, containing both letters and numbers, as charged with potential meaning and, over time, the potential for the interpretation and re-interpretation of meaning:

> What in the text is actually adequate to what is out there? Letters or numbers? The auditory or the visual? Is it the literal thinking that describes things or the pictorial that counts things? Are there things that want to be described and others that want to be

counted? And are there things that can be neither described nor counted – and for which science is therefore not adequate? Or are letters and numbers something like nets that we throw out to fish for things, leaving all indescribable and uncountable things to disappear? Or even, do the letter and number nets themselves actually form describable and countable things out of a formless mass? (Flusser 2011a: 25)

This can be contrasted with McLuhan's (2001: 119) contention that 'the electric age brings number back into unity with visual and auditory experience', or numbers into unity with the alphabet. In *Into the Universe of Technical Images*, Flusser (2011b: 4) also argued that the rising 'dominance of technical images', or 'telematic society', is irreversible. But he speculated about the different forms that this could take in the future: 'One moves toward a centrally programmed, totalitarian society of image receivers and image administrators, the other toward a dialogic, telematic society of image producers and image collectors'. Preferring the 'dialogic' to the 'totalitarian', Flusser (4) argued that human beings 'are still free at this point to challenge these values'.

Where both Flusser and McLuhan anticipated a wholesale reconfiguration of humanity's relationship to its media, for McLuhan, the specific form that this will take is fixed in a way that remains somewhat more open for Flusser. In a 1970 lecture on the subject of the coming 'acoustic' or 'electric' world in which the alphabetic and numeric converge, one way that McLuhan distinguished between the visual phase of human history (which for him begins roughly with the spread of the Western phonetic alphabet) and the coming acoustic world is in terms of a diminished human capacity to focus attention, take positions and make decisions: 'It's hard to have a fixed point of view in a world where everything is happening simultaneously. It is hard to have an objective in a world that is changing faster than you can imagine the objective being fulfilled' (McLuhan 1970: n.p.).

As a way to understand the transition presently underway, the alphabet was looked back upon as a kind of force that, once unleashed, transformed 'Western man' iteratively over hundreds of years to the extent that it is on the cusp of a radical transformation, or to use McLuhan's language, a 'big flip'. In the same 1970 lecture McLuhan speculated about how this transformation might play out in Eastern cultures (while claiming not to be 'making value judgements'):

The Japanese today are introducing Western literacy into their own culture and spending $6 billion to get rid of their own alphabet and put in our alphabet. Little do they know what is going to happen to them or to us as a result. But the alphabetic man is very aggressive and very specialized. The Japanese world is likely to manifest an enormous increase of energy and aggression when they get our alphabet installed. It will also wipe out their whole culture – their ideogrammatic forms of writing and culture will be destroyed [...] So if the Chinese or the Japanese were to take on our alphabet seriously, they would be in great trouble, and we would too. I don't think they understand what's involved. (McLuhan 1970)

Although it is indisputable that McLuhan considered the phonetic alphabet to be the cornerstone of western civilisation, his particular prose style makes slippages between placing this idea as the basis of a further claim of superiority, or merely an amoral observation, difficult to track across the breadth of his writings. The passion inherent in McLuhan's writing and speaking makes it difficult to accept that there are no 'value judgements' – though what motivates him or what he advocated for specifically in relation to the transformations he described remain open questions. What can be gleaned, however, is a sense of the phonetic alphabet itself as a force which has irrevocably been unleashed in a way that will ultimately colonise human culture with its own media.

Media theorist and scholar of German literature Chadwick Truscott Smith (2014) offers a reading of Flusser's (2002: 165–71) essay 'Celebrating', that responds to the question, which has been raised by other scholars, of whether either or both Flusser and McLuhan are engaged with the post-human in their speculations about the future of communication. Although Flusser gives a great deal of consideration to the reconfiguration of inter-relations between humans and machines, Smith interprets Flusser's writings as ultimately maintaining the possibility of the human as a participant in future process and/or dialogues that question and reconfigure media beyond the end of alphabet and history:

> Flusser retains the belief that even as new technologies emerge to prompt further changes, however, something called the human – with 'marrow and bone in the margin between 10^{-5} and 10^{5} cm' – will still remain. The retention of the word is necessary, even if we don't know what it is, because something threatens this subject of the process of humanization [...] It leaves open the process whereby the human (or humanities) have the capacity to redefine the apparatus (or the digital), even as the former is conditioned by the latter (Smith 2014: 13).

To summarise, Flusser's conceptualisation of the alphabet operates concurrently in two inter-related ways. First, it provides a way to talk about history as a function of the discursive relationship between human beings and their media, a relationship that is presently being drastically reconfigured to the point that it will give rise to a new condition of being or 'telematic society' in which writing and history are at an end and technical images dominate. Second, building here on Smith, it facilitates an identification, foregrounding and valuation of the dialogic as what humans could potentially contribute to the quality of this reconfiguration. Whereas for the Toronto School, the alphabet was associated with a kind of colonisation by the visual to which all humanity is increasingly subject, for Flusser it was associated with both producing and resisting the coming of the technical image as well as positioning humanity with regard to how it might interact with and through technical images in the future.

II.

At the time of Google's launch in 1998, its founders Larry Page and Sergey Brin declared the company's mission as 'to organise the world's information, making it universally accessible and useful' (Google 2019). Following the success of their internet search engine, their initial offering as a publicly traded corporation (IPO) in 2004 brought with it an exploration of how this principle could be elaborated and scaled up. Business decisions following the IPO, such as movements into the book publishing and spatial data sectors, suggest their starting point was to consider the limits of internet search in achieving their bold, if under-defined, proposition of universally-accessible information. Their search engine was powerful but could only ever reach digital information stored on computers connected to the internet. However, their mission statement had specified 'the world's information' without differentiating between internet-based information and information more generally. From this point, two questions began to emerge through their activities and public statements: What information is not available on the internet? Where can the best quality of information be found and what makes it better?

Both Brin and then Google product manager Marissa Mayer were interviewed for a 2007 article in the *New Yorker*, covering Google's legal disputes with publishers of out-of-print books, which they had begun digitising in partnership with several large English-language, mainly American, university library collections in 2004. Regarding Google's motivations for initiating such an ambitious scanning and indexing project, Mayer cited the quality and reliability of information: 'Google has become known for providing access to all of the world's knowledge, and if we provide access to books we are going to get much higher-quality and much more reliable information' (Toobin 2007). Communications scholar Siva Vaidhyanathan (2011: 173) argues that Google Books, as it interacted with entities ranging from universities to local public libraries to scanning equipment to the legalities of copyright, was a move toward the 'privatisation of knowledge', with many associated implications of great concern given its growing role as a corporate 'mediator, filter, and editor' of all information. It is useful to place this important concern in the context of a question which, though seemingly-obvious is not as straightforward as one might intuit, of what it is about books in particular that makes them high quality information. Vaidhyanathan points out that Google's poor standard of reproduction was not up to archival standards maintained by the library community. For example, images were often poor in quality and physical variations of books, such as fold-outs, were treated expediently. However, my question addresses the more mundane. How did selection, scanning, optical character recognition (OCR), file formats, and indexing for search terms interact with the 'high-quality' of books as information?

In the same 2007 article in the *New Yorker*, Bryn offers slightly more detail about Google's specific understanding of the value of books:

> We really care about the comprehensiveness of a search [...]
> And comprehensiveness isn't just about, you know, total number
> of words or bytes, or whatnot. But it's about having the really
> high-quality information. You have thousands of years of
> human knowledge, and probably the highest-quality knowledge
> is captured in books. So not having that – it's just too big an
> omission. (Toobin 2007)

For Google, books were seen as repositories of specifically-'human knowledge' developed and extended over millennia in a way that is not expressed sufficiently in terms of quantities of words or bytes, but that are nevertheless 'too big an omission' to exclude from their search. This resonates with the earlier discussion of Flusser's formulation of history as produced through writing in tension with the numeric. Writing is dialogic in a way that facilitates the continuous production of new knowledge. It is not clear precisely how this relates to the standard of 'really high-quality information' that Bryn associated with books in the first place, but it does provide a way to put the subsequent development of Google Books in context.

Google Books ultimately developed into a search platform with results that can appear arbitrary compared to, for example, a visit to a library or bookshop. Only books published during the early twentieth century and earlier, and which fall outside the scope of various copyright laws, are available as complete texts in downloadable PDF or Google Play formats. So, searching from the UK, for example, without an affiliation with a contributing university library, the first results for 'capitalism' are the full version of 'A Circular from the Commissioner of Emigration to the Agriculturists, Manufacturers and Capitalists of India' by John Wilstach, published in 1866, or the first few pages of the second edition of David Schweickart's *After Capitalism* (2011) – with no mention of the likes of Adam Smith or Karl Marx. The majority of books published from the mid-twentieth century onwards are available in either 'preview' or 'snippet' mode. This means that the searcher is granted access to a limited number of paragraphs (snippet view) or pages (preview view) or in some cases only meta-data, such as the title, containing instances of the search terms. A large majority of information accessible on Google Books is thus presented to most searchers in disorganised and discontinuous fragments. Copyright questions and the need for legal settlements with publishers meant that this aspect was probably a compromise of the intended end-user experience of Google Books. However, as then-president of the French National Library Jean-Noël Jeanneney (2008: 68) argued, the entire premise of 'discovering books only through pages that are separated from one another and located by a search engine, according to the unique criteria of a search for related hits, is not necessarily a good way – and certainly not the most beneficial way – to approach books or make use of them'. Jeanneney identified a basic contradiction between what he saw as an unrealistic, unachievable, and distracting ambition of comprehensiveness, and the aspiration to high quality. Whether through the behind-the-scenes logic of its search algorithm or through the deals it makes with certain university libraries or publishers, Google prioritises information in a way that is inseparable from its business interests. And Google's business interests are not the same as 'the richest, the most intelligent, the best organised, the most accessible of all possible selections' (67).

Google Books may have been set up with the idea of indexing and providing access to 'thousands of years of human knowledge, and probably the highest-quality knowledge'. However, the subsequent development of the project exemplifies the way in which the logic of techno-capitalism places the value associated with distinctly-'human knowledge' at risk. In Jeanneney's view, a 'selection' performed by human beings will always be of higher quality than one carried out as a function of a market-driven algorithm. This difference can also be understood in the terms of Flusser's distinction between alphabetic and encoded media. Books as a medium are easily understood as alphabetic, but in their transposition into Google Books, they become something more encoded in a way that undermines their dialogical or human value. The story of Google Books makes Google's later adoption of the moniker of Alphabet seem ironic. Moreover, it is an example of a Google project that demonstrates that the association of the alphabetic with the discursive is important in a way that must be reflected upon actively, even if Google's services, in which people and their associated data become products, are reconfiguring humanity in a way that sets these values aside (Powers and Jablonski 2015: 74–98).

Google Maps, which ultimately became a more successful venture than Google Books, was launched in 2005, a short time after book-scanning commenced. In certain ways, it arose out of an ambition of comprehensiveness similar to that which motivated the development of Books. In a 2010 interview looking back on Google's history, then Google Street View UX designer Andy Szybalski commented on Google's decision to develop Maps and Street View following the widespread success of its search engine technology.

Szybalski (2010) offered, 'Spatial [maps and later street view] built upon Google's broader mission to organise, or index, all information that exists by acknowledging that most of it is not inside computers but rather visible everywhere in the world.' The project began with the 2004 acquisition of the three-year old Keyhole Corporation, a company which had gained a reputation for supplying immersive fly-through maps composed by stitching together satellite images and aerial photographs (Google 2004).

The premise of stitching together otherwise disparate fragments is where Google Maps differed significantly from Books. Where Books encoded established assemblages of knowledge – bound printed pages – as separate fragments of text and image, Maps gathered disparate images and addresses into a coherent continuous association of tiles and layers. The novelty of this was such that Google felt compelled to explain, in a 2005 blog entry introducing Google Maps, that when panning or zooming, 'there's no wait for a new image to download':

> We think maps can be useful and fun, so we've designed Google Maps to simplify how to get from point A to point B. Say you're looking for 'hotels near LAX'. With Google Maps you'll see nearby hotels plotted right on a crisp new map (we use new rendering methods to make them easier to read). Click and drag the map to view the adjacent area dynamically – there's no wait for a new image to download. Or get step-by-step directions to where you're headed. If a particular intersection on the route looks tricky, click on that step in the directions to see a magnified view. Play with the keyboard shortcuts (arrow keys to pan or the +/- keys to zoom in and out) too. The tour shows you even more. Happy trails. (Google 2005)

Google Maps also differs from standard Google Search because search queries are specifically about location, and search results are presented as maps rather than lists of links. Google Maps incorporates and utilises of a range of pre-existing spatial indexes and organisational systems: twentieth century postal codes, transport maps, fire and tax surveys; latitude and longitude as well as other standards of measure, which date back to the nineteenth century; street names, which can date back thousands of years, and building numbers, which came into use during the eighteenth century; political boundaries that are the product of thousands of years of power struggle and negotiation; as well as features of landscape and topography that pre-date humanity itself. These indices, among others, are cross-referenced to answer specific kinds of questions such as: 'What's the best way to get from Cupertino to Mountain View?'; 'How far is it from Cupertino to Mountain View?'; 'Where is the nearest bookshop [to where I am now]?'; 'Are there any bookshops in the vicinity of 1600 Amphitheater Parkway in Mountain View, CA?'

Rather than dismantle established 'high quality' approaches to knowing about location, by integrating and synthesising a diverse range of well-established and tested methods, Google Maps facilitated new kinds of dialogue with location. This was exemplified by the many unanticipated 'Google Maps Hacks' independently published even before the release of the Maps API in late 2005. These hacks ranged from tools for comparing the prices of nearby gasoline stations to mapping political donations or crime data (Schuyler and Gibson 2006). While images such as maps can generally be understood as encoded in Flusser's terms, Google Maps brought with it an array of unexpected interpretations and subsequent developments exhibiting characteristics of the alphabetic and a wave of experimental engagement with cartography.

A number of recent applications of Google Maps, whether it be a map of 'where to cry in public in the Boston area', or one that coordinates the transformation of vacant lots into community gardens in New York, can be said to transmute location into an alphabetic medium in a way that verges on the literary. In his contribution to the introductory volume to this series on technographies, English literature scholar Steven Connor associates the designation of literary with 'active self-relation'. He argues that language's 'capacity to signify itself to itself' enables it 'to work on the world by working and reworking its own system of representation' (Connor 2016: 30). Taking a different but connected approach to interrelation of the textual and numeric to that of either Flusser or McLuhan, Connor develops the proposition that 'literature is a name for what lies between language and number' (32). For Connor, in a way that relates to Flusser's designation of alphabetic, literature occurs in the pursuit of a numeric/digital/machinic ideal:

> The mediation of other machines assists literature to imagine and start to become the ideal machine it is always aspiring to be. Literature is not any kind of rage against the machine: it is the name for this machinic desire, the desire of this ideal machinery. (31)

This concept is productive for understanding the ways in which location is becoming, in Flusser's terms, more alphabetic, or in Connor's terms, more embroiled with language and the facilitation of imaginaries.

Take the example of HYDESim, or *High-Yield Detonation Effects Simulator*, a Google Maps-based visualisation of the impact of a nuclear blast of variable explosive yield that can be quickly centred on any place in the world. An un-commissioned side-project of noted web coding expert Eric Meyer, HYDESim appeared at first to be primarily informational in purpose (Meyer 2006). However, the map was shared widely as a way to draw attention of British and American audiences to contemporary military deployments, for example 'how a 21,000-pound bomb like the one just dropped on ISIS in Afghanistan would affect your city' (Bertrand 2017). It functioned outside the original intended purpose of Google Maps, which was to provide useful information such as how to get from one place to another. Instead, it deployed location and situation to convey a critical position on a difficult subject in an unexpected form. And it did so in a dialogic way that furthered the development of location as a medium.

The consideration of the development of Google Books alongside that of Google Maps yields a number of useful observations. First, while the association made by Google's founders between books and 'high quality knowledge' seems rational because of the long and deep historical alignment of literature with books, in practice, the logic of Google Books is not conducive to advancing this history. Likewise, while Google envisioned their spatial products in primarily utilitarian terms, the subsequent use of Google Maps by independent developers, for a range of unanticipated purposes and expressions, demonstrates an association between the openly discursive qualities of a medium and the potential for 'high quality knowledge' to be produced. The story of Google Maps also reveals that in the contemporary context, at certain moments, location is beginning to take hold as a literary or alphabetic medium. Furthermore, the comparison sketches out relationships between the presumed a-situatedness – comprehensiveness, in Google's terms – of a global tech giant such as Google and the further potential for location as a medium; these relationships demand active reflection on situation in literally-geographic terms, as well as those more-figurative ways in which it has been used by humanities scholars in recent decades.

III.

Finally, what do these brief extracts from Google's history reveal about the meaning of alphabet for Google as it continues to develop in its new life as Alphabet, Inc.? One of Alphabet's younger companies, Jigsaw (previously Google Think Tank), is worth considering. Jigsaw proposes to provide 'technology to tackle some of the toughest global security challenges facing the world today – from thwarting online censorship to mitigating the threats from digital attacks to countering violent extremism to protecting people from online harassment' (Jigsaw 2018). According to its CEO, former US statesman Jared Cohen, rather than being philanthropic, as its vision statement might suggest, the primary value of Jigsaw to the rest of Alphabet is that it protects its other companies, such as Android, Gmail and YouTube, from vulnerability to digital threats. Alphabet executive and former Google CEO Eric Schmidt commented, 'I don't think it's fair to ask the government to solve all these problems – they don't have the resources [...]. The tech industry has a responsibility to get this right' (Carr 2017). Between the lines of these comments, there is a presumption on the part of Alphabet's executives that what's good for Alphabet is good for the world and vice versa, or at least a vagueness regarding distinctions between the technology sector and human interests. This echoes, in many ways, McLuhan's description of the alphabet as a colonising force to which humanity is increasingly subject and by which it is being transformed.

This sense of the inevitable also permeates the rhetoric surrounding contemporary concerns regarding the commodification of personal data by Google (and Facebook). Are human behaviour and movement becoming a new sort of alphabet out of which texts are unknowingly encoded and to which only partial access and limited control are retained? Is the true significance of Google becoming Alphabet that human beings are becoming subsumed as unwitting writers both facilitated by and in the service of Google? Will the full realisation of this mean the end of history, as Flusser has suggested? Or, as Flusser has also suggested, is it possible to maintain a dialogic stance in relation to the present phase of humanity's reconfiguration by its technology?

The comparison between Google Books and Google Maps provides some insight into the role of location, and situatedness, in the human potential to participate actively in the construction and reconstruction of meaning over time. As has been discussed, the two initiatives had in common an ambition toward the production of 'high quality knowledge', though closer scrutiny reveals that it is difficult to be explicit about what this entails precisely – this chapter has associated 'high quality knowledge' with alphabetic-ness, in contrast to encoded-ness by way of Flusser in relation to McLuhan. Where Google Books has placed many of the alphabetic qualities of printed books at risk by encoding them indiscriminately as a vast database of de-situated fragments, Google Maps integrates encoded data with location in ways that, at times, supports what has the potential to develop, in the long term, into 'high quality knowledge'. More an accident of capitalism, this is not a particular credit to Google. Rather, given the claim over humanity that Google's renaming enacts, this chapter has sought to foreground a thread of alphabet-ness within Alphabet in the hopes that it can be grasped more strongly.

Works Cited

Bertrand, Natasha. 2017. 'Here's how a 21,000-pound bomb like the one just dropped on ISIS in Afghanistan would affect your city'. *Business Insider.* https://www.businessinsider.nl/effect-of-moab-bomb-on-new-york-city-2017-4/.

Carr, Austin. 2017. 'Can Alphabet's Jigsaw Solve Google's Most Vexing Problems?' *Fast Company.* October 22, 2017.

Connor, Steven. 2016. 'How to Do Things with Writing Machines.' In *Writing, Medium, Machine,* edited by Sean Pryor and David Trotter, 18–34. London: Open Humanities Press.

Flusser, Vilém. 2011a. *Does Writing Have a Future?* Minneapolis: University of Minnesota Press.

Flusser, Vilém. 2011b. *Into the Universe of Technical Images.* Minneapolis: University of Minnesota Press.

Google. 2004. 'Google Acquires Keyhole Corp'. News from Google. https://googlepress.blogspot.com/2004/10/google-acquires-keyhole-corp.html.

Google. 2005. 'Mapping Your Way'. Official Blog. https://googleblog.blogspot.co.uk/2005/02/mapping-your-way.html.

Google. 2019. 'Our Company'. https://www.google.com/about/our-company/.

Grosswiler, Paul. 2004. 'Dispelling the Alphabet Effect'. *Canadian Journal of Communication* 29: 145–58.

Jeanneney, Jean-Noël. 2008. *Google and the Myth of Universal Knowledge: A View from Europe.* Chicago: University of Chicago Press.

Jigsaw. 2018. 'How Can Technology Make People In The World Safer?'. https://jigsaw.google.com/vision/.

Liu, Lydia H. 2015. 'Scripts in Motion: Writing as Imperial Technology, Past and Present'. *PMLA* 130: 375–83.

Logan, Robert K. 1986. *The Alphabet Effect.* New York: St. Martin's Press.

McLuhan, Marshall. 2001. *Understanding Media.* London: Routledge Classics.

McLuhan, Marshall. 1970. 'Living in an Acoustic World'. Lecture at University of South Florida. http://www.marshallmcluhanspeaks.com/lecture/1970-living-in-an-acoustic-world/.

Meyer, Eric A. 2006. 'Jackals and HYDEsim'. meyerweb.com. https://meyerweb.com/eric/thoughts/2006/10/11/jackals-and-hydesim.

Morison, Stanley. 1972. *Politics and Script: Aspects of Authority and Freedom in the Development of Graeco-Latin Script from the Sixth Century B.C. to the Twentieth Century A.D.,* edited by Nicolas Barker. Oxford: Clarendon Press.

Page, Larry. 2015 (updated). 'G is for Google'. Alphabet. https://abc.xyz.

Poster, Mark. 2010. 'McLuhan and the Cultural Theory of Media' *MediaTropes* 2. https://mediatropes.com/index.php/Mediatropes/article/view/11931.

Powers, Shawn M. and Michael Jablonski. 2015. 'Google, Information, and Power'. In *The Real Cyber War: The Political Economy of Internet Freedom,* 74–98. Urbana: University of Illinois Press.

Sampson, Geoffrey. 1985. *Writing Systems.* Palo Alto: Stanford University Press.

Schuyler, Erle and Rich Gibson. 2006. *Google Map Hacks.* Boston: O'Reilly Media.

Smith, Chadwick Truscott. 2014. "'The Lens is to Blame": Three Remarks on Black Boxes, Digital Humanities, and The Necessities of Vilém Flusser's "New Humanism"'. *Flusser Studies* 18 http://www.flusserstudies.net/node/480.

Szybalski, Andy. 2010. Interview by Ben Campkin and Rebecca Ross with then Google designer Szybalski. August 19, 2010.

Toobin, Jeffrey. 2007. 'Google's Moon Shot: The Quest for the Universal Library'. *New Yorker*, February 5, 2007.

Vaidhyanathan, Siva. 2011. *The Googlization of Everything (And Why We Should Worry)*. Berkeley: University of California Press.

9

Situated Data: Articulating Art Methods, Cultural Institutions and Infrastructure

I. It's Not Serendipity

If asked for a one-liner to summarise the contents of this chapter, I would be tempted to use these words the digital writing professor Casey Boyle posted on Facebook on 1 September, 2017: 'It's not serendipity, it's the Dewey Decimal System.' Even though blurbed with the casualness of a social media update, it does however capture something rather essential about the organising media of our knowledge systems and their historical lineages: one stumbles across data because somebody put it there in the first place. An articulation of a thing or a meaning is always, at least partly, already premised by the fact that a system articulated it to be discoverable. It has the same sort of revelation as Jacques Lacan's seemingly obscure note that the bunny is in the magician's hat only if you put it there in the first place (Lacan 1988: 81). Magic and serendipity, as well as all those things one is tempted to name under the broad rubric of knowledge, depend on the infrastructure that sustains them.

A more formal way of introducing this chapter would be to say that it concerns infrastructure, a central topic nowadays in media and digital culture studies. From submarine cables to satellites, information systems such as GPS to the logistics that underpin contemporary cultures of the circulation of things and data, the interest in materiality has taken a decisively infrastructural turn, which is inspired by earlier work in Science and Technology Studies (see, for example, Bowker and Star 1999; Parks and Starosielski 2015; Mattern 2017). Addressing, placement, circulation, search, articulation, and retrieval must be managed by a variety of procedures and protocols, materials, and architectures from the Dewey System to shelves, spine marks, trolleys, and intellectual furniture of other material kinds (Mattern 2014). The expansion of media theoretical questions from devices to infrastructures also establishes a further connection to current discussions concerning media and logistics, platforms and digital labour. But this infrastructural angle can also find a situated focus as institutional analysis.

It is in this sense that this chapter examines cultural institutions as mediated data infrastructures that are both in place and formative of that space. Working through the case study of the British Library, it investigates this infrastructural question through artistic methods. The project Internet of Cultural Things collaborated with the artist Richard Wright, known for his earlier work on data visualisation and critical media arts as part of the Mongrel-collective, to unfold questions of media and infrastructure that extend much beyond the current focus on digital institutions and discourses such as the Internet of Things. (The Mongrel and later Harwood, Wright, Yokokoji-collaboration included the MediaShed 'free-media' space in Southend-on-Sea, the 'Cross Talk' eco-media project, and the 'Tantalum Memorial' that won the transmediale 2009 award.) Even if technologically focused and often corporate-led investigation of digital cultural institutions is becoming the mainstream way of understanding the infrastructural possibilities of data analytics concerning library users, holdings, and the various other relationships that define cultural institutions, we were interested in more experimental questions: how have notions of publicness already been incorporated into libraries in earlier phases of data infrastructure before the digital? In what ways was the library always already a proto-computer specialised in addressing, retrieving, and processing data (that for a long period came in the form of books and printed material)? This approach to the library connects questions developed in contemporary media theory with artistic methods, and produces an interesting installation-based entry point for the investigation of contemporary issues around automation, labour, and what sustains institutions as knowledge systems that are dependent on their material infrastructures.

Obviously, this enters a territory that has been of special interest to the Digital Humanities in recent years. Instead of merely treading the same footsteps, this chapter proposes to use theoretical ideas, methods, and approaches both from the artistic field – critical and historicising investigations of data culture – and media theory, especially from work interested in logistics and automation, as well as cultural techniques of knowledge systems. In practice, this chapter will engage with the Internet of Cultural Things project (AH/M010015/1, 2015–16) Wright undertook as artist-in-residence at the British Library, examining the ways in which data becomes understood through infrastructural operations. The project was funded by the Arts and Humanities Research Council and involved King's College London, the British Library, and the Winchester School of Art at University of Southampton. Furthermore, contextualising this practice in relation to art methods about data and media infrastructural studies, this chapter will continue by discussing Wright's *Elastic System* (elasticsystem.net), a data visualisation and art installation that picks up the title term from the nineteenth-century librarian Thomas Watts and replaces it in current debates about data, media, and infrastructure. The *Elastic System* creates alternative imaginaries for libraries as media systems and offers an alternative to the more corporate-led technological futures that are part and parcel of the current discourse about digital institutions. As such, it sets itself against the particular fantasies of cultural institutions' effective data management and works to trigger other sorts of questions about labour and automation than those posed in some of the more mainstream discourses that will be the focus of the next section of this chapter – albeit if, in part, as fiction.

II. Fantasy Institutions

Fantasies hold institutions together: imaginaries articulate particular bodies, machines, processes, and procedures into a mission or a purpose. The sort of language that Benedict Anderson used to demonstrate the imaginaries that maintain nationalism also works as a way to describe institutions, including cultural institutions; many of them were, in any case, already projects closely tied to that of the nation state (Anderson 2006).

The current fantasies of cultural institutions are often painted in the grey hues of corporate infrastructures of metrics and analytics, as one can observe from even a casual look at what 'cultural data' has come to mean in these contexts. These discourses and uses also become easily adaptable to the 'New Public Management ethos and private sector interest' (Kitchin 2014: 62): data about the performance of so-called cultural institutions for various forms of statistically motored governance that demand comparative measurability to be established through numbers. Techniques of automation ('never click again'), centralisation, and data-driven behaviourism of user patterns that, importantly, are operational: 'Actionable insight and intelligence'. These quotes are from Dexibit (http://dexibit.com/), a company specializing in museum data and data-driven analytics.

It would be easy to extrapolate and offer a dose of speculative fiction about the 'grey media' of cultural institutions (see Fuller and Goffey 2012). Moreover, in this version, the future media landscape of institutions is one of multiple intensive relations of data that are aggregated and analysed in real time. Corporate customers buy access packages that are linked to a variety of back-end analytics processes and institutional databases. Besides user profiles for optimisation of experience (pre-emptive building guidance based on earlier use patterns), the data handling corporation also feeds relevant input across the ecology of information of the cultural-security-entertainment complex. For example, to the private security company on the premises whose job it is to be alert for various security issues based on a multi-scalar risk estimation chart of suspicious movement, body gestures, perspiration, and behavioural patterns: is the User a researcher after the rare manuscript collection or a homeless person loitering? Of course, there would be further potential to build it up as a cultural data version of the quantified self-movement. Instead of California and fitness, it finds its killer app developers in the cultural capitals of the world. The cognitive understanding of culture spreads to a different measure: to evaluate a cultural institution not merely by the way we gather information, educate ourselves, interpret the world through history books, literature, and such – the things one learned as *Bildung* as the German word signalled. But rather, how a user population's relation to a national institution is also about the measurement of the object-traffic – item requests, tracked object transport, warehouse solutions or then the measurement of the user itself through the involuntary reactions: microbial, nerve and skin-based, heart rate and other reactions where this data becomes part of the Key Performance Indicators of the institution. The correctly balanced microbial gut level of its users defines one version of the future biotechnological public sphere of the British Library circa 2048.

Speculative design fiction aside, the various tropes, narratives, and projections about data and infrastructure lead to the question: what are cultural institutions as media institutions? This also begs to ask how to start investigating those situations of media and infrastructure from the bottom-up: from the operational situations where one encounters infrastructure at work as in contemporary cultural institutions and starts to unfold both its historical paths and its connections to current discussions in labour and automation. This infrastructural view starts to look at data as part of the historical build-up of technologies that are part of the media infrastructures of knowledge, or as Shannon Mattern puts it succinctly: 'What ideas, values, and social responsibilities can we scaffold within the library's material systems – its walls and wires, shelves and servers?' (Mattern 2014). This awareness of the intellectual scaffolding leads us into questions where media become less about devices *per se*, and more about where they connect: library middleware (Mattern 2015; see also Drucker and Svensson 2016) and infrastructures that scaffold 'the public', as well as questions about how cultural institutions have for a longer period been computational machines operating with analogue server farms, as Jeffrey Schnapp termed it (Schnapp 2015) – referring particularly to the library institutions and the off-site warehouses that have constituted one central node in data operations since the nineteenth century.

Data can be understood in terms of its volume, velocity, variety and more (Kitchin 2014). Data emerges as relations which internally articulate data points as patterns that become meaningful, not necessarily in the humanistic sense of the term, but when handled as an input for governance, marketing and management. But this mobilisation of data and its relational existence in institutions, uses, and discourses must be approached in situated and context-specific ways as it extends outside a focus merely on data sets and data structures (Boyd and Crawford 2012). This means an interest in relations that start to define data in spatial, architectural and even geographical senses from library spaces to off-site storage depots. While the focus on data easily obfuscates the question of material, spatial sites, it is as necessary to understand that space changes in its meaning, reachability, and searchability through data that governs it (see Amoore 2016). We can easily claim that data is everywhere, but even this elusive everywhere is also somewhere – even if infrastructures are ways to mediate between specific situations, to enable transport across this and that particular space (Bowker and Star 1999: 287). The ways of approaching data as situated – not merely as an ephemeral cloud-based informational entity, but also as institutionally conditioned and conditioning – is what drives a sort of a critical insight to cultural data as a bundle of issues from questions about the public to its particular media and transport infrastructures.

Questions about location and the situated nature of data as a material articulation can also be approached through some experimental methods that build on research in media studies. This includes work that picks up on art methods to investigate the material realities of data and moves from celebratory accounts of data visualisation to how art methods can intervene in the business-as-usual discourses on what cultural data means.

Artistic Data Methods

Data visualisation that would be an effective artistic method in intervening in institutions has to take its aim at the political aesthetic of the situation, to follow Sean Cubitt's ideas. To avoid the dangers of celebratory practices or mere meta-representation that data visualisation might easily produce, Cubitt argues that 'critical data visualization arts occupy a third position, carefully marking the abstraction of data from its raw appearing as natural beauty or human behaviour, in order to explore the techniques through which that abstraction is perpetrated' (Cubitt 2015: 180). In this vein, one can start to see a methodological possibility: practices of data visualisation can become more than second-order representations or immediations of data already given (whatever the etymology of the word) and investigations into the mentioned sites and practices, techniques and situations in which the abstractions function and become operational. As such, data practices and art practices can function as ways to start to map the situations in which the ephemerality of data and its persistent real-world effectiveness, its material involvement in structuring reality, are articulated. This involves not merely pitching existing data as something to be made visible – but also turning the investigative method the other way round: how does data become articulated as data that then affords visualisations, patterns, operational procedures, management decisions and more? Through what routes, what sorts of methods of compilation, organisation, transmission, transport, and access does it become the sort of thing we take as, well, data – a given? (See Gitelman 2013.)

It is important to underline that artistic projects about data are not merely ornamental commentaries, pretty pictures of data worlds, 'beauty of data', or other form of aesthetics as anaesthetics, but can produce ways of being involved with data. Over the past years, we have seen inspiring takes that illuminate this point. While I cannot give a full list or engage in a lengthy discussion in this text, some good examples include Paolo Cirio and Alessandro Ludovico's *Face-to-Facebook* project, a part of their *Hacking Monopology* trilogy of works that used hacktivist methods in the grey zone of partly illegal data operations. This involved stealing profiles from Facebook, and remediating them as on a different, invented platform of a dating site, detaching profiles from personal identities and playing with the idea of the persona as a datapoint that can be transported across platforms, institutional terms and conditions, and particular interfaces that map into a variety of social situations and perceived expectations. Closer to the discussion about cultural institutions, James Bridle's installation and project *Five Eyes* at the Victoria and Albert Museum brought combinatory data analytics from military and surveillance contexts back to cultural data collections. As such it provides an inspiring example of engaging with the existing datasets and holdings of a cultural institution while demonstrating how data analytics produces much more than just 'cultural' data. Referring to the Anglo-block of Cold War and later-era surveillance networks, *Five Eyes* produces a further layer of search and analysis on the Victoria and Albert's digital objects, demonstrating the flexibility of data as material for multiple layers of operations, analytic and institutional uses, even big data apophenia, a term used by Benjamin Bratton and Hito Steyerl to refer to the paranoid drive of finding underlying patterns in data (see, for example, Steyerl 2016).

Another approach to the situated nature of data and art methods is found in Burak Arikan's work in critical mapping: using their Graph Commons platform, Arikan's work moves from data visualisation to the wider art-activist practices that engage in participatory work with collectives and workshop participants. The aim of the work that comes out, sometimes in art installations but often in a workshop-format, is partly to illuminate what data collecting is as a creative activity that feeds towards civic data initiatives by way of such art methods; mapping urban infrastructures and planning projects, corporate ownership ties, but also issues that relate to the archives of cultural institutions, providing a way to understand the graph as something of a central feature of data-based interactions. Art methods use, reuse, re-institutionalise data; practices such as Arikan's start to unfold an activist-inspired story of the question, 'What can you do with data', but also: 'What can you do with a cultural institution?' and 'What is a library good for?' Here cartography is not merely the art of mapping existing relations and creating visualisation but also a form of conceptual work: to map power relations across different institutional, geographical, and other parameters, a point that is central to the work of such theorists as Rosi Braidotti (2006). In addition, one should also note the work librarians have done to map their institutional networks and presented them with public-facing interfaces. (See a list of relevant projects

and resources collected by Shannon Mattern at http://www.wordsinspace.
net/booksdata/fall2016/portfolio/november-15-public-facing-interfaces.)
Cartographies are not only representations, but ways to articulate embodied,
situated, and multi-levelled movements of agency. One way to do that is to
engage with infrastructure, which will be the topic of the next section.

III. Art of Infrastructure

Richard Wright's work as artist in residence at the British Library addressed
the work of data in the infrastructures of an institution. The lead questions
emerging out of the residence – which included 'Where is the library?' and
'What can you do with a library?' – illustrated performative and situated ways
of understanding the institution (Wright 2016a and Wright 2016b). Wright's
observations included notes about the protocols of the digital management of
the library but also on how users interacted with the space in and outside the
reading rooms. At the British Library, like in many other libraries, most of the
books had been removed from public access to the storage:

> Up until the 1850s, the public were allowed direct access to
> the bookshelves. But after the Round Reading Room was
> constructed, Anthony Panizzi, the Principle [sic] Librarian,
> decided that the print collection had grown so large that it was
> no longer practical to allow readers to wander amongst the ailes
> [sic] themselves. Many of the items are still stored according to
> shelfmarking systems partially inherited from those days and so
> still reflect how they would have appeared to the public before
> being removed from view. (Wright 2016a)

The only exception stands at the centre of the British Library building at St.
Pancras: the Royal Library of George III that, since its donation in 1828, has
contractually always to be publicly available – or at least on display, as in this
case of the library tower as a spectacle. As Wright notes:

> This area in the middle of the British Library was originally
> designed to hold the printed catalogues and various library
> index cards. By the time the St. Pancras building opened in
> 1997 however, most of that material had been digitised and so
> the decision was taken to use this area to house the Kings [sic]
> Library instead. An object which is accessible but no longer in
> direct visible form was displaced by an object which is visible but
> no longer directly accessible. (Wright 2016a)

Questions of visibility and accessibility became central ways to tackle the
infrastructural angle to items. Wright's work included mobilizing his expertise
in data visualisation and experimental methods in electronic arts to the

Figure 9.1: 'The Large Room' at the new library space at the British Museum as depicted in the Illustrated London News, 1851. The British Museum Collections, used under license CC BY-NC-SA 4.0.

cultural institution, and examining work that starts to look at the layers of data as it is articulated through the infrastructure. Hence, it was meant to engage as a media art practice that demonstrated practice-based methods for involvement in those situations where data becomes an action – for example, in cultural institutions, themselves storing and collecting, distributing and safeguarding cultural data, and increasingly in infrastructures that are not of their own making. Data infrastructures of libraries and other cultural institutions often 'make use of hardware (i.e., conveyor and "sortation" systems) and software (barcodes and inventories) that originated in manufacturing, retail, and shipping' (Mattern 2015), emphasising the institutional link to wider media cultural questions: whose infrastructure governs data and towards what sorts of ends?

Wright's work was to provide an account of the function of infrastructural operations as already in-situ data operations, as well as to offer alternative imaginaries of *where, what, when* is data; how it is articulated as situations, as spatially conditioned interfaces, and to offer alternative ideas and imaginaries that can then feed back to the institutional work. At the core of the project was a productive tension: the situated nature of data in a cultural institution like the British Library and the manner of how data is constantly built up in relation to extra-institutional forces: standards, formats, the inter-operationality of datasets, which also allow the circulation of data outside the confines of institutions and hence also articulate the complex levels of stacked governance where the institution's boundaries are perceived through a cartography of its data infrastructure.

For Wright, and the project in which the media artist in residence was embedded, infrastructure formed a way to unfold data as operations across the institution and its habituated routines. Focusing on the British Library, while the building and its space had for a longer period acted as a hub of public citizenship, Wright investigated how data structures the British Library but also how to start building processes, practices, and habits on top of the already implemented and actioned situation. Instead of merely reproducing the usual functions of data circulation, Wright was interested in these questions: What are the affordances of its infrastructures? 'What could you use all the abilities of a modern library system for?' (Wright 2016b).

In more detail, Wright's method contextualised itself in relation to the institutional affordances and databases such as the ABRS (Automated Book Requesting System):

> [...] we also need to attend to the fact that such a practice forms amongst the relations between the data infrastructure, the actual conditions in which it is accessed and the significance that lives on from their pre-digital history. We have to attend to how to *situate* this born digital data in the wider context from which it takes shape and in which its affordances address themselves to a public. And we start with what we have got. It will be impossible to rewrite the software that governs the operation of a national library. So *intervention* is one key strategy here – diverting its current functioning, placing foreign bodies inside it, offering alternatives. We cannot do anything which prevents it from functioning, but we might create a situation in which people are motivated to use it in a non-functional way. (Wright 2016b)

Another way to phrase this would be to say that the BL functioned as an organism of data governed by protocols, actions, operations, transport, logistics, and more. Data was approached through its systematic appearance, such as through the Integrated Archives and Manuscripts System (IAMS), Anonymised Reader Records, book ordering data, the ABRS, etc. – and at the same time through creatively mapping what to do with a library and its particular affordances. Data became seen as a part of those operational activities that organise the institution – governed by standards, interfaces, classifications, etc. – and hence feed into the spatial settings that themselves structure what we understand and see as the 'public' side of a public institution. This is an especially interesting question when one starts to consider it from the point of view of data operations and datasets: all the individualised, anonymised, and aggregated data that in many ways adds up to one perspective on what the 'public' means in contexts of institutional data. The interesting question became how to understand data as an action, or readiness for an action, in particular spatial, architectural, and institutional situations (see Easterling 2011: 155). In Wright's artistic residency, this meant investigations into the logistics and spaces of the institution, both in central London and in Yorkshire at Boston Spa, which is where the library hosts their robotic retrieval system for the newspaper archives.

Data became seen and conceptualised as circulation across buildings, humans, interfaces, transport, and transmission systems. This circulation also included putting the observers in movement. The 'infrastructure tours' at the British Library worked as a guided insight into the architecture of the institution and how the vertical and horizontal passages are infrastructurally connected to what the user or the public understands its function to be as an institution of knowledge. Down into the basement and underground levels, the visitors gathered for a glimpse of those spaces where the cultural institution's work includes procedures like security clearances and data obfuscation – in other words, not snapping photographs, since the books should not be identifiable by their physical location. Data addresses needed to be kept masked from the visitors who were not library staff. But multiple levels of work and structure also became visible in new ways; electricity, data, data sets, holdings, catalogues, plastic book trolleys moving across the building on the mechanical delivery system that was governed by both human work and the electronic request system with its own interfaces and standards. This also included people as agents in the partly automated retrieval systems and other parts of the library system – even as metadata, when it comes to the work of cataloguing. Considering people as infrastructure is an idea from the urban ethnography suggested by AbdouMaliq Simone (Simone 2004: 407–29). But in recent art theory, similar arguments have also been elaborated that start to point to already existing practices as elaborating something important: not merely to transport art methods to cultural institutions like archives – to make administration art with other means – but to elaborate the practices of archives, libraries, and museums as the grey, administrative strand of art practice that arrives in the wake of the earlier avant-garde, and in the context of conceptual art too.

In recent discussions in art theory and methods, Jane Birkin from the Winchester School of Art has analysed how the practices and techniques of bureaucracy such as archives turn into art methods of description; the idea of not merely transporting art methods into a cultural institution, but cultivating the bureaucratic practices itself into an art method that has to do with some key modern formations of knowledge. This also resonates with discussions concerning the performativity of art methods in such institutional settings.

Birkin goes on to quote Iversen to reiterate that this sort of performativity is picked up on the labouring operations of repetition, iteration, and other such mundane operations, and not on the art of spontaneity or self-expression (Birkin 2015; see also Birkin 2021, Buchloh 1990, Foster 2004, and Spieker 2008).

The project and Wright's method, in the process of observing the library staff and their systems, also transformed them. The actual operations started to form a different sense of data that is not merely digital or embedded in the datasets and their prescribed sets of possibilities, actions, and guidance. In other words, the project expanded the question of the cultural institution as a media institution to include the interaction of multiple sorts of agency from the human to the infrastructural. Methodologically, this participant observation was a form of spatial mapping, to use Mattern's ideas. Data started to unfold as a relation in and across spaces and multiple forms of agency. To quote Mattern: 'To visit the sites that are producing our networked experiences is thus an attempt to understand these new entanglements, sensations and practices, these network-associated changes – this new way of being' (Mattern 2013).

Can data and infrastructure be conceived as a way of being? Can such situations of data start to inform both artistic and theoretical ways of connecting experience with infrastructure? (see Bhowmilk and Parikka 2021). In many ways, that is what infrastructure is supposed to do silently anyway. It must offer the necessary categories, affordances, and support to interface with the library as an infrastructural organism, a data entity that feeds on those actions: digital search to the retrieval systems via human hands, electro-mechanic systems and, at times, even notes on paper slips back to the user who is hailed as part of the delivery/addressing system that constitutes the institution. The screen opens up to a multiplicity of actions invisible behind the interface (on categories as infrastructure, see again Bowker and Star 1999).

Wright's artistic output devised an additional interface that was built on top of the existing British Library search and delivery systems, and which opened a different way of understanding the search as a cultural technique that defines the institutional boundaries. Cultural technique is used here in the same manner it has been done so during the last 10 to 15 years of German media theory. Cultural techniques produce anthropological differences, such as inside/outside and sacred/profane, and are, as such, epistemological machines or the medial conditions of what then becomes known (and one might add, felt). Bernhard Siegert writes: 'However, it is crucial to keep in mind that the distinctions in question are processed by media in the broadest sense of the word (for instance, doors process the distinction between inside/outside), which therefore cannot be restricted to one or the other side of the distinction. Rather, they assume the position of a mediating third, preceding first and second' (Siegert 2015: 14).

The *Elastic System*, a search system and an installation, was created by Wright for visual browsing at a time when most searches for knowledge take place in interfaces and search strings instead of on open shelves. The *Elastic System* parasites the searches, locations, indexes, and catalogues of items that are already included in the catalogue systems of the BL. Thus, it becomes an additional layer on top of the existing data search and retrieval system. It borrows its name and main image from the nineteenth century librarian Thomas Watts, who worked at the British Museum's library (the forerunner of the British Library). Watts himself is rather unknown outside certain library studies circles, but he is revealed as the developer of what he at least himself was convinced would be a nineteenth-century revolution in data management: the elastic system. Watts's obituary, however, did not think much of this particular innovation. His short posthumous fame in a newspaper recounts the carriage accident that took his life and that, besides his library work, he published some essays in periodicals – nothing of the sort that would mark him as a great forerunner of the twenty-first century data organisation society (Thomas Watts's Obituary 1869). Hence, by way of a media archaeological rediscovery, another side of Watts comes to light. Richard Wright's system is described as follows:

> Elastic System is a database portrait of the librarian Thomas Watts. In 1838 Watts invented his innovative 'elastic system' of storage in order to deal with the enormous growth of the British Library's collections.
>
> The mosaic image of Watts has been generated from 4,300 books as they are currently stored in the library basements at St. Pancras, an area not normally accessible to the public. Each one is connected live to the library's electronic requesting system.
>
> The Elastic System functions allows people to visually browse part of the British Library's collections, something which has not been possible since Watts's time. When a book is requested it is removed from the 'shelf' to reveal a second image underneath, an image that represents the work that goes on in the library's underground storage basements, the hidden part of the modern requesting system. (From the Elastic System project description, part of the temporary installation at the British Library in Autumn 2017. See also http://elasticsystem.net/.)

Wright's *Elastic System* is not so much a reconstruction as a nod to an early grey innovator of indexing and search infrastructure. Wright's work points to Watts's innovation and records the changes since. But it also signals subtly to the idea of cultural institutions as data organisations. The *Elastic System* is a playful prototype that demonstrates a historical lesson about pre-digital machines of information management – cards and catalogues – and the institutions which become such computational machines organised by these cards and catalogues, as Markus Krajewski points out (Krajewski 2011). Card catalogues were already imagined as universal machines for data storage and efficient management, and as such, they occupied the spot that computers would later occupy. As Krajewski suggests, 'The possibility of rearranging its elements makes the card index a machine: if changing the position of a slip of paper and subsequently introducing it in another place means shifting other index cards, this process can be described as a chained mechanism' (Krajewski 2011: 7). The focus on the paper slips as the elements of flexible rearrangement was actually central to Watts's original work, and the *Elastic System* carries a particular media historical theme with it. In May 1855, in a letter addressed to the Principal Librarian of the BL, Anthony Panizzi, Watts proposes to radicalise the use of the bibliographic slips (letter sourced from the British Library archives and collections). As Watts recounts, the usual four slips recorded the information about the author, the title, the place and date of imprint, and the pressmark (location); the typical use of those was primarily to organise the catalogue as per the author slip, but Watts's letter proposed to speculate the benefits of separate catalogues organised by titles, by place, even by physical location of the item. The benefit was meant to be a more flexible and varied way of cataloguing and searching. This idea of an expanded notion of multiple combinatorial systems might seem not so special considering the ease of reorganising our search with current interfaces, digital data, and Boolean search operators, but to think of this as a paper slip machine was in itself something peculiar: the librarian's version of Victorian steampunk, even. To add to the aura of Watts himself, according to legend, in his role as 'Placer' he was able to remember the location of some 100,000 titles, performing the role of ideal search engine in his own living persona as part of the library system (Wright 2016b). Indeed, he was hailed as 'a gentleman with prodigious memory and encyclopaedic learning' (Garnett 1878).

Obviously, Watts and his prodigious capacities as a search engine would itself be a suitable starting point for speculative fiction about library infrastructures that would offer an alternative to the corporate versions we started with. It would also offer such tempting potential for speculative media theory. In many ways this is an opportunity to raise Watts to the same status that Daniel Paul Schreber has occupied within media theory: as a central figure, for Friedrich Kittler, through which to understand the threshold of the discourse networks of 1800 and 1900 (see Kittler 1990). But in Watts's case, he would become the figure that stands at the threshold of data management and searching, the key media functions of the library. With or without Watts, his idea of the Elastic System carries forward imaginaries of smoothness of information management, recombinatorics, flexibility, and innovations that have become the infrastructural enabling condition for the later digital media that runs as part of the library. Whether that machine is digital or not is in this case secondary to the elasticity of searching as a cultural technique.

THE ARCHED ROOM.

Figure 9.2: 'The Arched Room' at the new library space at the British Museum as depicted in the Illustrated London News, 1851. The British Museum Collections, used under license CC BY-NC-SA 4.0.

Wright's version of the Elastic System includes access to only a small part of the BL's holdings that he selected and photographed, using the spine as an index of the visual sign of searchability. Despite the limitations, as practical exposition it taps into issues of the visibility of holdings that start to form a web of questions about public space, cultural data, and the historical precedents to data indexing and searching. The art installation starts to unfold this important story about the infrastructural, and data-operation-reliant nature of what counts as 'public' and also what sort of operations of labour maintain such systems: sorting, cataloguing, placing, retracing, fetching, transporting, and handling, to name some of the cultural techniques that imply the labour of infrastructure. As such, it also becomes a reminder of those multiple other sorts of machines and imaginaries of data organisation that are stacked as part of institutional histories before the digital.

The Elastic System becomes a way to articulate a media historical moment: the removal of items from public hands-on-access to the storage depot (both in London and at Boston Spa) and the entry of infrastructural support systems, such as book trolleys, as part of the search and delivery of holdings. This sort of replacement of items with data about items and locations is part of the particular information glut since the nineteenth century and the emergence of the delivery systems that are designed to mediate between the card indexes offering the catalogue order of the holdings and the actual physical locations – two sorts of address spaces that define the library or archival data relations as a combination of symbolic and material conditions of access. A similar theme was present in other institutions too, including in some key research libraries. In the telling words of Harvard University's library services in the early twentieth century, shifting items out of immediate access and into request only was a question of how to make access 'less convenient and attractive', as a way to manage this informational situation and the user's relation to the system (Charles William Eliot, quoted in the documentary *Cold Storage*, metaLAB at Harvard University, 2015).

Museums have for a longer period functioned as media that govern the public's attention, behaviour, and movements – and, as such, formed various surfaces, interfaces, channels, and other modes of governance (see Bhowmik 2019). The sort of aesthetic governance of what you see, in what order, in what space, was part of the infrastructure of the public since the nineteenth century, as Michelle Henning has demonstrated (Henning 2006). In parallel, one can see how this formed part of the imaginary of the library too: a public space and, in some ways, also a spectacle of visual display even before the King's Tower at the current BL location, as the *Illustrated London News* from 1851 visualises the British Museum Library (now the BL). The library was a place for a Victorian-era stroll into the atmosphere and space of knowledge. It is this sort of an imaginary of public hands-on access that is also the subject of what happens offsite: the storage holdings where mediation happens by way of search and request and the infrastructure that continues to maintain the retrievability for the user. Hence, one starts to pay attention to how the offsite is managed as a part of search systems and starts to form the other part of the logistical story that includes how the user of the public library needs to be kept at a distance with the mediation of the logistics systems and database services. Furthermore, the offsite itself is increasingly becoming automated, which is emblematic of a further set of changes that include a wider political economic aspect that begins to speak to questions of automation and labour as well.

IV. Server Space

Automation has become one way to understand the changes in the institutional infrastructure of libraries. It is also a topic that connects particular institutional changes to a bigger picture of the transformations in work, economy, and logistics (see, for example, Scrnicek 2016 and Rossiter 2016). These changes also pertain to the library sector and tie in with the various sorts of real and speculative futures we started with that deal with labour costs, efficiency, and data-based management of the traffic of knowledge, items, and people. Hence, the British Library site in Boston Spa is far from being a solitary example of automation in the form of robotic retrieval facilities. Similar systems are in place in various countries from Norway to the US where humans are evacuated from the logistical library space, which functions in low-oxygen conditions and is also optimised to pack items more densely; in short, the cultural institutional site is becoming 'more data-center-like in its storage logic, labor logistics, and ambience', as Mattern puts it (Mattern 2015). This includes priming the space for machine-based scanning and handling of items, as well as, increasingly, priming the space for machine-based entities. This angle would have been one way to pitch a futuristic narrative creation about the posthuman holding retrieval systems which, even after climate change had made much of Britain uninhabitable, would continue working. Now already it was sustained in an environment of low oxygen and devoid of humans, creating an eerie sense of future logistics systems for cultural data.

The automation of library operations and services is a major topic when set as part of the far-reaching discussion on work and employment in digital culture. But it is also part of a parallel set of interesting media theory discussions concerning what enables this transformation in terms of the management systems of the library. The sort of work that Watts excelled at, and that became the human-embodied version of search and discovery in libraries, is here one reference point in a chain of transformations that are often referred to by way of their technological determinants (from the automated library to the digital library), but which actually involve a range of techniques at the level of bodies, shelves, stacks, and many other levels of the library machine. Aptly, when the Swedish National Library in the mid-1990s completed its study of a future library set in 2045, it referred to how 'robots, or 'butlers' would help students and researchers to access the archived material by retrieving it from the basement' (Hjerpe 2016). Interestingly, what remains less investigated is that the terminology of butlers – even if automated ones – itself stands apart as a different kind of media history of the labour of service with clear gendered and class dimensions. This aspect concerning the media history of service is demonstrated by Markus Krajewski and offers a different connotation to the set of changes that also pay attention to the various levels of how cultural techniques operate in the library space (Krajewski 2018). Besides the cultural techniques of library work, contemporary labour also includes multiple kinds of other aspects that put library staff at the centre of often-feminised immaterial and affective labour. Furthermore, service was in many ways already always automated as a technique and was reliant on protocols of behaviour and responsiveness, a fact that was for a long time made visible in the computer-optimised walking routes created for human employees in the large Amazon warehouses searching for items requested for delivery (Wohlsen 2014).

But of course, when it comes to technological servers, a different set of protocols enter the scene in discussions of networked systems. Indeed, here one can start to investigate the changes in place that enabled this continuing servantry at the core of the computational search-systems called libraries. This includes changes such as Machine Readable Cataloguing, RFID systems (Lewis 2016), and other developments that allow an alternative coordination system that can bypass human eyes, hands, and feet in the work. Thus, Wright's seemingly obsolete implementation of a visual search system is set to open up an investigation, from a media historical sense, on the transformation from the visual component of shelf marks and book spines as part of the address system of the library to the automation of such procedures towards a 'smart shelf' that becomes one component in new RFID antenna media infrastructure of knowledge (see Li et al. 2015: 6100). Some experimental library systems have already employed ideas that are reminiscent of Watts's and Wright's elastic systems but taken to the next level. Foremost of these examples would be the Sitterwerk Art Library which uses RFID tags to enable a dynamic organisation of the items as part of a continuous inventory that does not require items to be placed in their original location, since the digital catalogue is constantly updated:

> The principle of serendipitous discoveries is depicted and broadened on the level of the digital catalogue: groups of books that have been brought together are documented in the database and represented graphically as a virtual shelf. This also results in the creation of new search options in the digital catalogue: in addition to conventional searches according to author, keywords, etc., it has recently also become possible to search in the Sitterwerk according to the context of a book. ('Kunstbiblithek' n.d.)

In the Sitterwerk, the user is incorporated as part of the dynamic organisation of the system. Wright's Elastic System articulates library labour in different ways. Pixel by pixel, every requested item unfolds another image under the mosaic portrait of Watts. This other image depicts the labour that takes place downstairs at the library institution's backend, representing the human staff as part of the server-based, partly automated machine of the library. This interface effect works as a way to tap into the questions where labour and

Figure 9.3: The interface of the Elastic System (web version): a mosaic of books and labour.
Used with permission, image courtesy of Richard Wright.

bureaucratic systems are tackled by way of art methods. It also raises the
wider question about automation of storage. While specific technologies such
as RFIDs are making the knowledge space scannable, offsite storage deserves
further attention before we move to our conclusions.

In other words, the different national examples such as the British
Library or the National Library of Norway's automated facilities are ways
to further elaborate what storage means in the context of media theoretical
investigations of knowledge. While digital libraries and repositories are one
crucial part of the imaginary of the future library, we should pay attention to
what automation and robotics mean in this projected transformation. In fact,
the two – digitality and physical robotics – are tightly linked when it comes
to managing storage. This connection to the digital management of space
and traffic starts to unfold much more than what concerns 'just libraries', and
it becomes part of the discussion about the logistical turn that occupies the
attention of contemporary critical scholars of capitalism, media, and labour

– as has been noted above. Indeed, software governs space and allows a more extensive (e.g. higher stacks) and intensive use of storage (see Olney 2014). The British Library adopted their system in the wake of some inspiring examples from North American research libraries such as the Widener at Harvard and also the Norway National Library. The rail systems in place at such automated sites are part of the legacy of the nineteenth-century transport system for books and other items, but also a feed-forward to what constitutes part of the current logistical system binding libraries to the massive business of warehouse management, transport, and cloud service platforms. In Norway's case, the automated repository library includes '43,500 steel boxes in racks, and between the three rack sections there are three automatic cranes on rails', but what characterises the organisation of the repository items and boxes is Automatic Storage and Retrieval System (ASRS) that is governed by the Warehouse Management System (WMS).

> Chaos storage is the main principle for storage in the ASRS, and is used for the books. Chaos storage means that the books have no permanent box in the stores, and the boxes have no permanent place in the stores. A book is stored in any vacant folder in any steel box in any of the stores. All publications, folders and boxes are identified by barcodes, and this enables the ASRS to keep track of in which folder and in which box any given publication is stored. (Sakrihei 2016)

As Mattern noted, the library systems increasingly resemble data-server systems where the butler or servantry as a cultural technique is not limited to the trained human skill but in addition includes the protocological data operations that link ways of seeing as scanning (barcodes, RFID) to intensifying the use of space. This space is however not mapped (only) according to the shelf arrangements in the Dewey System, but to the digital logic that uses space more effectively when read and controlled by machines. The other, more familiar, example of this is the Amazon 'Fulfillment Center' with its KIVA robots doing similar work. Aptly, the library transformation finds its counterpart in the warehouse management where robotics can help cut operating costs, reduce the amount of floor space that would be otherwise needed for human workers, and hence utilise space effectively for the management of items in, items out (Bhattacharya 2017). These are cultural techniques for the compression of space.

Amazon Wish Fulfillment Centers seem to easily allow a sort of grey logistical science fiction to emerge, considering how quickly *Wired* turned the description of one Phoenix warehouse into somewhat modern futuristic language: 'Also known by the codename PHX6, the place radiates a non-human intelligence, an overarching brain dictating the most minute movements of everyone within its reach' (Wohlsen 2014). If one would still be in the futuristic mood, it would be tempting to continue this line of thought further to discuss cultural institutions becoming mere subsets of warehouse logistics platforms and robotics, but I will leave further speculative fiction for some other occasion. Instead let us focus on what is at the back of this brain that governs both human and robotic movement: we find something that is also the parallel of what the library offsite servers have been dealing with. Hence, from Dewey to chaos storage, a different set of protocols start to govern the address space and movement inside it:

> The inventory at PHX6 is made up largely of 'smalls', merchandise small enough to be stored on shelves about the size of those at a typical library, which is exactly how Amazon refers to the levels of seemingly endless metal shelving at PHX. Each shelf is divided into small cubbies, and each cubby gets a barcode and an alphanumeric ID, much like the Dewey Decimal System. (Wohlsen 2014)

'Much like the Dewey' does not however mean the Dewey. Alternative address systems govern this space that has a financial cost attached to it. Indeed, the discussions about the poor labour conditions of Amazon workers is one indication of the sort of technical protocols that govern the financial understanding of space and logistics that are made to function primarily as the true non-human force. Indeed, as Cubitt aptly put it referring to the planetary scale corporations of digital culture, '[a]ctually existing cyborgs are huge agglomerations of technologies with human implants' (Cubitt 2017: 34).

One cannot avoid the sense of media historical irony that can sometimes be triggered by a mere mistyped URL. A minor mistype in the URL address for the online version of the Elastic System (www.elasticsystem.net) leads to the Amazon's Elastic File System (www.elasticsystem.com) – 'simple, scalable file storage' – part of the Amazon Web Services that offers cloud platform services for a variety of customers and corporations from Netflix to Coursera. Hence the sort of elasticity that was meant to become part of the institutional set of affordances at the proto-computer address, index and search techniques of the library is nested inside the planetary-scale management of data and goods, things and their addresses that stand at the centre of the operations of corporations such as Amazon. At two very different kinds of scales, the operations of an Elastic System demonstrate, besides the appeal of the term, the attractiveness of how such systems of organisation and management are crucially about the elasticity of the management of addressing as a cultural, media technique and the relation of addresses to physical space. Indeed, as Louise Amoore has well argued, the particular critical imaginaries of data geographies have to also take into account how data management affects the ways in which space is perceived, localised, addressed and, for example, securitised (Amoore 2016).

V. Conclusions

Libraries are media systems in multiple ways: libraries help to articulate how media infrastructures work in particular institution settings, while the media studies angle helps to articulate how libraries have already incorporated the link between space and data in different historical solutions. This chapter has aimed to elaborate this work of articulations by way of discussing the art installation and project that involved artist Richard Wright. Besides an art project that deals with cultural techniques of data and search in cultural institutions, it also connects to current questions debated in media theory and digital humanities about infrastructure and agency. In this case, the British Library offered one situation to investigate both the imaginaries of the future library and the discourses of the digital management of efficiency and the production of historically situated and spatially bound ideas of how libraries function – and have functioned – as already machinic systems. These paper machines – and paper machine institutions – as Krajewski, Mattern and others have shown, are already complex entities of data-management that, in engaging with themes of automation, have included the human as part of their operations. Hence, questions of labour and political economy are not far removed from the media theoretical questions concerning the conditions of existence of the library as media – not merely containing media of various sorts, but functioning as a device for addressing, searching, retrieving, transporting, communicating, and storing.

Mattern outlines well the stakes in looking at the media of cultural institutions like libraries. As she poignantly points out:

> It's hard to wrap one's head around the breadth of these distributed systems – all the far-flung truck routes, database subscriptions, interlibrary loans, and protocols. But acknowledging this complicated logistical network makes visible the labour, equipment, and expertise required to build and maintain our libraries, one of our society's few remaining intellectual and cultural commons. (Mattern 2015)

In other words, questions of data include also that longer backstory of various levels of procedures. Of interest in this chapter was the question of transport – both within an institution and outside it – that dealt with how items are addressed and located both by way of visual knowledge (shelf marks, placement, retrieval) and in the age of chaos storage and automated optimised use of scannable space. From user query and request via a digital interface through the system to the electro-mechanic conveyor belt and barcode enabled tracking to the automated robots to the transport system from Boston Spa to London via hands and digital interfaces, the data stack is an assemblage that includes labour and data management, physical transport, and information protocols. The *Elastic System* becomes a fascinating entry point to infrastructures of data in the sense which Keller Easterling notes, that infrastructure is about management and the creation of action, whether when mobilising robotic assistants or people as infrastructure (Easterling 2011). A similar emphasis is found in the activist literature of the Invisible Committee: 'Power no longer resides in the institutions [...] power now resides in the infrastructures of this world' (quoted in Rossiter 2016: 145).

This chapter proposed that art methods dealing with data and cultural institutions need to investigate the infrastructures of the cultural institution as the programming of potentials of action – both human and data based. Indeed, art and other creative cross-disciplinary methods are 'device[s] in the practice of transdisciplinary research', as Ned Rossiter puts it (60), underlining that visualisation can also still function as one useful technique in the bundle of complex methods that link data, labour, and infrastructure together. This sort of inventive artistic-academic-activist work is geared both towards addressing conditions of data, and towards the invention of relevant methods, where the idea of a 'substitute interface' (60) became also one central part of the operational toolbox for this project at the British Library. It was not merely a visualisation of what is already determined and handed down as data, but a further layer of the existing infrastructure and an operation that then exposes the other sorts of holdings and data that travel in an institutional space that is a logistics space (see also Bhowmilk and Parikka 2021). One stumbles across data because somebody put it there in the first place. It's articulations all the way down.

Acknowledgements

A warm thanks to Shannon Mattern for her incisive and helpful feedback. The research for this text was supported by the AHRC-funded project Internet of Cultural Things (AH/M010015/1).

Works Cited

Amoore, Louise. 2016. 'Cloud Geographies: Computing, Data, Sovereignty'. *Progress in Human Geography* 42: 4–24.

Anderson, Benedict. 2006. *Imagined Communities: Reflections on the Origins and Spread of Nationalism,* revised edition. London: Verso.

Bhattacharya, Ananya. 2017. 'Amazon is Just Beginning to Use Robots in its Warehouses and They're Already Making a Huge Difference'. *Quartz,* June 17. https://qz.com/709541/amazon-is-just-beginning-to-use-robots-in-its-warehouses-and-theyre-already-making-a-huge-difference/.

Bhowmik, Samir. 2019. 'Thermocultures of Memory'. *Culture Machine* 17. https://culturemachine.net/vol-17-thermal-object/.

Bhowmik, Samir and Parikka, Jussi. 2021. 'Memory Machines: Infrastructural Performance as an Art Method.' *Leonardo* 54 (4): 377–381.

Birkin, Jane. 2015. 'Art, Work and Archives: Performativity and the Techniques of Production.' *Archive Journal,* November. http://www.archivejournal.net/essays/art-work-and-archives/.

Birkin, Jane. 2021. Archive, *Photography and the Language of Administration.* Amsterdam: Amsterdam University Press.

Bowker, Geoffrey C. and Susan Leigh Star. 1999. *Sorting Things Out: Classification and Its Consequences.* Cambridge, MA: MIT Press.

Boyd, Danah and Kate Crawford. 2012. 'Critical Questions for Big Data.' *Information, Communication & Society* 15: 662–79.

Boyle, Casey. 2017. Facebook, September 1. https://www.facebook.com/casey.boyle/posts/10155682505472612.

Braidotti, Rosi. 2006. *Transpositions: On Nomadic Ethics.* Cambridge: Polity.

Buchloh, Benjamin H.D. 1990. 'Conceptual Art 1962–1969: From the Aesthetic of Administration to the Critique of Institutions'. *October* 55: 105–143.

Cold Storage (documentary). 2015. metaLAB at Harvard University. http://www.librarybeyondthebook.org/cold_storage/.

Cubitt, Sean. 2015. 'Data Visualization and Political Aesthetics'. In *Postdigital Aesthetics: Art, Computation, and Design,* edited by David M. Berry and Michael Dieter, 179–90. Basingstoke: Palgrave Macmillan.

Cubitt, Sean. 2017. *Finite Media: Environmental Implications of Digital Technologies.* Durham: Duke University Press.

Drucker, Johanna and Patrik Svensson. 2016. 'The Why and How of Middleware'. *Digital Humanities Quarterly* 10. http://www.digitalhumanities.org/dhq/vol/10/2/000248/000248.html.

Easterling, Keller. 2011. 'The Action is the Form'. In *Sentient City: Ubiquitous Computing, Architecture and the Future of Urban Space,* edited by Mark Shepard, 154–158. Cambridge, MA: MIT Press.

Foster, Hal. 2004. 'An Archival Impulse.' *October* 110: 3–22.

Fuller, Matthew and Andrew Goffey. 2012. *Evil Media.* Cambridge, MA: MIT Press.

Garnett, Richard. 1878. *On the System of Classifying Books on the Shelves Followed at the British Library.* Conference of Librarians, October 1877. London: Chiswick Press.

Gitelman, Lisa, editor. 2013. *'Raw Data' is an Oxymoron.* Cambridge, MA: MIT Press.

Henning, Michelle. 2006. *Museums, Media and Cultural Theory.* Maidenhead: Open University Press.

Hjerpe, Annika. 2016. 'Robots, Holograms and Libraries.' *Scandinavian Library Quarterly* 49. http://slq.nu/?article=volume-49-no-4-2016-12.

Kitchin, Rob. 2014. *The Data Revolution: Big Data, Open Data, Data Infrastructures and Their Consequences.* Los Angeles: Sage.

Kittler, Friedrich. 1990. *Discourse Networks 1800/1900,* translated by Michael Metteer, with Chris Cullens. Stanford: Stanford University Press.

Krajewski, Markus. 2011. *Paper Machines: About Cards & Catalogs, 1548–1929,* translated by Peter Krapp. Cambridge, MA: MIT Press.

Krajewski, Markus. 2018. *The Server: A Media History from the Baroque to the Present,* translated by Ilinca Iurascu. New Haven: Yale University Press.

'Kunstbiblithek.' Sitterwerk Art Library website. http://www.sitterwerk.ch/en/art-library/dynamic-order/rfid-technik.html.

Lacan, Jacques. 1988. *The Seminar of Jacques Lacan: Book II, The Ego in Freud's Theory and in the Technique of Psychoanalysis,* translated by Sylvana Tomaselli. Cambridge: Cambridge University Press.

Lewis, David W. 2016. *Reimagining the Academic Library.* Lanham: Rowman & Littlefield.

Li, Renjun, Zhiyong Huang, Ernest Kurniawan, and Chin Keong Ho. 2015. 'AuRoSS: An Autonomous Robotic Shelf Scanning System.' *IEEE/RSJ International Conference on Intelligent Robots and Systems (IROS)*: 6100–05.

Mattern, Shannon. 2013. 'Infrastructural Tourism.' *Places* (July). https://placesjournal.org/article/infrastructural-tourism/.

Mattern, Shannon. 2014. 'Library as Infrastructure.' *Places* (June). https://placesjournal.org/article/library-as-infrastructure/.

Mattern, Shannon. 2015. 'Middleware: Landscapes of Library Logistics.' *Urban Omnibus* (June). https://urbanomnibus.net/2015/06/middlewhere-landscapes-of-library-logistics/.

Mattern, Shannon. 2017. *Code and Clay, Data and Dirt: Five Thousand Years of Urban Media.* Minneapolis: University of Minnesota Press.

Olney, Dawn. 2014. 'A UK First; An Automated, High-Density Solution for the British Library.' *Where Shall We Put It? Spotlight on Collection Storage Issues,* National Preservation Office Conference: 4–14.

Parks, Lisa and Nicole Starosielski, editors. 2015. *Signal Traffic: Critical Studies of Media Infrastructures.* Urbana: University of Illinois Press.

Rossiter, Ned. 2016. *Software, Infrastructure, Labor: A Media Theory of Logistical Nightmares.* London: Routledge.

Sakrihei, Helen. 2016. 'Using Automatic Storage for ILL – Experiences from the National Repository Library in Norway.' *Interlending & Document Supply* 44: 14–16.

Schnapp, Jeffrey. 2015. 'Cold Storage Hots Up', blog post, January 6. http://jeffreyschnapp.com/2015/01/06/cold-storage-goes-live/.

Scrnicek, Nick. 2016. *Platform Capitalism.* Cambridge: Polity.

Siegert, Bernhard. 2015. *Cultural Techniques: Grids, Filters, Doors, and Other Articulations of the Real,* translated by Geoffrey Winthrop-Young. New York: Fordham University Press.

Simone, AbdouMaliq. 2004. 'People as Infrastructure: Intersecting Fragments in Johannesburg.' *Public Culture* 16: 407–29.

Spieker, Sven. 2008. *The Big Archive: Art from Bureaucracy.* Cambridge, MA: MIT Press.

Steyerl, Hito. 2016. 'A Sea of Data: Apophenia and Pattern (Mis)Recognition.' *E-Flux* 72 (April). http://www.e-flux.com/journal/72/60480/a-sea-of-data-apophenia-and-pattern-mis-recognition/.

Thomas Watts's Obituary. 1869. *The Times,* September 10.

Wohlsen, Marcus. 2014. 'A Rare Peek Inside Amazon's Massive Wish-Fulfilling Machine.' *Wired,* June 16. https://www.wired.com/2014/06/inside-amazon-warehouse/.

Wright, Richard. 2016a. 'Where is the Library?' Elastic System project website. http://www.elasticsystem.net/.

Wright, Richard. 2016b. 'The Elastic System: What Can You Do with a Library?' British Library's Living Knowledge Blog, November 24. http://blogs.bl.uk/living-knowledge/2016/11/the-elastic-system-what-can-you-do-with-a-library.html.

Author Bios

Caroline Bassett is Professor of Digital Humanities in the Faculty of English at the University of Cambridge and a Fellow of Corpus Christi College. She is the Director of Cambridge Digital Humanities. Her work explores technological cultures, critical theory, feminism and AI. Publications include *Furious*, a co-authored monograph written with Sarah Kember and Kate O'Riordan (Pluto, 2020), and *Anti-Computing: Dissent and the Machine*, on the history of refusal and automation anxiety (Manchester University Press, 2021). Recent work includes 'The Construct Editor. Tweaking with Jane, Writing with Ted, Editing with an AI?' for *Textual Cultures*. Public writing includes 'Feminism, Refusal, Artificial Writing' for the Transmediale festival and the *AI Level Study Guide*, written with human and machine collaborators.

Renée Farrar is an Assistant Professor of English at the United States Military Academy at West Point. Her academic interests center on the constraints that digital media places on interdisciplinary creativity. She uses digital media as a means for exploring possible methods and modes of disobedience, as creators function within systems of control (both in the digital realm and not). Renée's article "Word Processor Art: How 'User-friendly' Inhibits Creativity," published by *Digital Humanities Quarterly*, explores the limits of the digital page and its unseen influence on the user. Renée received a Master of Arts in English from the University of Colorado at Boulder. She lives north of Salt Lake City, Utah, working as a freelance editor, poet, and consultant. Additionally, Renée is a combat veteran, serving as a Major in the United States Army Reserves as a Foreign Area Officer.

James Gabrillo is an assistant professor of music at University of Texas at Austin. Previously a lecturer at The New School and a postdoctoral fellow at Princeton, he earned his PhD at the University of Cambridge. His research has been published in the *Journal of Popular Music Studies*, *Musical Quarterly*, *Rock Music Studies*, *American Music Perspectives*, and the *Routledge Companion to Radio and Podcast Studies*. Gabrillo previously worked as a journalist and editor for various publications including *The National* and *Al Jazeera English*. His multimedia work has also appeared on *Rolling Stone Italia*, *Wired*, and *The Japan Times*.

Bernard Dionysius Geoghegan is a Reader in the History and Theory of Digital Media at King's College London. Duke University Press recently published his book *Code: From Information Theory to French Theory*. He can be reached online at www.bernardg.com.

Emma McCormick Goodhart, based in New York City, is an artist who experiments across media, timescales, and modes of practice. Interested in fathoming deep-time developments of sensing, especially in sound, alongside technosensory futures, she has presented work at Belmacz (London), Bergen Assembly (Norway), Haus der Kulturen der Welt (Berlin), Kunsthalle Zürich, Le Musée d'Art Moderne de la Ville de Paris, Montez Press Radio (New York), Pioneer Works (New York), Storefront for Art & Architecture (New York), The Merchant House (Amsterdam), and elsewhere. Her writing has been published by e-flux Architecture, Flash Art, frieze, Goldsmiths CCA, Kunsthaus Zürich, Luncheon, MOLD, PIN-UP, Sternberg Press, The Plant, and Vestoj. She was recently an artist resident at Sitterwerk Foundation in St. Gallen, Switzerland, and dramaturge for William Forsythe's sonic intervention at Kunsthaus Zürich in 2021. Two commissions – a sound piece, with Jessika Kenney, and a moonmilk-derived scent climate, evolved with Barnabé Fillion x Arpa, in *Hollow Earth: Art, Caves & The Subterranean Imaginary* – will travel from Nottingham Contemporary to The Glucksman (Cork) in 2023.

Melle Jan Kromhout is an independent scholar from Amsterdam, The Netherlands, working on the intersection of musicology, sound studies and media studies. His research focuses on the conceptual relations between music, sound, and media from the nineteenth century to the present. After obtaining his doctoral degree at the Amsterdam School for Cultural Analysis (ASCA), University of Amsterdam, he worked as a Postdoctoral Research Fellow at the Faculty of Music and Corpus Christi College, University of Cambridge. His first book, *The Logic of Filtering. How Noise Shapes the Sound of Recorded Music* was published by Oxford University Press in 2021. More information: www.mellekromhout.nl.

Jussi Parikka is Professor in Digital Aesthetics and Culture at Aarhus University as well as visiting professor at FAMU (Prague) and Winchester School of Art (UK). Some of his books include *Insect Media: An Archaeology of Animals and Technology* (2010), *A Geology of Media* (2015) as well as several publications on media archaeology, including *What is Media Archaeology?* (2012). Recently, he co-edited (with Tomáš Dvořák) *Photography Off the Scale* (2021) and he co-authored (with Lori Emerson and Darren Wershler *The Lab Book: Situated Practices in Media Studies* (2022). More information: http://jussiparikka.net.

Rebecca Ross is the director of the graphic communication design programme at Central Saint Martins, University of the Arts London. Her interdisciplinary and multimedia practice spans across fields including graphic design, media studies, history of technology, and urbanism. Ross is co-founder and co-editor, since 2012, of the publication *Urban Pamphleteer*. In 2015, she created the digital billboard installation, *London is Changing*. She recently contributed a chapter, 'Making Academic Publishing More Public', to *Transverse Disciplines* and is currently working on a book about addressing.

Louisa Shen was educated in Auckland and Cambridge. She trained originally in literature, film, and history in New Zealand, with a significant apprenticeship in writing studies. Prior to returning to research, she worked as technical author in the software sector. Her professional and academic experience therefore sits at the intersection of the arts and sciences, with a significant emphasis on the history of technology and the phenomenology of sensory engineering (19th century – present). Other areas of research interest thus include the intersection between media and technology, the cultural constructions of electronic and computational culture, and the portrayal and refraction of technology in visual texts, broadly conceived.

Bernhard Siegert is Gerd-Bucerius Professor for the History and Theory of Cultural Techniques and the Director of IKKM, Bauhaus Universität Weimar. From 2008 to 2020 he was co-director of the International Research Center for Cultural Techniques and Media Philosophy at Weimar (IKKM). Since 2021, he has led the project 'The New Real – Past, Present, and Future of Computation and the Ecologization of Cultural Techniques' funded by the NOMIS Foundation. Siegert was Max Kade Professor at the University of California at Santa Barbara (2008 and 2011), Phyllis and Gerald LeBoff Visiting Scholar at the Department for Media, Culture, and Communication at New York University (2015), International Visiting Research Scholar at the Peter Wall Institute for Advanced Studies, University of British Columbia, Canada (2016), Eberhard Berent Visiting Professor and Distinguished Writer in Residence at the Department of German, New York University (2017), Guest Lecturer at the Department of Culture and Aesthetics, Stockholm University, Sweden (2018), and Visiting Professor at the Department of Visual and Environmental Studies at Harvard University

(2019). His many publications have drawn upon disciplines including the histories of science, technology, art, literature, anthropology, data processing and bureaucracies to reflect various cultural phenomena in terms of a history of mediums and cultural techniques. Translations in English of his work on media theory and history have appeared as *Relays: Literature as an Epoch of the Postal System* (Stanford University Press, 1999) and, most recently, *Cultural Techniques: Grids, Filters, Doors, and Other Articulations of the Real* (Fordham University Press, 2015).

Nathaniel Zetter is a College Teaching Associate in English at Selwyn College, University of Cambridge. His articles on literature, technology, and critical theory have appeared in *Textual Practice, Humanities*, and *Critical Quarterly*, and in the collection *Surveillance, Architecture and Control* (2019). He is currently at work on his first monograph, a cultural history of the rhetoric of war and sport.

www.ingramcontent.com/pod-product-compliance
Lightning Source LLC
Chambersburg PA
CBHW031432270326
41930CB00007B/666